THE NATIONAL INSTITUTE OF
ECONOMIC AND SOCIAL RESEARCH

Economic and Social Studies

I

STUDIES IN THE NATIONAL INCOME 1924–1938

CAMBRIDGE
UNIVERSITY PRESS
LONDON: BENTLEY HOUSE
NEW YORK, TORONTO, BOMBAY
CALCUTTA, MADRAS: MACMILLAN

STUDIES IN THE NATIONAL INCOME

1924–1938

Edited by

A. L. BOWLEY, Sc.D.

Emeritus Professor of Statistics in the University of London

CAMBRIDGE
AT THE UNIVERSITY PRESS
1942

PRINTED IN GREAT BRITAIN

Contents

CORRIGENDA

p. 7, line 6 from bottom, *for* the *Quarterly Economist Journal* read *The Quarterly Journal of Economics*

p. 14, *substitute for present footnote* According to Colin Clark, *The Conditions of Economic Progress*, p. 31.

p. 39, line 28, for *Richess* read *Richesse*

p. 43, line 10, for *Statistisk* read *Statistik*

p. 139, line 10 from bottom *for* Laspeyrc's *read* Laspeyre's

Introduction

In 1938 the National Institute of Economic and Social Research delegated to a Committee of the London School of Economics the task of reporting on the National Income of the United Kingdom in any detail that should be found possible. I was appointed Director of the investigation with Mr H. S. Booker as Secretary and principal investigator. It was intended to make a comprehensive study of income as a whole and of its distribution, together with examination of definitions and of such special topics as depreciation. Owing to the outbreak of war, several of the investigations were necessarily suspended. The staff was transferred to other work and it became impossible to obtain information other than that already published relating to the period under consideration, namely 1924–38. Since September 1939 the investigation has proceeded, but intermittently as circumstances permitted. The Committee whose task it was to superintend the undertaking was unable to give more than a perfunctory attention to it. Consequently I have had to carry on the direction of the work as time and circumstances permitted without the advantage of discussion. The result is that the opinions expressed and the method followed in this book are my responsibility alone.

Since the investigation has been thus curtailed and some important aspects omitted altogether, the book is termed 'Studies in the National Income'. It may serve some useful purpose to publish it in this incomplete form; at any rate there is no prospect of making it more complete.

Though the whole is my responsibility, particular chapters are mainly due to others. Thus the main table on earnings in Chapter II is Mr Booker's work, with slight modifications; also the study of income for the years 1937 and 1938 in Chapter II was mainly prepared in consultation with Mr Campion. Mr Campion and Miss Marley compiled the section on salaries. The Chapter of definitions is the work of Dr M. J. Elsas, who took over the bibliography prepared by Miss Dessauer. Chapter III on the Census of Production is Dr A. Neumann's work so far as the main tables and their explanation are concerned. The Index was compiled by Miss B. Lawrence.

It will be seen from Chapter I that the concept of national income is by no means simple. A questionnaire containing 31 queries with 36 sub-divisions was hypothetically addressed to some dozen principal writers on the subject. A rough computation suggests that the possible alternative definitions would number over 200 milliards, i.e. more than half the number of sixpences in the national income. The authors, however, were not found to give explicit answers to very many of the questions. It would have been an advantage to frame the estimates of income in such a way that they could be matched with any possible definition, but in fact only a limited number of variants could be included. When decision is reached on definition there still remains a complete lack of statistics on some classes, and an element of approximation in nearly all classes. In the treatment here followed an effort has been made to indicate clearly the origin and nature of other factors involved and to give some estimate of its precision. It will be clear that there is no simple answer to the question: What constitutes national income? and no precise answer to the question: How great is the national income?

The treatment in Chapters II and III follows conventional lines, but when in Chapter IV we come to the question of the measurement of real income new methods have been adopted. Hitherto the custom has been to estimate money income over a series of years and then adjust it by a series of index-numbers of prices to obtain real income. In fact this process is only an indirect way of forming an index of quantity, and in Chapter IV the procedure is to estimate changes in quantity of the principal classes and weighting them by their importance at fixed dates to obtain the measurement of the change of the quantity of goods and services available to the nation in successive years. It is not possible to give any unique and consistent definition of real income; we can only show the result of following selected hypotheses. Apart from this there is a fundamental difficulty which necessitates a considerable element of uncertainty in the result. Half of the national income is received not in return for physical products that can be measured objectively, but in return for services for which in general there is no definite measurement of change. Consequently one can only show the result of particular hypotheses on the amount of services rendered per week, for example, in transport, in teaching, in clerical work, in administrative work, and incorporate it with the estimate of physical production.

In some cases great detail of the statistics and working is shown, while in others the treatment is summary. Where fresh information was collected or unfamiliar methods were used, the whole operations are exhibited, even if the effect on the main totals was slight. But where the data were already published in accessible reports, it was thought to be sufficient to give references to the originals and to indicate only briefly the way they were treated, especially if it was evident that variation of treatment could not have any significant effect. There are, however, many quantities for which there are no definite statistics—for example, depreciation or the cost of transport or selling—here rough approximations are necessary and are a matter of judgment; all that can be done is to show the results of various methods on the final figures.

While this book was passing through the press, new information was published about the distribution of Income among income-tax payers, in the White Paper Cmd. 6347 (referred to on pages 53, 121 below) and in a statement in the House of Commons *circa* July 23, 1942. The former was discussed in the Bulletin of the London and Cambridge Economic Service, April 1942, p. 32; it is intended to analyse the latter in the Bulletin of the Institute of Statistics, Oxford, due August 29, 1942. If these reports had been available, the treatment on pp. 115–17 below would have been modified and extended; but it remains impossible to show the distribution of wage-earners' and other incomes under £250 per annum, either per head or per family, or in relation to sex or age.

A. L. B.

30 *July* 1942

Chapter I

THE DEFINITION OF NATIONAL INCOME

By Dr M. J. Elsas

1. *INTRODUCTION*

This study tries to give a survey of the literature on national income, or on parts of it. In the bibliography, Appendix, pp. 201–247, an attempt is made to catalogue the different authors in different countries. The arrangement provides for classifying the books and articles according to the specific topics on national income. Some of the authors have covered the whole field but others have only dealt with some of the items which come under the heading of national income.

This list of books and articles, substantial as it is, cannot be considered complete, for the number of publications which in one way or another are related to national income is so great, that their treatment would require a very great expenditure of time, and be too extensive to include here.

Our next aim was to show the difference between the various definitions of national income. Only if we are sure of the exact definition which underlies a given estimate are we able to make full use of it.

No one of the estimates is based upon quite the same method as any other, unless it is built up purposely on the method introduced by one of the leading authors on national income. The differences in method we try to sum up in a question list, composed of 31 questions and 36 sub-questions, in all a total of 67 questions. The questions are naturally not all of the same importance; some are trifling compared with others. Some of them, on the other hand, are of outstanding importance and so relevant that an omission or insufficient definition of these points would make an estimate valueless for the purpose of comparison with others. For instance, an estimate should answer the questions whether indirect taxation or depreciation and the services rendered by unpaid domestic work are included or not.

The relative importance of an item does, however, not always correspond with the length of space some authors have devoted to it. Some modern authors have sometimes dwelt on minor items which, interesting though they may be, would not alter an estimate to a great extent, whether included or not in the total of national income; and sometimes it looks as if the definition of national income has become hairsplitting, and one cannot help wondering whether this way of treating problems has not infrequently taken more the form of a hobby.

Section 2*d* contains the answers of the principal authors to the questions. Besides their estimates there are others either by authorities or semi-officials or failing these often by private statisticians; those estimates are dealt with in Sections 3*a* and *b*. In Section 3*c* we have given the answers deduced from British official publications to the questions with which they implicitly deal.

In Section 2*c* we have tried to give an account of the differences in the methods used. We have furthermore tried in a few instances to clarify the problem or to give our own answer to some points which it seemed to us have not yet been sufficiently treated.

2*a*. *LIST OF BOOKS AND ARTICLES*

OF THE PRINCIPAL AUTHORS ON NATIONAL INCOME

A. L. Bowley. *The Change in the Distribution of the National Income*, 1880–1930. Oxford, 1920.

—— *The Division of the Product of Industry*. Oxford, 1919.

—— The Definition of National Income. *Econ. Journ.* March 1922.

—— Discussion to Stamp's paper on 'Methods used in different countries'.

Bowley and Stamp. *The National Income*, 1924. Oxford, 1927.

Edwin Cannan. *Wealth*. 3rd ed. 1928.

Colin Clark. *National Income and Outlay*. London, 1937.

—— *National Income*, 1924–1931. Cambridge, 1932.

W. H. Coates. *The Citizen's Purse*. Manchester Statistical Society. Dec. 1931.

M. A. Copeland. *Concepts of National Income. Studies in Income and Wealth*. National Bureau of Economic Research. Vol. I. New York, 1937.

S. Fabricant. *Capital Consumption and Adjustment*. New York, 1938.

F. v. Fellner. Le revenu national de la Hongrie actuelle. *Bull. de l'Inst. Int. de Stat.* XIV, 3, p. 30.

I. Fisher. Der Einkommensbegriff im Lichte der Erfahrung. In *Die Wirtschaftstheorie der Gegenwart*. Ed. by H. Meyer. Wien, 1928.

—— *The Nature of Capital and Income*. New York, 1912.

A.W. Flux. Discussion on Stamp's paper on 'Methods used in different countries'.

C. Gini. La determinazione della Ricchezza e del Reddito delle Nazioni nel dopo Guerra e il loro confronto col periodo prebellico. *Bull. de l'Inst. Int. de Stat.* 1931, xxv, 3, p. 358.

—— Di alcuni circostanze che nei tempi moderni tendono a fare apprire l'incremento del reddito nazionale maggiore del vero. *Bull. de l'Inst. Int. de Stat.* 1931–32, Tome xxviii, 2, p. 248.

J. R. Hicks. *Value and Capital.* London, 1939.

S. Kuznets. *Changing Inventory Valuations in Studies in Income and Wealth.* National Bureau of Economic Research. Vol. i. New York, 1937.

—— *Commodity Flow and Capital Formation.* New York, 1938.

—— *National Income and Capital Formation,* 1919–1935. New York, 1937. (See *Addendum,* p. 53 below.)

H. Leak. Discussion of Stamp's paper on 'Methods used in different countries'.

E. Lindahl. *National Income of Sweden,* 1861–1930. London, 1937.

Alfred Marshall. *Principles of Economics.* 8th ed. 1922.

Matolcsy-Varga. *The National Income of Hungary,* 1924/25–1936/37. London, 1938.

W. C. Mitchell and S. Kuznets. Current Problems in measurement of national income. *Bull. de l'Inst. Int. de Stat.* 1935, xxviii, 2, p. 280.

K. Mori. Estimate of the National Wealth and Income of Japan proper. *Bull. de l'Inst. Int. de Stat.* 1931, xxv, 2, p. 179.

A. C. Pigou. *The Economics of Welfare.* London, 1929.

Lord Stamp. *British Incomes and Property.* London, 1920.

—— Methods used in different Countries for Measuring National Income. *Journ. of the R. Stat. Soc.* 1934, xcvii, p. 423, 541.

—— *See also* Bowley and Stamp.

U.S.A. Department of Commerce. *National Income in the United States,* 1929–1935. Washington, 1936.

C. A. Verijn-Stuart. Volksvermögen und Volkseinkommen in den Niederlanden. *Bull. de l'Inst. Int. de Stat.* 1931, Tome xxv, 3, p. 457.

A. Wagner. Statistik des Volks- und Nationaleinkommens. *Bull. de l'Inst. Int. de Stat.* 1905, xiv, 3, 4, p. 1.

2*b*. *LIST OF QUESTIONS*

CONCERNING THE DEFINITION OF NATIONAL INCOME

1 *a*. Is National Income that produced within the area of the nation?

b. Is National Income that accruing to Nationals (home produced and from abroad)?

c. Is National Income that consumed within the Area?

d. Is National Income that consumed by Nationals?

2. Valuation of the Product subject to Taxation.
   a. Are Excise Duties included in the value of the product to which they apply?
   b. Are Import Duties included in the value of the product to which they apply?
   c. Are rates on house property included in the value of the product to which they apply?

3. Valuation of commodities, production of which is subsidized,
   (*a*) at cost (including profits),
or (*b*) at selling price.

4. Valuation of commodities and services provided freely by the Government from the proceeds of taxation.
   a. How is public education valued?
   b. How are health services valued?
   c. How are police services valued?
   d. How are defence services valued?
   e. How are the services of tax collectors, customs and excise officials valued?
   f. How are the services of the clergy valued?
   g. How are the services of State officials valued?

5. Is allowance made for changes in the value of stocks and shares and other paper titles?
   a. Is any distinction made for services which are rationed or have the consumption controlled in ways other than by prices?

6. Is a value added for the services of houses occupied by owners?

7. Is a value added for the services of other durable consumers' goods (not houses), e.g. furniture?

8. Is allowance made for the value of services rendered to oneself or one's family?
   (*a*) Domestic services rendered by wives.
   (*b*) Produce of gardens and allotments.
   (*c*) Produce of farms consumed by farmers' families.
   (*d*) Services rendered by oneself which could be done by paid work.

9. Is allowance made for gifts
   (*a*) from or to persons in other countries,
   (*b*) between individuals within a country?

10 *a.* (i) Treatment of income from Government debt.
   (ii) The case of war loans.
   b. Treatment of income from pensions, payments to the unemployed, etc.
   (i) Contributory.
   (ii) Non-contributory.
   (iii) Special cases of pensions.

10 *b*. (iv) University teachers, etc.
(1) Is contribution out of salary or addition by employer counted as income, as savings or omitted?
(2) After employment: consumption of capital or income?
(v) Is income out of annuities counted as income, as savings or omitted as consumption of capital?

11. Is any distinction made between Government expenditure from direct and indirect taxation?
a. Government income from indirect taxation (local rates, health insurance, etc.).

12. The valuation of income in kind for lodging, board and other perquisites
(i) when in return for services rendered,
(ii) when charity.

13. Is any attempt made to value the net advantages of particular employments?

14. Are increments or decrements in the money value of
(*a*) durable capital,
(*b*) materials,
(*c*) stocks of finished goods,
(*d*) goods in process of manufacture,
allowed for, when quality and physical condition remain unchanged?

15. Are undistributed profits included?

16. Is allowance made for the destruction of irreplaceable commodities?

17. How are insurance losses by fire, wrecks, etc. and personal injuries treated?
a. Insurance and saving.

18. Is any allowance made for different costs of living in different parts of the country?

19. How are savings defined and valued?
The relation of income to expenditure and of these to production.

20. The distinction between the production of capital and of consumption goods.

21. The distinction between the production of material goods and of services rendered directly to consumers.

22. Is advertisement included as a cost or as an investment?

23. Treatment of depreciation of
(*a*) capital goods,
(*b*) materials,
(*c*) partly finished goods,
(*d*) finished goods.

24. Is Government expenditure divided into expenditure on goods and services and transfer expenditure and is the former divided into services rendered to entrepreneurs and consumers?
25. Treatment of incomes of societies and other corporate bodies.
26. Is any attempt made to sum up expenditure on particular commodities to derive a figure for national income?
27. Totals arising from various sources.
    Comparison of inventory and aggregate method.
28. Division of income among factors.
29. Division of income among persons.
30. Gross and net income.
31. Price changes.
    Measurement of real income.

2*c*. *SUMMARY AND CRITICISM OF ANSWERS*

Although there is a vast literature about national income, only a few authors have dealt even with all the main problems of the subject thoroughly. Among those we call the principal authors are a few who have not cared to give a full definition of national income, but have taken part in the discussion on papers on national income read by principal authors. The main authors do not all agree even on the chief points; it is therefore obvious that their estimates on national income are only comparable if these differences are taken into consideration. Estimates on the other hand may be based on similar definitions, but the data for certain items may not have been available in a country and the author had therefore to impute figures if he did not choose to omit them altogether. Such a procedure only provides rough estimates for national income.

Only a small number of authors, who rank according to our definition amongst the principal authors, and even fewer authors of less importance, have given an estimate of national income which can be compared with other estimates without substantial amendments or adjustments. Estimates for the same countries but for different periods also need careful examination whether comparison is permissible without corrections; it may be that the definition of income has undergone relevant changes in the meantime. This change may be due to different or changed opinion on the inclusion or exclusion of an item. It may be that the data for an item, which could not be included before because the figures were not available, have in the meantime been computed by the authorities. Comparison has of course also to take into account the change in territory of a country as well as a change in the number of inhabitants. Finally an item, thought to be trifling in earlier periods, might have become an important one in later periods (e.g. war loans and war pensions or old age pensions).

Had there been the same or similar method underlying the various estimates of national income in all countries concerned, even then not all the estimates would be comparable without corrections. In countries with different standards of living various items are of quite different importance. That also applies to the same countries for estimates of different periods, if the standard of living has changed in the meantime to any extent.

Furthermore, in countries with large external debts or countries in which the profits of important industries or transport undertakings are paid to foreigners, or at least non-residents, the definition of national income must be different. Here the Inventory method has to be adjusted accordingly.

Finally, in a country like Soviet Russia a quite different concept of national income is applied by the authorities. In Russia the incomes derived from so-called unproductive occupations are not included in the total national income; therefore professional services, although paid for, are excluded. Evidently comparison of the national income of Russia with that of other countries would necessarily be misleading.

As to *real* national income, comparisons between different countries or different periods are beset with pitfalls. Besides, no wholly satisfactory method has been applied to turn the nominal value of national income into a real one.

In a recent book on economic progress we are told that the ancient Greeks in Athens had been not worse off (at least those who were free men) than the people of to-day. The statistical data on which this statement is based are, however, neither plentiful nor convincing. In a review (the *Quarterly Economist Journal*, 1923) Professor Bowley wrote: 'Though there is every reason that the facts should be known, whether they are pleasing to us or not, it is inadvisable that very doubtful estimates should be given currency, whether they make for complacency or for discontent.'

WHAT ARE THE CHIEF DIFFERENCES BETWEEN THE DEFINITIONS OF NATIONAL INCOME?

Most of the principal authors adhere to the definition 1 *b*, which Bowley-Stamp termed income accruing to residents. Colin Clark deducts from the total of national income 'income belonging to foreigners'. Bowley-Stamp think it necessary to add an estimate for the income of soldiers and sailors abroad. Lindahl excludes services of foreign vessels in Swedish waters from Swedish national income.

Bowley-Stamp (*The National Income*, 1924) give estimates for different types of income.

Aggregate income; including war pensions, old age pensions, and employers' contribution to insurance funds.

Disposable income;[1] home and foreign, less income belonging to foreigners.

Individual and corporate income; including undivided profits.

Earned and unearned income; ignoring foreign debt and reparations.

Social income; that is, aggregate income minus transfers (transfers are pensions and national debt interest).

Taxable income; this equals total income arising within the United Kingdom plus income from abroad.

2*a*. Whereas practically all main authors include excise and import duties, Fellner excludes them. Lindahl and Stamp both exclude excise duties in a closed community. The authorities in Germany include them also in official estimates but deduct cost of service.

In Great Britain customs and excise duties amounted to roughly 28 per cent of total net tax revenue in 1931–32, in Canada to 25 per cent, in Belgium to 28 per cent. In the Irish Free State and in India customs and excise duties amounted to 62 per cent of total net tax revenue in the same year, 1931–32.[2]

2*c*. Only Lindahl refers to rates on house property. He points out that 'the agents of production employed in private production processes should be calculated inclusive of all rates and taxes paid but with a general deduction for the costs of the State' (*National Income of Sweden*, Vol. I, p. 19).

1 Disposable in the sense that the income comes into the possession of individuals or corporations in the United Kingdom, and can be disposed in private or public expenditure or saved at their choice.

2 *Tax Systems of the World*, New York State Tax Commission, 5th ed. 1934.

3. The literature about national income is not large as far as subsidies are concerned. Some writers who deal with this question are not certain how to treat it. Amongst the principal authors Copeland excludes subsidies as a transfer payment, so does Lindahl and Matolcsy-Varga, the latter as far as the grain certificate funds are concerned. The British Census of Production excludes custom and excise duties from total net output but includes subsidies (but see Chapter IV below).

4. Stamp includes Government services provided freely only when they are met by direct or tax payments charged on industry and reducing its profits, as it otherwise would be a problem of duplication. Bowley leaves the question open.

Colin Clark includes all Government services provided freely at cost price. He refers to Marshall and points out: 'Marshall also seeks to exclude the services supply by public enterprise (road, water supply, education, defence and the like) but modern economists in every case now include the value of such services in the national dividend.' But Marshall spoke only of public property. He wrote: 'The benefit which he derives from using his own personal goods or public property such as toll-free bridges are not reckoned as parts of the national dividend but are left to be accounted for separately' (*Principles of Economics*, p. 524). Clark's reference to Marshall therefore seems erroneous.

4*a*. Kuznets and Matolcsy-Varga think that public education eludes statistical approach. Lindahl includes it and gives detailed computation. Colin Clark reckons it at cost price.

Fellner excludes the services of State officials.

5. Only a few of the principal authors answer the question whether allowance is made for changes in the value of stocks and shares and other paper titles. Colin Clark excludes the increase in value as part of national income, just as declining value is not debited. On the other hand, the income authorities in many countries are interested in this question. France, Germany, U.S.A., Austria and Italy, most of them with some reservation to lapse of time, take the increase of value into account; whereas the United Kingdom does not, except in death-duty assessment at current value. The tax authorities in those countries which take this item into account are not so much interested in the logic of taxation as they are in the efficiency in regard to the amount it yields.

6. The majority of the main authors include the value of services of houses occupied by the owner, with the exception of Fellner and most of the American authors. For instance, Irving Fisher thinks it wise to exclude the services of dwellings just as we exclude the service of a piano. Kuznets excludes owned farmhouses. W. I. King (*The National Income and its Purchasing Power*, 1930) includes imputed rent of owned houses. The tax authorities of U.S.A., Canada and New Zealand exclude owned houses in their income estimates. German authorities include them.

A house ranks amongst durable consumption goods as one which is generally used for more than one generation; in that it differs considerably from other durable consumption goods, which have a more limited period of existence. The inclusion of this item seems therefore justified. On the other hand, where the annual service of a house is very small and where the habitation of the native should more suitably be termed a hovel (as in India and Africa), in these cases one might be justified in excluding the imputed value of its service, as this is neither of great money value nor the service rendered for a great length of time.

7. There is much divergence of treatment in connection with the exclusion or inclusion of services of durable goods other than houses. Matolcsy-Varga considers this question negligible. Amongst those who think it necessary to include it are Mori (Japan), Lindahl, Irving Fisher and Verijn-Stuart. The last named thinks that it makes no difference in money income whether somebody furnishes a house himself or rents a furnished house. Lindahl includes it or not according to the durability of the goods. Fellner, Colin Clark and Pigou exclude the item and so does Kuznets; Mitchell in collaboration with Kuznets are not decided. They are doubtful about the services of furniture, cars and clothing and they think no hard and fast rule can be established.

None of the named authors in the various countries include this item. W. I. King gives two alternatives, with and without imputed income from durable consumers' goods. He applies an interest rate of 6 per cent of the market value of goods other than houses. Lindahl takes as the value of the annual service rendered 5 per cent of the value of durable consumers' goods other than houses. As the standard of living has been raised, and therefore the equipment of the homes as well as the number of motor cars, the trend of the value of services rendered by 'other durable goods' has increased considerably in inter-war years.

8. Practically all principal authors exclude services rendered to oneself. Fellner thinks these services should be included and so does Gini; no estimate, however, follows this advice.

8*a*. Domestic services rendered by wives are excluded by Bowley, Stamp, Mitchell-Kuznets and Verijn-Stuart. Fellner and Matolcsy-Varga include them. Gini thinks they should be included. Lindahl includes women over 15 years of age, but thinks excluding this item might be preferable. He gives alternative estimates with and without unpaid domestic work. The difference between these two estimates is rather substantial.

	National Income of Sweden excluding unpaid domestic work Million kroner	National Income of Sweden including unpaid domestic work Million kroner
1921	7,296	9,181
1922	6,459	8,044
1923	6,482	7,987
1924	6,690	8,245
1925	6,916	8,451
1926	7,048	8,588
1927	7,210	8,760
1928	7,367	8,932
1929	7,862	9,447
1930	7,744	9,324

The first estimate, excluding unpaid domestic work, differs from the estimate including it by about 25 per cent in the years 1921–25 and about 20 per cent in the years 1926–30.

The total income from paid domestic work in Sweden amounts to not much more than 10 per cent of the imputed income of unpaid domestic work in Sweden.

In the *Measurement of Social Phenomena*, Bowley points out:

The only basis for valuing this (women's household work) would be to reckon the cost of having it done by paid help if the wife did none of it; but apart from the fact that much of it would be different—e.g. the difference between a mother's and a nurse's handling of children—the valuation would not be reasonable, for the paid work would not be directed in the same way to satisfy the most urgent needs, nor fitted into odd times. I do not think that any general attempt to value these services would result in valid measurement. We may evade the difficulty, however, by using two methods of reckoning simultaneously and applying that which is most suitable to any problem or classification in hand. One is to regard family income of two parts—one measurable and the other composed of incommensurable services; so long as we are dealing only with a class in which the practice of having servants or of not having servants is universal, no difficulty arises in comparison. The other method is to subtract the expenses of domestic help; this applies where the women go out to work, or work for gain at home, and in consequence pay for such help,[1] which they would otherwise not need. Then the expenses of the help may be subtracted.

In 'The Definition of National Income', *Economic Journal*, 1922, Bowley writes:

The ignoration of the value of women's domestic services has been less plausible in recent years. During the war the domestic staffs of many houses decreased and well-to-do women rendered more services to their own households. If the housemaid left and made munitions and the housewife did her work, the total of goods and services was increased by the value of the munitions, but part is cut out of the reckoning because no longer paid for. If in 1920 the former servant helped in her own home, when her wages were no longer needed, the total of services is still greater than in 1914 if her former mistress is still doing the housemaid's work, but since there is no payment to either income is decreased. Dr Dalton[2] points out that though services rendered within the households can be omitted for some comparisons, yet in many measurements of the inequality of incomes proportional differences are involved and therefore the complete totals are needed.

In consequence of these and other ways in which elements of income, which were ignored before the war as not affecting comparisons, have become of some importance, I question whether Sir J. Stamp's[3] dictum that 'the sum total of wages, salaries, profits and interest presents a fairly comprehensible idea, free from important ambiguities, for ordinary comparative purposes, is valid as between 1914 and 1921'.

Some authors have avoided taking sides in the discussion by stating that the services of wives and other family dependants are invaluable, and therefore have to be omitted. We cannot help feeling that such an answer is somewhat hypocritical; an infinite value is not nought. There are better arguments why this item could be excluded. True, a country, formerly predominantly agricultural, which has become an industrial one, seems on account of the decrease in unpaid domestic work and of the increase in paid jobs to have become richer than is really

1 If a servant is kept only because there are lodgers, her expenses should be deducted from family income.

2 *Inequality of Incomes*, p. 168.

3 *British Incomes and Property*, p. 416.

the case. Many of those who formerly worked without pay are working for pay now. However, the whole concept of national income is based on the principle that only those goods and services are to be taken into account which are bought and sold, or can be exchanged for money, but on the other hand to omit all those which are not. We have to keep to this rule, otherwise the definition of national income would become inconsistent. Those who are not satisfied with this, as far as unpaid domestic work is concerned, should remember that the exclusion of unpaid domestic work and the inclusion of the same job, if paid, is on the whole quite sound and logical, as the greater or smaller number of paid jobs available in a country is in itself one of the best yardsticks of national prosperity. Kitchen work, formerly done by the housewife, but now taken over by the cook, is usually proof of greater prosperity of the family.

The trade cycle manifests itself in the ups and downs of the numbers of available jobs, and would become meaningless if this criterion was not considered. The change from unpaid to paid work is by no means an illusionary increase of national income, if such a change is the expression of an increase of independence which is generally denied to those who have to perform unpaid jobs. In normal times the change from unpaid to paid work does not take place erratically. On the other hand, Bowley quite rightly questions whether between the years 1914–20 this criterion was still as valid as before ('The Definition of National Income', *Economic Journal*, 1922). The answer to this is perhaps that rules and laws are often not applicable under abnormal conditions. Even in physics some vital laws, gas laws for instance, do not hold good in extreme cases.

Rao, in his estimate for *The National Income of British India*, 1940, deals with income of members of family workers in the family concern. He includes services of 'working dependants'. Working dependants are defined as 'dependants following any occupation which contributed to the family maintenance and not themselves receiving the wage or controlling the means of subsistence gained'. The last class really corresponds to the dependants engaged in—to borrow Mr Colin Clark's phrase—family occupations, and presumably have an imputed income. Rao assumes that the earnings of a working dependant, as also the earnings of one who follows agriculture as a subsidiary occupation, is one-third of that of one who follows it as his principal occupation.

8*b*. It seems that the German tax authorities alone include produce of gardens and allotments in national income.

Bowley (*Measurement of Social Phenomena*, 1923) points out:

> Where vegetables, food, or flowers are grown in a garden or allotment their value is income, but before reckoning it, the rent of the ground (if that can be determined apart from the building) and expense of seeds and tools should be subtracted; in amateur gardening it might easily happen that the remainder was negative, though possibly balanced by the pleasure obtained in anticipation and the health invigorated by cultivation. Practically the only important cases are allotments and cottage gardens of the nature of allotments, and in these cases estimates are not difficult to make correctly, within, say, six pence per week.

8*c*. Farm products consumed by farmers' families are as a rule included. Differences, however, exist as to how they are valued. Colin Clark includes them at wholesale prices, Lindahl at market prices, which one may assume are identical with wholesale prices. The German official estimates also include them at wholesale prices. King (U.S.A.) includes them at average prices, a not quite clear definition. Poland and Eire[1] include this item at retail prices.

This item is open to major error. Most likely in agricultural countries, or countries with a large proportion of farming population, we may expect in the value of this item the comparatively largest under-estimate of all items included.

Rao computes the produce of farms in India by the formula (obtained by the Department of Agricultural Statistics of India)

$$\text{Standard yield} \times \text{seasonal factor} \times \text{area under cultivation.}$$

Harvest prices are used for the purpose of valuation.

8*d*. Services rendered by oneself which could be done by paid work are generally excluded by the main authors. Lindahl, who also excludes it, thinks it might be included if it could be done at market price. Stamp considers services of mutuality by co-operatives might be included. It is surprising that this item, services rendered by oneself, is discussed at such length in the literature, though in practice it is hardly of relevance. One man may stop going to the barber and shave himself, but another may just do the opposite. Besides, if he shaves himself

1 According to *Statistik des Deutschen Reiches*, Sonderheft 23, International tax comparison.

he might spend nearly as much money for blades and other tools (electric shaver). The problem is, though theoretically of interest, comparatively trifling if it comes to putting it down in figures. If we start to add the value of service by shaving oneself, why not, if one wants to be consistent, add an imputed value for the service done to oneself by dressing oneself without the help of a valet, whom a certain number of people employ for that purpose? Other services of similar nature could be cited to show the absurdity of creating problems where there are none.

9*a*. Nearly all principal authors include gifts from abroad. Lindahl seems to include only gifts from emigrants to the U.S.A. Copeland, however, excludes gifts.

9*b*. All authors seem to exclude gifts within the country, as this is a transfer of income.

The tax authorities in Great Britain consider this item for death duties, but only if a certain number of years has not elapsed between the date of the gift and the benefactor's death. In Germany, on the other hand, all gifts are taxed above a certain amount.

10*a*. (i) (ii) The American authorities, Copeland, Coats and Colin Clark include income from Government debts. Verijn-Stuart includes it also, but he excludes interest from loans issued for covering deficits in the ordinary budget and Pigou excludes if loans have been employed unproductively. Lindahl excludes income from Government debts, Bowley-Stamp exclude interest of Government loans from total 'social income', treating this item as transfer, but they include it in 'aggregate income'.

All main authors exclude war loans.

One might be doubtful whether it is sound to differentiate between productively and unproductively employed loans. The term 'productive' is open to discussion. Why should the production of defensive weapons, say, 5,000 British aeroplanes, if we had produced them in the years 1935–39, and which would most likely have prevented this war, be called unproductive, but on the other hand the production of a pair of silk stockings, a luxury perhaps not lasting longer than a week, be termed productive?

War loans, as mentioned before, are excluded by all authors, but not loans, spent for the same or similar purposes, issued before the outbreak of war. Germany, for instance, spent and borrowed more for armament purposes between 1934 and 1939 than in the first year of the present war. To differentiate between peace and war loans seems somehow arbitrary and not always justified.

10*b*. (i) The American authorities, as well as Colin Clark, include employers' social insurance charges; Bowley-Stamp also include employers', but not Government, contributions.

10*b*. (ii) The majority exclude non-contributory social insurances, amongst them Mitchell-Kuznets; Kuznets, without collaboration, seems to include this item.

10*b*. (iii) Lindahl, Matolcsy-Varga, Colin Clark, Copeland and Irving Fisher include pensions. Fellner excludes them. Bowley-Stamp exclude pensions derived from public funds, except old age pensions, unless they are above the tax limit. They include it, however, as 'other income' in aggregate total income.

11*a*. Services from indirect taxation are included in estimates by German authorities; the cost of these services is deducted. Colin Clark adds the proceeds of indirect taxation to total individual income. Flux includes it in the value of product. See also No. 2*a*, p. 8.

12. (i) All authors include income in kind, but often not in its full value. Lindahl, therefore, suggests that addition should be made.

12. (ii) The main authors exclude board and lodging, when charity, and treat this as transfer of income.

14. Bowley, Matolcsy-Varga, Irving Fisher and the American authorities exclude increment in the money value of goods. Bowley thinks one may deal with this item in a supplement. Gini includes it, though with reservations.

The tax authorities in most countries allow the choice between current market prices or cost prices, whichever is the lowest. The tax authorities in Germany and France include this item if a firm is sold or liquidated.

Kuznets points out (*Commodity Flow and Capital Formation*, Vol. 1):

It was considered advisable to see what results would be obtained if no effort were made to allow for changes in the ratio of construction materials to total value of construction.

First, it may be assumed that the ratio of value of construction materials to total value of construction is constant when both are measured in fluctuating current prices. The implication is then either that both prices and quantities of materials, as compared with those of labour and of other production elements, change from year to year in exactly the same fashion or that if changes in prices and in quantities of the two groups of production elements are divergent, they are equally divergent in opposite directions. The latter implication is reasonable if it is assumed that the two groups of productive elements can be easily substituted for each other....

The other possible assumption is that the ratio of construction materials to total value of construction is constant when both are expressed in terms of a constant price level. This assumption, a direct opposite of that suggested above, implies that the technical conditions of construction activity are quite rigid with respect to the relative amounts of materials consumed as over against the amounts of the other groups of production goods used; and the variation of the ratio of the value of materials to the total value of construction, when both are expressed in current prices, results exclusively from divergent changes in prices of these two groups of production goods.

15. Bowley-Stamp, Colin Clark, Lindahl, Wagner and Kuznets include undistributed profits. Tax authorities in the United Kingdom, Germany, New Zealand, New South Wales and Japan include this item, provided they know of it.

As undistributed profits may be book profits and may not be ready for distribution in form of dividends, their inclusion in the total of national income may sometimes lead to over-statement; for instance, when the trade cycle has turned and depression has set in which have used up the reserves.

16. Lindahl, as well as Pigou, thinks allowances should be made for wasting assets of irreplaceable commodities. Matolcsy-Varga and Colin Clark disregard them in accordance with the practice of the tax authorities.

18. Colin Clark, Lindahl, Matolcsy-Varga and Copeland think it advisable to make allowance for different costs of living in different parts of a country.

There are, however, great difficulties, and division might therefore be impracticable. If a distinction should be made, the division into urban and rural districts would perhaps be the most important one.

20. Distinction between production of capital and consumption goods is not frequent. Kuznets differentiates between

A. Consumers' Goods

I. *Perishable*	II. *Semidurable*	III. *Durable*
1. At destination	1. At destination	1. At destination
a. Finished—bread, coal used by households, etc., in hands of households	*a*. Finished—shoes, clothing, etc., in hands of households	*a*. All finished—passenger cars, jewellery, furniture, in hands of households *aa*. Residential buildings *bb*. All other
b. Unfinished—none	*b*. Unfinished—none	*b*. Unfinished—none
2. In circulation	2. In circulation	2. In circulation
a. Finished—same as under A I, 1 *a*, but in hands of producers and distributors	*a*. Finished—same as under A II, 1 *a*, but in hands of producers and distributors	*a*. Finished—same as under A III, 1 *a*, but in hands of producers and distributors
b. Unfinished—raw materials, fuels, supplies, so far as they are used for production, transportation and distribution resulting in A I, 1 *a*	*b*. Unfinished—raw materials, fuels, supplies used for production, transportation and distribution resulting in A II, 1 *a*	*b*. Unfinished—raw materials, fuels, supplies used for production, transportation and distribution resulting in A III, 1 *a*

B. Producers' Goods

I. *Perishable*	II. *Semidurable*	III. *Durable*
None	None	1. At destination
		a. Finished—industrial, farm machinery, buildings, trucks, etc., in hands of business units who will use them
		b. Unfinished—none
		2. In circulation
		a. Finished—same as under B III, 1 *a*, but in hands of producers and distributors
		b. Unfinished—raw materials, fuels, supplies, etc., used for production, transportation and distribution resulting in B III, 1 *a*

Lindahl (*National Income of Sweden*) points out:

A general differentiation has been made between non-durable and durable goods. All goods that may be assumed to have been consumed within a year are non-durable goods. These include all raw materials and fuel, and—of consumers' goods—provisions, clothing and household utensils of brief duration. All services come under this heading. Durable goods include all plants, dwelling-houses, machinery, implements, and generally all goods, the durability of which exceeds one year.

See also No. 20 in Section 3*c* (United Kingdom).

22. Bowley, Colin Clark and Lindahl treat advertisement as a cost. Kuznets finds it impossible to distinguish which part is expense and which part is goodwill.

23. The treatment of depreciation is beset with ambiguity. So far as ordinary depreciation takes place, deduction—equal amounts spread over several years—is generally accepted by the main authors as well as by the tax authorities. There is, of course, a variety as to the percentage allowed for the different items.

Things, however, look quite different if replacement is concerned. A comparatively new machine, or even a new plant, has sometimes to be replaced only because technical progress or new inventions makes its further use uneconomic. In such a case many tax authorities, as for instance, the British, are open to a compromise. But there is, of course, no hard and fast rule about the procedure. This item sets problems to the entrepreneurs as well as to the tax authorities.

24. In regard to the division of Government expenditure Mitchell-Kuznets point out:

In estimating total income produced at its source in the business establishment, one has the alternative of either deducting taxes or leaving them undeducted. In the first case, taxes are deducted because they constitute payments by business establishments to the government for services rendered, and are thus on a par with other business payments of the firm (for materials, labour, etc.). It is then necessary to cover separately the service activity of the government, i.e. to include in the national income total the value of services rendered by government employees and government creditors (in the form of wages to government employees and interest payments on government debt). In the second case, taxes are not deducted; but on the other hand, no allowance is made for any income produced by government labour or government capital. This last procedure, however, raises two difficulties: (1) it does not yield a proper industrial allocation of income produced, unless it is considered that government activity is a non-productive type of pursuit, constituting a pure draft upon the economic system of the country, (2) it is impossible to segregate income produced from income paid out. For both reasons the first procedure, namely, the deduction of taxes paid by business establishments and the independent estimate of income arising from government activity, seems to be preferable.

But if this procedure is followed the possibility that some relief expenditures are paid by the government out of taxes on business establishments gives rise to a difficult problem. To the extent that relief is paid out of these business taxes, and the latter are subtracted from the net income of the business establishments, it constitutes a part of income produced but not accounted for, a part which is paid by business establishments to individuals via the government channels. This part should be included in both income paid out and income produced, preferably as a separate item. But any student who has ever worked with government data showing government receipts and expenditures can readily visualize the maze one gets into in any attempt to trace a specific government expenditure back to some distinct source.

See also Lindahl, Question 2*c*.

25. The income of societies, charities and other corporate bodies is often omitted in official and other estimates. The great part, however, is included in the British accounts.[1] Colin Clark suggests that these incomes have to be added back, when tax exemption has been made to charities and educational institutes.

Fellner advocates that, when subjective method is used, not only the incomes of individuals have to be considered but also income of societies, corporations, communities, municipalities, foundations, churches and State, in other words 'des personnes morales'.

Lindahl thinks income from capital, owned by idealistic associations, can be regarded as the income of the members of the associations.

Stamp points out that the main difference between total income assessed and the aggregation of individual income is the income of clubs and societies not traceable to individuals.

26. A. E. Feavearyear[2] analyses the national expenditure for the average of the years 1924–27, and 1932. He divides

1 But see H. Campion, *Public and Private Property in Great Britain*.

2 'The National Expenditure, 1932', *Economic Journal*, 1934. See also A. E. Feavearyear, 'Spending the National Income', *ibid.* 1931, and Myra Curtis, 'National Income and Expenditure and the Measurement of Saving', *ibid.* 1935.

expenditure into food, maintenance of the home, clothes, direct taxation, liquor, smoking, trade, entertainments and sport, sickness, and accidents and State insurance, religions, reading, miscellaneous expenditure, saving including new houses and furniture.

27. Kuznets compares distribution of national income

(*a*) according to industrial organization,
(*b*) according to type of income.

In *National Income*, 1929–32, he divides national income paid out into total labour income, total property income, total entrepreneurial income (net rents and royalties and entrepreneurial withdrawals). Then he gives figures for income produced by industrial divisions, and income paid out by industrial divisions.

Colin Clark (*National Income and Outlay*, p. 125) shows a table for the distribution of the Product of Industry divided first into wages, salaries below and above £160 and rent, interest and profits. At the same time this table is split into manufacture, mining and building, railways, agriculture, ownership of dwelling-houses, other transport, commerce and services. This division into income arising from various sources shows also the number of persons occupied in the different industries. This table combines the answers to our Questions 27, 28 and 29.

28. Bowley[1] divides total gross income into

Actual income:
(1) Schedules A, B, C; (2) Schedules D, E.
Wages and earnings.
Unearned income.
Sundries: (1) Pensions; (2) Employers' contribution; (3) Others.

Bowley-Stamp, in *The National Income*, 1924, make the following division among factors:

Aggregate income.
Disposable income.
Individual income and Corporate income.
Earned and Unearned income.
Social income.
Taxable income.

1 'Some Constituents of the National Income,' *Journal of the R. Stat. Soc.*, 1940.

In *The Income of the United States, its Amount and Distribution*, 1909–19 (by the Staff of the National Bureau of Economic Research), Vol. I, an analysis is made of the estimate by sources of production.

In the second volume (*Income of the People of the United States*, 1922) the national income is divided among persons receiving income under and over $2,000.

See also No. 27, Colin Clark and Kuznets.

29. Division of income among persons is shown for U.S.A. by W. I. King (*The Wealth and Income of the People of the United States*, 1915) in an estimate of the distribution of income among families of the Continental U.S.A. in 1910.

The table shows (*a*) the thousands of dollars income, and (*b*) the number of families classified according to income classes. Bowley, in an article 'The British Super-tax and the Distribution of Income' (*Quarterly Journal*, 1914), quotes super-tax yields and shows how it is divided among persons chargeable. The diagram of frequency, shown in this publication, corresponds to Pareto's Law also for higher incomes between £5,000 and £55,000 (for the year 1911–12), but not above income limit of £55,000. Colin Clark gives a similar table of surtax progress for a later year (*National Income and Outlay*, p. 105). See also No. 27, Colin Clark and No. 28, *Income of the People of the United States*, by the Staff of the National Bureau of Economic Research, Vol. II, 1922.

In the 36th Report of the Commissioners of H.M. Inland Revenue for the year ended on 31 March 1920 there is a table showing income classes, and number of persons having the income of the especial class. See also No. 29 in Section on British answers, p. 51.

30. 'Gross' and 'net' income: these terms are not always used in the same sense. Kuznets point out:

> Gross national product includes, besides income payments to individuals and net savings of enterprises, the amounts deducted by the users of durable capital goods as an allowance for the current consumption of these goods in the productive process. If these deductions, which appear largely as depreciation and depletion charges, are added to net savings of enterprises, the resulting total represents the share of gross national product retained by enterprise. If we designate this share as gross savings of enterprises, then gross national product, at the point of distribution, is equal to income payments to individuals plus gross savings of enterprises.

Colin Clark defines net national income = gross national income − maintenance and depreciation.
See also No. 1 *b*, in Section on British answers.

31. Real income is generally measured by using cost of living index or wholesale index as the denominator of money income, though this is, as every statistician knows, rather a rough method. Stamp points out that it would seem that a more detailed effort to suit the sectional indices to sectional parts of income is very desirable, and the use of cost of living index is also worth consideration. The recent official American estimate indicates that it requires an all-inclusive index covering wholesale and retail, and all groups of people, and such an index is not available.

Colin Clark says:

The basic idea is that such an index should incorporate an index-number of the current prices of goods and services for consumption, and that weighted additions should be made for the prices of visible and invisible exports and of home investment goods, and that then a negative weight should be given to the price of imports.

According to Lindahl:

As it is impossible to obtain a satisfactory price index, one of the available index series will, therefore, have to do. The choice has fallen on the cost of living index, as this is based on prices more in conformity with the prices of the finished products than the other indices, which are based on the prices of raw materials and semi-finished products.

W. I. King recommends the use of five indices, the first for measuring the income for earned manual and clerical workers, the second for farm labourers, the third for farmers, the fourth for families spending for direct goods $5,000 and over, and the fifth for families spending $25,000 and over.

Mitchell-Kuznets point out:

Whatever price indices may be selected for making price adjustments, be they wholesale commodity and services indices in the case of national income produced, or cost of living indices in the case of national income consumed, we are faced with greater difficulties not only because of drastic price changes which upset the price 'system' and make reliance on sample price quotations most dangerous; but also because rapid shifts are occurring in the quality of what appear to be identical commodities, and marked substitution of one commodity group for another in the total output of our economy as well as in the consumption of its individual members.

In the official estimates of Germany's national income the cost of living index is applied, in that of Canada the wholesale price index is used.

In the *Measurement of Social Phenomena* Bowley writes about real income:

An obvious, if crude, correction would be by the use of index-numbers of the purchasing power of money; but, even if we can get over the trouble of deducing retail price changes from wholesale, index-numbers still refer to commodities and not to services directly rendered. In particular ordinary index-numbers do not include rent, which affects all classes, and the poorer more closely than the richer; nor domestic or professional services, which affect the rich rather than the poor....

Again, as the country becomes more densely populated, the free gifts of nature are appropriated and become marketable and their annual value is included in somebody's income. Allowance is made in estimates of agricultural labourers' wages for the free fuel they used to have; but no allowance is made for scarcity of blackberries, nuts, mushrooms, etc., when they are improved away by building for closer cultivation, nor for the greater or less enjoyment of fresh air or scenery....

It should be observed that in all measurements of this kind changes in totals or averages may be so great as to make it certain that qualifications and corrections would not over-ride the change; while the small changes might easily be nullified by such corrections. The trouble from the point of view of scientific measurement is that we cannot always estimate any limit to the margin of error, so that an element of complete uncertainty or guesswork may remain.

In Chapter IV below this subject is discussed in detail.

2*d*. *ANSWERS OF THE PRINCIPAL AUTHORS*

TO SUCH OF THE ABOVE QUESTIONS AS THEY CONSIDER

	A. L. Bowley	Lord Stamp	Bowley-Stamp
1 *b*.	Defines it as income accruing to residents.	Adheres to it.	See Bowley.
2 *a*.	Includes.	—	—
2 *b*.	Includes.	Excludes in a closed community.	—
2 *c*.	Includes.	—	—
4.	Leaves question open.	Includes where met by direct or taxing payments reducing industrial profits.	—
4 *a*.	Includes.	—	Not counted.
4 *b*.	Includes.	—	Counted only under employers' contributions to insurance funds.
4 *c*.	Includes.	—	—
4 *d*.	Includes.	Includes.	—
6.	Includes.	Includes.	—
8.	Excludes.	Excludes.	Exclude.
8 *a*.	Excludes.	Excludes.	Exclude.

	A. L. Bowley	Lord Stamp	Bowley-Stamp
8 *b*.	Excludes.	Excludes.	Exclude.
8 *c*.	Includes.	Includes.	Include.
8 *d*.	Excludes.	Generally excluded; possible exception: co-operatives.	Exclude.
9 *b*.	—	Excludes unless business expense.	—
10 *a*.			
(i)	Excludes [1919 publication].	Excludes.	Exclude from 'social income' but include in 'aggregate income'.
(ii)	—	—	
10 *b*.			
(i)	Excludes, but somewhat undecided.	Includes.	Exclude receipts but include employers' contributions.
(ii)	—	—	Exclude.
(iii)	Includes; also soldiers pensions, but is somehow reluctant.	—	Exclude.
11 *a*.	—	—	Include health insurance but do not count insurance paid out to recipients.
13.	—	Omits it; follows Coates.	—
14 *a*.	Should be treated separately.	—	—
14 *b–d*.	Undecided regarding lowest value principle.	—	—
15.	Includes under Schedule D (income tax).	—	Include.
17.	Premiums to be deducted from net output figures.	—	—
21.	—	Includes services rendered direct to consumers.	—
22.	Treated as cost.	—	—
23.	Gives a rough system.	—	Refer to 68th Report of Commissioners of Inland Revenue.
25.	—	Not always possible to include.	—
27.	—	Scheme for subjective and objective method.	—
31.	Suggests computing index-numbers out of budgets for calculating real income.	Sectional indices for sectional parts of income and also considers cost of living index.	Computation should be corrected by a number related to wholesale price and cost of living index.

Colin Clark

1 *b*. Adheres to it. 'Goods and services which are customarily exchanged for money.'
4. Includes at cost price.
4 *a*, *b*, *c*, *d*. At cost price.
4 *g*. Includes, gives no details.
5. No allowance made.
6. Includes.
7. Excludes.
8 *a*. Excludes.
8 *c*. Includes at wholesale prices.
9 *b*. Excludes.
10 *a*. (i) Includes.
10 *a*. (ii) Excludes.
10 *b*. (i) Includes charges paid by employers.
10 *b*. (ii) Excludes as relief payments.
10 *b*. (iii) Includes pensions to retired employees of the State or firms, but excludes old age and widows pensions.
11 *a*. Includes; changed his opinion since 1932 regarding rates on business premises.
14. Yes; but has doubts about decrements.
15. Includes.
16. No; on account of technical difficulties.
17 *a*. Insurance is a kind of savings; expenses are to be deducted.
18. Yes; four areas in the U.K.
19. Savings = excess of income over consumption.
22. Treated as cost.
23 *a*. 4 per cent compound interest over 60 years for buildings, other property according to inland revenue allowance.
24. Yes.
25. Includes.
26. Yes; where exemptions have been made they must be added.
27. Yes. Checks his results by Feavearyear's figures and refers to an article by Myra Curtis.
30. Gross income – cost of repairing and replacing of capital instruments = net income.
31. Suggests price index for comparison and makes various other proposals.

M. A. Copeland

1 *b*. Adheres to it.
3. Treats it as transfer payment.
6. Includes.
9 *a*. Excludes.
9 *b*. Excludes, but treats only college fees.
10 *a*. (i) Includes.
10 *b*. (ii) Undecided.
10 *b*. (iii) Includes pensions.
15. Includes undistributed profits as far as non-corporate companies are concerned.
17. Does not take into consideration.
18. Thinks it advisable, but cannot recommend any method.
19. Social income – consumption = savings.

23 *a*. Follows accountants' procedure.
24. Takes subsidies as kind of transfer items.
28. Suggests three indices: consumption index, index of wealth, index for inventories, etc.
29. Gross social value − depreciation and depletion = net social value product.

IRVING FISHER

1 *b*. Adheres to it, but does not stress the point regarding nationals.
7. Includes.
10 *b*. (iii) Includes.
14. Excludes.
19. Savings are not income. Interest of savings is income.
23. In case of depreciation fund, uses it to reduce realized income to earned income.

S. FABRICANT

17. Treated as losses on capital account.
23. Takes the value of the current services rendered by capital goods and used up in production.
31. Measures capital and capital consumption in current prices, but allows constant prices for the purpose of time comparison.

F. V. FELLNER

1 *b*. Adheres to it.
2 *a*. Excludes.
4 *g*. Excludes from private income.
6. Excludes as not produced in the period.
7. Excludes as not produced in the period.
8. Should be excluded.
9 *a*. Includes.
9 *b*. Excludes.
10 *a*. (i) Includes.
10 *b*. (ii) Excludes, but not quite decided.
10 *b*. (iii) Excludes, but not quite decided.
23 *a*. Depreciation percentage for machines 1·72 per cent of value of gross production, or based on horse-power.
25. Must be added when using subjective method.
27. Compares subjective and objective methods.
31. Proposes to measure in constant prices, for instance in pre-war prices, so as to be able to eliminate changes in the value of gold.

Interest. Interest due inside the country balances and has to be left out.

EDWIN CANNAN

6. Includes.
7. Excludes as a rule.
8 *a*. Excludes as a rule.
8 *d*. Excludes as a rule.
9 *b*. Excludes to avoid double counting.
11 *a*. Excludes.
23 *a*. Deducts sum paid into the depreciation fund.
25. Includes ordinary net income, but excludes gifts and legacies.

C. A. Verijn-Stuart

1 *b*. Adheres to it.
6. Includes.
7. Includes.
8 *a*. Excludes because not quantitatively definable.
10 *a*. (i) Includes generally.
10 *b*. (iii) Includes.
21. Includes direct services to consumers.
31. Cost of living index seems the best although not satisfactory.

Conrado Gini

1 *c*. Adheres to it.
3. Deducts Government subsidies from its expenditure.
4 *a*. Deducts from public expenditure.
4 *c*. Deducts from public expenditure.
4 *d*. Deducts from public expenditure.
6. Includes.
8. Should be included.
8 *a*. Should be included.
10 *a*. (i) Interest should be computed in the private income of the nation, just as it is computed in individual incomes, and should be deducted consequently from the amounts paid in taxation.
10 *b*. (i) Excludes.
11. Includes both generally.
11 *a*. Includes, unless it raises public revenue.
13. Deducts railway fares.
14 *a*. Includes changes in value which can be forecast, but with some doubts on revenue figures.
17. Premiums are not to be deducted, but insurances paid out are to be deducted.
31. Is not content with any existing index, as they do not consider services, but does not offer solution.

	S. Kuznets	W. C. Mitchell-S. Kuznets
1 *b*.	Adheres to it.	Adhere to it.
1 *c*.	—	Give definition. (See also 1 *b*.)
4 *a*.	Excludes.	—
6.	Includes.	Include.
7.	Excludes.	No hard and fast rule.
8.	Excludes.	No hard and fast rule.
8 *a*.	—	Exclude.
8 *c*.	Includes.	—
10 *b*. (ii)	Includes. (See Mitchell-Kuznets.)	Exclude. (See Kuznets.)
12. (i)	Includes (no details given).	—
14 *a*.	Calculates in current as well as in constant prices.	—
14 *b*.	Gives two alternatives in fluctuating and in constant prices.	—
15.	Includes.	—
17.	Fire losses = capital consumption.	—

	S. KUZNETS	W. C. MITCHELL-S. KUZNETS
19.	Gives definition for gross and net savings.	Income consumed + savings by individuals = income paid out. Income paid out + net savings by business firms = income produced.
20.	Consumers' goods = commodities used by ultimate consumers. Producers' goods = used by business firms.	—
21.	Includes (1) industries dealing with the production of commodities, (2) commodity handling, (3) service industries.	—
22.	Thinks it impossible to distinguish between cost and goodwill.	—
23 *a*.	Uses 'cost or market whichever lower' principle for valuation of capital goods.	Conservative accountant practice may mislead during times of violent price changes.
24.	—	If taxes are deducted from business incomes, the different Government services are to be separated.
27.	Distribution by industrial organization and type of income.	—
28.	Division by labour income, etc. See p. 21.	—
30.	Gross national income − value of commodities consumed in the process of production = net national product.	—
31.	Applies revaluation by means of various indices.	Wholesale price index for national income produced and cost of living index for national income consumed.

ERIK LINDAHL

1 *a*. Adheres to it; excluding services of foreign vessels in Swedish waters.
2 *a*. Includes.
2 *b*. Excludes (in a closed community).
3. Not considered in calculating the value of commodities produced, but deducted from public expenditure.
4. Includes with certain exceptions. (See 4*b*, *f*, 10*a*.)
4 *a*. Gives a detailed system.
4 *b*, *c*, *d*, *e*. Valued under the heading public administration.
4 *f*. Values at the sum of the expenses occurred.
4 *g*. Includes at cost.
6. Includes.
7. Includes.

8 *a*. Includes all women over 15 years, but thinks exclusions would be preferable.
8 *b*. Not quite decided.
8 *c*. Includes at market price.
8 *d*. Excludes unless measurable at current prices.
9 *a*. Excludes generally, but includes gifts from emigrants to U.S.A.
10 *a*. (i) Excludes.
10 *b*. (iii) Includes pensions.
12. (i) Includes, based on special enquiry.
12. (ii) Excludes when charity.
13. Adds allowances for public servants.
15. Includes.
16. Gives formula.
18. Differentiates only regarding dwellings.
20. Refers only to durable and non-durable goods.
22. At cost.
23 *a*. Gives list of depreciation ratios for buildings and machinery.
23 *b*, *c*, *d*. Calculates it as capital gains or losses which must be debited or credited to the income.
25. Includes.
27. Compares national income inclusive and exclusive of income from buildings and inclusive and exclusive of unpaid work.
30. Gross national income – (services which have been double counted + raw materials and the goods used in the production process) = net national income.
31. Uses cost of living index, and for real investments the best available price index, but is not satisfied.

Entrepreneurial income. Entrepreneurial incomes are the amount by which the exchange value of the productive contribution exceeds the total of the contractual income.

K. Mori

1 *a*. Adheres to it. (See also 1 *b*.)
1 *b*. Adheres to it. (See also 1 *a*.)
7. Includes.
12. (i) Includes; doubles money wages.
28. Multiplies total number of units with estimated average market price.

W. H. Coates

8 *d*. Excludes.
10 *a*. (i) Includes.
10 *b*. Includes.
11 *a*. Includes employers' contributions.
13. Omits as too difficult to find out.

J. R. Hicks

1 *b*. Adheres to it.
19. Saving = income – consumption.
23 *a*. Thinks exact calculation will hardly be possible to match expenditure and consumption.

Alfred Marshall

1 *a*. Adheres to it regarding his main concept, but on account of his treatment of foreign investments may also be counted under 1 *b*.
1 *b*. See also 1 *a*.
8, 8 *a*, *d*. Not reckoned as part of the national dividend, but should be reckoned separately.
9 *b*. Excludes.
10 *a*. Excludes.
23 *a*. Allows for depreciation, but does not specify.
30. The net income is found by deducting the outgoings that belong to its production from gross income.

M. Matolcsy-StVarga

1 *b*. Adheres to it.
2 *a*. Includes.
3. Adds net receipts of state monopolies (Grain Certificate Fund not added).
4. Excludes when objective system applied.
4 *a*. Includes theoretically as immaterial wealth, but thinks itstatistically not approachable.
4 *g*. Includes if paid out of indirect taxation.
6. Includes.
7. Considers it negligible.
8 *a*. Includes.
9 *a*. Includes; also remittances of emigrants.
10 *b*. (iii) Includes, but excludes it from taxes.
11. Makes no distinction.
11 *a*. Includes taxes which tend to raise prices.
12. (i) Includes for farm workers.
14. Excludes.
16. No; on account of statistical difficulties.
18. Differentiates between rural and urban areas.
23 *a*. Deducts 10 per cent from house values.
27. Makes comparison between seven concepts.
31. Valueing has been carried out at current prices, and revaluated in the 1925–26/27 price level.

A. C. Pigou

1 *b*. Adheres to it.
2 *a*. Includes main part.
4. Excludes.
4 *d*. Includes.
6. Includes.
7. Excludes.
8, 8 *a*, *d*. Excludes, but should be accounted for separately. (See Marshall.)
9 *b*. Excludes; also allowances received by children from their parents.
10 *a*. (ii) Excludes.
10 *b*. (iii) Excludes old age pensions, but includes pensions received by civil servants.

11. Makes a distinction between income from public services and income tax and death duties.
16. Yes, with reservations.
23 *a*. Depreciation is made good by the provision of the original money value of new machines.
28. Suggests corrections, but makes no proposal.

A. W. Flux

1 *a*. Adheres to it.
11. Includes only customs and excise duties, but does not deal with direct taxation.
11 *a*. Includes.
21. Wants to include derivative services.
27. Compares factors of production and goods and immaterial services produced.

A. Wagner

1 *b*. Adheres to it. Defines it as the income of a population of a certain area.
4. Includes.
9 *b*. Excludes.
11 *a*. Excludes.
15. Includes.
25. Includes.
31. Computation in one and the same unit seems impossible. (Makes no suggestion.)

3*a*. *OFFICIAL ESTIMATES*

COUNTRIES WITH, AND AUTHOR'S INTERPRETATIONS

Canada

1 *b*. Adheres to it.
2 *b*. Includes.
6. Rental value of owned houses are not included in income-tax returns.
7. Excludes.
8. Excludes.
8 *a*. Excludes.
8 *b*. Excludes.
8 *c*. Only included if persons derive their main livelihood from such activities.
12. (i) Includes.
23. Certain deductions have been made to arrive at the net national income regarding the material consumed in the process of production.
28. The official wholesale price index has been used to compute the real national income.
29. Net income = gross income − deductions connected with the maintenance of the industrial equipment of the country, not only providing for depreciation but also for obsolescence and replacement by new and improved apparatus of production.

Explanatory Notes:

Sources:

Dominion Bureau of Statistics, the *Canada Year Books*, particularly the *Canada Year Book* for 1934/35 giving the national income for 1920–32.

Statistics of service and repair work were not collected after 1922, and to effect comparability, the totals for the year were repeated in 1923 and 1924. The totals for 1925 and 1926 were estimated according to the percentage change in data for manufacturing.

The survey of production does not include transportation, refrigeration and merchandising. Personal and professional services, for instance teachers and doctors, are also not included in the survey.

Germany

1 *b*. Adheres to it.
2 *a*. Includes excise duties.
2 *b*. Includes import duties.
4 *a*, *b*. All expenditure for public services are to be considered at cost.
5. Increments in the value of stocks and shares are included (with certain exceptions).
6. Includes.
7. Excludes.
8. Excludes services rendered to oneself.
8 *a*. Excludes.
8 *b*. Includes.
8 *c*. Includes.
9 *a*. Excludes.
9 *b*. Excludes.
10 *a*. (i) Includes.
10 *b*. (i) Includes unemployment assistance. Also includes contributions of employers towards social insurances.
10 *b*. (iii) Includes pensions (and war pensions); also those paid by the Government and by local authorities to foreigners wherever their domicile may be.
11 *a*. Includes government income from indirect taxation, but deducts cost of services paid out of indirect taxation.
12. (i), (ii) Includes.
14. Includes profits derived from increments in the money value of assets when a firm or corporation is sold or liquidated.
15. Includes.
17 *a*. Savings are included.
22. Advertisement is reckoned as a cost.
23. Depreciation of goods is deducted.
25. Includes.
31. To arrive at real income for 1928 cost of living index is applied.

Explanatory Notes:

Sources:

Einzelschrift zur Statistik des Deutschen Reiches. Nr. 23: *Internationaler Steuerbelastungsvergleich*. Nr. 24: *Das Deutsche Volkseinkommen*.

Statistisches Jahrbuch für das Deutsche Reich, 1936.

Wirtschaft und Statistik, Nr. 22. Das Deutsche Volkseinkommen, 1932.

The definition of income refers to the years 1925 to 1931. That of the *Statistisches Jahrbuch* to the years 1913 and 1927 to 1935.

Payment for 'reparations' resulting from the peace treaty are also included as income.

According to *Wirtschaft und Statistik* the major error in the estimates results from the valuation of agricultural produce consumed by farmers' families, owing to the difficulty of assessment.

The agricultural produce consumed by farmers' families is included at wholesale prices.

National income, spent by the Government on certain public services, are excluded from Germany's official estimates. These items are expenditure for the sole use of the state and for purposes other than production. Thus, for instance, expenditure for road maintenance and for armament, spent out of taxation, are not included [see *Statistisches Reichsamt,* Sonderheft 24]. Up to the year 1933 these items were relatively small, compared with the total national income; later on, however, they became more important, when expenditure for armament etc., spent out of taxation, increased.

JAPAN

1 *b.* Adheres to it.
4. Earnings of public services are included.
7. Excludes.
8. Excludes.
8 *a.* Excludes.
9 *a.* Remittances from nationals abroad are included.
10 *a.* (i) Includes income from Government bonds.
10 *b.* (iii) Pensions and annuities are included.
12. (i) Includes.
25. Income of State undertakings and State properties are included.

Explanatory Notes:

The above refers to the estimate of the national wealth and income of Japan proper (*Bulletin de l'Institut International de Statistique,* 1931) by K. Mori, chief statistician of the Bureau of Statistics in the Imperial Cabinet, Tokyo.

The estimate is for the year 1925.

The estimate includes income entirely evading the income tax. Mori assumes this to be 10 per cent of the total income below the exemption limit.

The above estimate gives little detailed explanation although it is authoritative. It can be supplemented by definitions given by Professor A. Shiomi as follows:

2 *a.* Excludes excise duties from industrial net profit.
2 *b.* Taxes are included.
15. Undistributed profits of corporations are included.
23. Depreciations of plant and equipment are allowed for.

Explanatory Notes:

Sources:

S. Shiomi, 'On Japan's national wealth and income', *Economic Review,* Kyoto University, Vol. IV, No. 1.

S. Shiomi, 'Survey of the distribution of the people's incomes in the light of the household rate', *ibid.* Vol. VIII, No. 1.

'Japan's national income in 1930', *ibid.* Vol. IX, No. 2.

The first two articles refer to the income of the year 1924/25.

NEW ZEALAND

6. Excludes.
7. Excludes.
8. Excludes.
8 *a*. Excludes.
9 *b*. Gifts from parents or relatives are excluded.
10 *b*. Pensions under the Pension Act, superannuations and such like are included.
11 *a*. All forms of public income are excluded.
12. (i) Payment in kind, free housing, etc. is excluded.
12. (ii) Gratuities are included.
15. Undistributed profits of companies (inclusive state taxation) are included.

Explanatory Notes:

Sources:

Dominion of New Zealand Population Census, 1926, Vol. II, Incomes 1930.
New Zealand Official Year Book, 1935.

In the *Population Census* we find the following explanation:

This is not the total private income of the population but only an aggregate derived from Census data in the case of lower incomes and from the statistics of incomes of persons and firms assessable for income-tax purposes in the case of higher incomes.

The income of the Maoris is estimated as being £3 mn.

The *Official Year Book* of 1935 explains:

In the two later estimates, although not in that derived chiefly from the 1926 Census records, certain non-monetary emoluments (e.g. free housing, free fuel and lighting where such are in reality part payments for services) are given a monetary equivalent and treated as income.

1 *a*. National income within the country (outflow to other countries not deducted, nor income added coming to New Zealand).
6. Includes owner-occupied dwellings.
7. Excludes.
8. Excludes.
8 *a*. Excludes.
10 *a*. (i) Includes income from Government debts.
10 *a*. (ii) Excludes interest on war loans.
10 *b*. (iii) Excludes pensions.
15. Includes undistributed profits.
17 *a*. Includes savings of companies in the form of reserves.
25. Includes profits of municipal State trading services of clubs and charitable societies.
30. Net income = total income − war loan interests and pensions.

Explanatory Notes:

The above estimate refers to F. B. Stephens (Department of Internal Affairs, Wellington), *National Income of New Zealand*, 1937, reprinted from the *Economic Review*, 1936.

The estimate does not deal with incomes awaiting income tax.

The income estimate for farming is 'rough', according to the author's explanation.

Two-thirds of the interest on the national debt are State trading ventures.

U.S.A. Department of Commerce

1 *b*. Adheres to it. (See Kuznets.)
4 *a*. Includes. (Gives no detail.)
6. Excludes.
7. Excludes.
8. Excludes. Thinks there is no satisfactory basis.
8 *a*. Excludes. Thinks there is no satisfactory basis.
9 *b*. Excludes.
10 *a*. (i) Excludes.
10 *b*. (i) Includes.
10 *b*. (iii) Excludes.
12. (ii) Excludes.
14. Excludes. Exception, professional dealers in assets whose profits and losses are held to measure the compensation for their services.
17. Public insurance treated as transfer of income.
19. When income produced exceeds income paid out, the business enterprises of the nation retain the residual portion of the net product, which is termed 'positive business savings'.
30. Income produced is derived by adding positive business savings to, or deducting negative business savings from, income paid out (except for agriculture).
31. Price index of finished products for gross product of industry, cost of living index for income paid out.

Entrepreneurial income. Net rent royalties and entrepreneurial withdrawals are entrepreneurial income payments.

3*b*. *SEMI-OFFICIAL ESTIMATES*

COUNTRIES WHERE INFORMATION IS INDEFINITE

Australia

1 *b*. Uses income method.
6. Includes 5 per cent of capital value, less repair and maintenance.
7. Excludes.
10 *b*. (i), (ii), (iii) Includes pensions and superannuation, but excludes Commonwealth old age pensions and invalid pensions. Excludes also retiring gratuity.
5. Includes undistributed profits.
25. Includes income of institutions, as churches, schools, literary institutes and sports clubs, and gives the total estimate for these items as £600,000.

Explanatory Notes:

The above refers to G. H. Knibbs, *The Private Wealth of Australia and its Growth*, published under the direction of the Commonwealth Bureau of Census and Statistics in 1918. The material is based on the war census of 30 June 1915. There is an income estimate for Australia by Colin Clark and G. Grawford, *National Income of Australia* for the years 1901–3, 1914–15 up to 1937/38. It refers to real national income at 1923–27 prices.

1 *b*. Refers to income of residents.
2. Includes indirect taxation.
4. Includes salaries of civil servants.

6. Includes.
7. Excludes.
10 *a*. (i) Interest of national debt paid in Australia is deducted so as to avoid double counting.
10 *a*. (ii) War debt interest is excluded, as transfer.
15. Includes undistributed profits of companies.
27. Gives two methods: (1) income produced, (2) income available.[1]

BELGIUM

1 *b*. Adheres to it. (Income method.)
2. Land tax is included.
4. Salaries of officials are included.
6. Includes.
7. Excludes.
10 *a*. (i) Includes income of state loans.
15. Includes undistributed profits of limited and public companies.

Explanatory Notes:

The estimate refers to Fernand Baudouin, 'Le revenu national en 1930', *Bulletin d'information et de documentation, banc national de Belgique*, Vol. v, No. 10, and F. Baudouin, 'Les finances Belges en 1937', *Bulletin de l'institut de recherches économiques*, 1937/38.

The latter publication gives estimates for the years 1934, 1936 and 1937.

BRITISH INDIA

1 *b*. Adheres to it; but owing to the lack of statistics uses a mixture of inventory and income method.
2 *a*. Includes excise duties.
2 *b*. Includes import duties.
6. Includes houses occupied by owners. As rental value of huts in villages Rupees 6 is taken; most of the houses in villages are, according to the author, hovels and command no rental value.
8. Excludes value of services rendered to oneself.
8 *a*. Includes services rendered by dependants.
10 *a*. (i) Includes, but deducts part of the debt used for unproductive purposes.
10 *b*. (iii) Includes pensions.
11 *a*. Includes.
23. Deducts depreciation of goods.

Explanatory Notes:

Sources:

The estimate is computed by V. K. R. V. Rao, 1940. The estimate refers to 1931/32.

As the nature of Indian statistics is inadequate, the available official statistics have been supplemented by the results of enquiries.

1 Available income is equal to income produced less amount payable overseas as interest or dividends on public or private account, plus the (considerably smaller) sums drawn by Australian interest or dividends from capital invested overseas.

The income of urban and rural unskilled workers is reckoned under the assumption that the income of two males equals the income of three females.

Four working dependants are assumed to have the same income as one principal earner; and three part-time workers (subsidiary workers) the same as one principal worker.

The estimate of the income of earners engaged in professions and liberal arts is full of pitfalls, of which the author himself is aware.

The estimate per capita income of 206,000 people occupied in letters, arts and science comprises 16,000 who were horoscope casters, astrologers, fortune-tellers, wizards, witches and medicine men and 14,000 conjurers, acrobats, reciters and exhibitors of curiosities and wild animals.

France

1 *b*. Adheres to it.
2 *b*. Includes.
4 *g*. Valued at salary cost.
6. Includes.
7. Excludes.
8 *a*. Excludes unpaid domestic services.
10 *a*. (i) Includes.
10 *b*. (iii) Includes pensions in national income, but excludes it in 'social income'.
12. (i) Includes food for domestic servants, but excludes lodging and tips.
17. Insurance for fire accidents at work, etc. has to be deducted, also special insurances for the harvest and stock, in order to arrive at the gross production of agriculture.
30. Net agricultural production = gross production − general expenses and − seed.
31. Real income is computed by using cost of living index.

Explanatory Notes:

The above refers to *La population de la France pendant la guerre avec un appendice sur les revenus privés avant et après la guerre*, by Michel Huber, director of the Statistique générale de la France.

Sources:

This estimate is based on Revenus du travail des ouvriers industrielles et agricoles (La statistique générale de la France). Published for 1911 and 1921 and every year since 1924 in October.

Les contributions directes pour l'établissement de l'impôt foncier, publiés par l'administration.

Salaire des employés de commerce: Tribune des employés; Salaire des domestiques: des enquêtes de la statistique générale de la France.

Salaire de chemin de fer: la Statistique officielle des chemins de fer français.

Huber computes the total of 'revenus privés' for the years 1913 and 1920–28. This total he calls 'conception fiscale'.

Furthermore, he computes 'social national income' in the sense as employed by Bowley-Stamp. Social income = total income − interest of state loans and − war pensions.

Two other estimates for France are by Dugé de Bernonville, 'Les revenus privés' and 'Les revenus privés et les consommations', *Revue d'économie politique*, 1933 and 1935.

Dugé de Bernonville is Sous-directeur à la Statistique générale de la France. His first estimate refers to 1913 and 1920–32, his second refers to 1913 and 1920–34. The estimate of 1913 refers to the pre-war territory of France and from 1920 onwards to the post-war territory. His definition, although less complete, tallies with that of M. Huber.

France

1 *a*. Adheres to it.
2 *a*. Includes excise duties.
2 *b*. Includes import duties.
4. Includes salaries of officials.
6. Includes annual value of owned houses.
7. Excludes.
8. Excludes.
8 *a*. Excludes.
8 *b*. Excludes.
8 *c*. Excludes.
10 *b*. Includes pensions.
12. (i) Includes board and lodging and calculates lodging as 10 per cent of the money wage, but lodging for farm labourers is excluded.
15. Excludes undistributed profits of limited companies.
31. Thinks that index figures could be used to arrive at real income but only uses food indices to compare income of 1903 with income of 1911.

Explanatory Notes:

The estimate refers to René Pupin, *La Richess de la France*, 1916. The estimate is for the year 1911.

There were 4·8 mn. farmers in 1911. Their consumption together with that of their families of farm products is given as 3,500,000,000 francs. This amount is excluded, as pointed out in 8*c*.

Greece

1 *b*. Adheres to it.
4. Public services are included.
7. Excludes.
9 *a*. Includes remittance from emigrants.
10 *a*. (i) Includes interest on public loans.
10 *b*. Includes pensions.
27. Apart from the estimate of commodities produced and services rendered there is also an estimate of the consumption of commodities by the Greek people.

Explanatory Notes:

The estimate refers to Pericles D. Rediades, 'The Greek National Income and Wealth in 1929', *Metron*, 1930. The estimate of the income of industry is based on the figures of the Ministry of National Economy for 1928. The income from houses is based on taxation figures on income from houses.

Hungary

1 *b*. Adheres to it. Defines 'pure' national income = total − interest of debts to foreign countries.
6. Excludes.
7. Excludes.
6 and 7 are not considered to be income, but derived from wealth.
8. Excludes.
8 *a*. Excludes. Gives figures for it separately, but does not add it.

Explanatory Notes:

F. v. Fellner, *Das Volkseinkommen Oesterreichs und Ungarns*, 1917.

Personal services (doctors, lawyers, clergy, teachers, judges, officials, etc.) are not considered to be elements of national income. Figures are given for it but not added to national income.

Source:

Many data are taken from the *Statistical Year Book for Hungary*.

Fellner also gives an estimate for Austria and uses the same method.

Irish Free State

1 *b*. Adheres to it. (Income method.)
4. Cost of public administration is included.
6. Includes.
7. Excludes.
8 *a*. Excludes.
9 *a*. Includes remittances from emigrants.
9 *b*. Excludes charitable gifts.
10 *b*. Pensions to army, police and civil officers are included; old age pensions are excluded as transfers.
12. (ii) Excludes.
17 *a*. Insurance premiums paid to companies abroad are included in the gross total but excluded in the net total.
30. Net income = gross income − assurance premiums paid to companies abroad and − profits remitted abroad.

Explanatory Notes:

The estimate refers to T. I. Kiernan, *National Income of the Irish Free State.*

The material is based on the Census of Industrial Production of 1926 and 1929.

The evasion of income tax, the author suggests, can be estimated to amount to 4 per cent of the income of Schedules C and D combined.

The remittances from emigrants for 1926 are assumed to amount to £3 mn.

Pensions paid by the United Kingdom to Irish Free State residents (ex-soldiers) are included. And pensions paid by the Irish Free State to residents in the United Kingdom are deducted.

Italy

1 *b*. Adheres to it.
6. Includes income from urban buildings.
7. Excludes.

8. Excludes.
8 *a.* Excludes.
9 *a.* Includes remittance from emigrants.
10 *a.* (i) Includes interest from Government debts.

Explanatory Notes:

The estimate is by Conrado Gini, *A Comparison of the Wealth and National Income of Several Important Nations before and after the War*, 1925. In former publications by Gini (see list of references and Gini's answers in our list of the principal authors) he answers 8 and 8*a* differently, 'should be included'.

See also Leonardo Meliadó, *Il reddito privato degli Italiani, nel* 1928.

New South Wales

1 *a.* (i) Net income of resident individuals and also (ii) income accruing to absentees (*a*) from private investment and property and (*b*) from investment in Government loans.
10 *a.* (i) Includes interest from Government loans.
10 *b.* (iii) Includes old age pensions and invalid and war pensions.
15. Includes undistributed income of local companies.
31. Existing data as to price levels are insufficient to enable a satisfactory measure of comparison.

Explanatory Notes:

Source:

The *Official Year Book of New South Wales* (1936/37).

Appreciable amounts of income derived by various Governments from State lands, forests, and mines, and from Governmental business enterprises are excluded from account.

Spain

2 *a*, *b*. Import and excise duties are included (the revenue due to the Government on tobacco is deducted from the income of the tobacco industry).
6. Includes. Takes 4 per cent of the value of houses as rent.
7. Excludes.
8. Excludes.
8 *a.* Excludes.
10 *a.* (i) Interest from internal debts of Government and municipalities only are included.
30. Net income = gross income − the debit of balance of payments.

Explanatory Notes:

The above reference refers to the estimate of José A. Vandellós, 'La richesse et le revenu de la Péninsule Ibérique', *Metron*, 1925. It refers to the year 1913.

The income of trade is taken as 20 per cent of the income of agriculture and mines and 30 per cent of the industrial production.

The second estimate is given for the year 1923. This is obtained by a rough estimate that the value of production increased from 1913 to 1923 in the ratio 100 : 225.

Sweden

In the *National Income of Sweden*, by Erik Lindahl, Vol. 1, p. 318, there is a table of the national income of Sweden for the years 1930–34, giving an estimate which has been made in the Department of Finance. It should, therefore, be considered as an official estimate.

Lindahl points out that for this estimate the same method was employed for the main part as was used by the Institute. Lindahl says the method differs only in one or two points, but he does not mention the points in question. But this difference in method has caused a difference of about 700 mn. kronor, or 8 per cent[1] between the two estimates for the year 1930. In considering these figures allowance must be made for the net contribution of certain industries having, in this calculation, been assumed to be constant throughout the period. Nor has, in this calculation or in that of the Institute, any allowance been made for changes in the stocks, which in some industries were of importance during these years.

The estimate gives figures for gross income as well as for net income.

Soviet Russia

The estimate of the national income for the U.S.S.R. excludes personal services, also domestic services and professional services.

It excludes services performed by public authorities. It excludes rents of dwellings, and finally it excludes non-productive services.

This refers to the *U.S.S.R. Handbook*, London, 1936. It is pointed out in the preface: 'This book has been compiled from the latest information received from the U.S.S.R. and our special thanks are due to the following distinguished Soviet scientists and writers, who have kindly supplied the material for the present volume (here thirty-two names are quoted).'

The estimate gives the national income in 1926–27 prices. The share of the socialized sector of national economy in the national income since 1928 is shown in the following table:

Percentage of National Income

1928	44
1929	56
1930	74·3
1931	90
1932	93
1933	95
1934	96
1935	97·5

(See also Colin Clark, *A Critique of Russian Statistics*, 1939.)

Switzerland

1 *b*. Income method used includes income of Swiss capital abroad.

4. Includes salaries of officials.

6. Excludes income of houses where the owner is the sole occupier, because there is no revenue from such property.

1 Compared with Lindahl's *National Income of Sweden*, alternative 2, Vol. 1, p. 237.

8. Excludes.
8 *a*. Excludes.
8 *c*. Includes farmers' consumption of agricultural produce.
10 *a*. (i) Includes loans of the State, Cantons and Municipalities.
10 *b*. (iii) Excludes pensions.
15. Excludes undistributed profits.
12. (i) Includes cost and lodging in return for services rendered.

Explanatory Notes:

This estimate is by P. Mori (Berne), 'Das Schweizerische Volkseinkommen', *Zeitschrift für Schweizerische Statistisk und Volkswirtschaft*, 1926.

The estimate refers to the years 1913 and 1924. The method for 1913 differs from that of 1924 in so far as the incomes of institutions are omitted in the estimate for 1913.

Union of South Africa

1 *b*. Adheres to it. (All goods and services produced.)
4. Includes Government services.
6. Houses owned by farmers included, as it is part of national income.* The rent of farm houses for the year ending 30 June 1918 is estimated at £13 mn. (The value of farm houses = £162 mn.)
7. Excludes.
8. Excludes.
8 *a*. Excludes.
23. Takes 2 per cent depreciation allowances on the value of buildings including land, and 6 per cent on plant and machinery; for other deductions £1 mn. is allowed.

Explanatory Notes:

Estimate is made by R. A. Lehfeldt, *The National Resources of South Africa*, 1922. It relates to the national income for the year 30 June 1917 until 30 June 1918.

Nearly all interest on capital invested in railways was payable to bondholders abroad. Incomes therefore, derived by South Africa from railways, consisted chiefly of salaries and wages.

Another estimate was made by S. Herbert Frankel and S. D. Neumark, 'Note on the National Income of the Union of South Africa', *The South African Journal of Economics*, 1940.

1 *b*. Adheres to it.
4. Includes public services.
6. Includes.
10 *b*. Includes Union Government contribution to pension funds as well as the pensions.

Explanatory Notes:

This estimate refers to the years 1927/28, and 1932/33 and 1934/35. No allowance is made for amounts payable overseas as interest or dividends on public or private account or sums drawn on by South Africans from investment or income outside the Union.

* 7 to 8 per cent of the valuation of houses are considered as an average imputed rental for urban and rural districts. Most of the houses, occupied by the owners, have no recorded rent.

UNITED STATES OF AMERICA

6. Includes owned houses.
7. Gives alternative estimates: (*a*) including imputed income from durable consumable commodities, valued at 6 per cent of the market value, and (*b*) excluding imputed income from this item (apart from residential property).
8. Excludes services rendered to oneself or to one's family.
8 *a*. Excludes domestic services rendered by wives.
8 *c*. Includes farm products used by owner, valued at the average price at a given date.
10 *b*. Includes pensions.
12. (i) Includes income in kind.
17. Includes compensation for injuries.
27. Gives two kinds of estimates (see 7 above).
31. Five different price indices used for different classes of the population: (*a*) urban manual and clerical workers, (*b*) farm labourers, (*c*) farmers, (*d*) families spending for direct goods, $5,000 annually, (*e*) families spending for direct goods, $25,000 annually.

Explanatory Notes:

The estimate refers to W. I. King, *The National Income and its Purchasing Power*, published by the National Bureau of Economic Research, 1930. It refers to the income for the years 1909–28. It also gives an estimate for the same years but in terms of dollars' purchasing power of 1913.

He excludes income from odd jobs, that is to say, jobs outside regular duties. The term 'realized income' which he uses is applied only to the income of individuals and not to that of business enterprises.

See also W. I. King, *The Wealth and Income of the People of the United States*, 1915. In this book he uses the wholesale index to arrive at real income. This estimate is based on the United States Census. The 1850–60 Census did not include slaves as persons, therefore the income per capita = output of free men.

3*c*. *OFFICIAL PUBLICATIONS*

UNITED KINGDOM

HOW BRITISH AUTHORITIES DEAL WITH THE QUESTIONS WITH WHICH THEY ARE CONCERNED

Reports of the Commissioners of H.M.'s Inland Revenue
Reports on the Censuses of Production

Agricultural Statistics.

1 *b*. Adheres to it.

Inland Revenue Report divides incomes from abroad to British residents into three groups:

Group I. Dominion and foreign interests and dividends paid through paying agents in this country or received by encashment of coupons through bankers, etc. in this country.

Group II. Income arising from business controlled in this country but mainly carried on abroad and with assets situated abroad, interest and dividends payable abroad (not included in Group I) and income from other foreign possessions.

Group III. Income arising from trading operations carried on abroad by British concerns trading mainly at home but partly abroad.

The Inland Revenue Report points out that Group I is identifiable; Group II is in part identifiable; Group III cannot be identified. The Inland Revenue Report, 1930, explains: '...the following estimates of the actual income of this group (i.e. Group II) as distinct from the statutory income as assessed have been made for the last nine years:

	Actual income in £000,000
1920/21	124
21/22	70
22/23	70·5
23/24	93·5
24/25	96·5
25/26	120
26/27	135
27/28	130
28/29	130

It should be borne in mind that these estimates, which are based on annual samples of representative cases, may be subject to an appreciable margin of error, and that they include income arising abroad which, although chargeable to tax here, may not be remitted to this country.' Group III is included in assessed income and in taxed income.

2*a*. Excise duties are excluded in aggregate income method but are included in inventory method.

2*b*. The same applies to import duties.

Totals from the Census of Production in £mn.

	Net Excise (Finance Accounts)	Net Customs (Finance Accounts)		Total Net Output of large firms (Finance Accounts)*
1923/24	126·0	90·4	1924	1,548·6
1929/30	15·3	94·1	1930	1,505·2
1934/35	89·8	126·5	1935	1,599·5

* Excluding laundry and excise customs, but including subsidies.[1]

1 Subsidies in £mn.

1923/24	15·4
1929/30	27·9
1934/35	28·6

They include coal-mining, sugar and road funds.

4*g*. Salaries of State officials are included in Tax Schedule E. They amounted in the year 1926/27 to 9·5 per cent of the gross income (arising out of Tax Schedule E), and 7·2 per cent for the year 1937/38.

5. Change in value of stocks and shares is, as a rule, not taken into consideration; except as part of profits of professional dealers.

6. The value for services of houses, occupied by owners, is included. Property vested in, and in occupation of, the Crown, cathedrals and churches, etc. is not subjected to valuation of income tax under Tax Schedule A.

Farm houses of an annual value of £20 and upwards which are occupied by persons other than tenant farmers or their farm servants are included as houses; other farm houses are assessed under 'lands, etc.'

7. The value for services of other durable consumers' goods (not houses) is excluded.

8. The value of services rendered to oneself or one's family is excluded.

8*a*. Domestic services rendered by wives are excluded.

8*b*. The produce of gardens and allotments is estimated in some accounts of the Censuses of Production, but is excluded from the usual agricultural statistics.

According to the report on the work of the land division in the year 1936 (quoted by the Agricultural Register for 1937/38, Oxford, 1938), the Ministry of Agriculture and Fisheries points out: after making due allowance for four authorities who failed to make a return, it is estimated that the total number of allotments in urban areas in England and Wales at the end of year 1936, excluding railway allotments, was 606,000, covering an area of 59,250 acres. In 1934 railway allotments amounted to 75,887 plots on 4,677 acres both in urban and rural areas.

8*c*. Produce of farms consumed by farmers' families are included implicitly in Tax Schedule B, as profit from the occupation of land is equal to the annual value, with certain exceptions, since 1924/25. Formerly they were reckoned to be equal to one-third of the rent. In the Census of Agricultural Production allowance is made for produce consumed on the farms.

9*a*. Gifts from or to persons in other countries are excluded. Gifts may be included in balance of payments.

9*b*. Gifts between individuals within the country are excluded; but they are subject to death duty if a certain period has not elapsed.

10*a*. (i) Income from Government loans is included.

10*a*. (ii) Income from war loans is also included.

10*b*. (i) Pensions and amenities are included.

10*b*. (iii) Voluntary pensions are included as well as war pensions.

10*b*. (iv) (1) Contribution out of salary in the case of University teachers, etc. is counted as income. Its addition by employers is not counted as income.

10*b*. (iv) (2) After their employment has ended recipients have the choice whether to receive a capital sum or annuity. Annuities are treated by the income-tax authorities as income. It goes without saying that interest on capital sums is taxed.[1]

10*b*. (v) Income out of annuities is counted as income.

11. In the case of the road fund in its early years, and possibly other cases, distinction is made between Government expenditure from direct or indirect taxation; excluding cases where Central or Local Government collects payments for services rendered.[2]

11*a*. See answer to Question 2*a* and 2*b*.

12. (i) On the whole, board and lodging, provided by the employer and which cannot be exchanged into money by the employee, is not taxed and is therefore not included in the income-tax assessment. Where, on the other hand, the terms of employment stipulates that the salary is paid gross, less deduction for board or lodging (e.g. a teacher at a boarding school), the assessment is based on the gross amount.

A house occupied rent free is assessed under Schedule A on the annual value.

12. (ii) Income in kind, when charity, is not included as income.

14. See No. 23.

15. Undistributed profits are included.

1 This is a case of double taxation (see C. W. Guillebaud, 'Income Tax and the Double Taxation of Saving', *Economic Journal*, 1935).

2 Such as B.B.C.

16. No allowance is made for the destruction of irreplaceable commodities; for instance, the products of mines.

17*a*. Savings are included in actual income, but, in some cases, income tax is reduced.

18. No allowance is made for different costs of living in different parts of the country.

20, 21. In the Report on the Census of Production (Cd. 6320, pp. 21–34)[1] the national income is estimated by adding up the value of goods produced, services and net imports. The following table shows the various items, which are admittedly only approximate:

Income, 1907

	£mn.
Gross output of industry, mining, and agriculture, excluding duplicates, but including imported materials to value of £380 mn.	1,370
Carriage, merchanting and retailing of home goods	430
Duties on home goods	50
Imports ready for consumption, valued at ports	220
Duties on carriage, merchanting and retailing of imports ...	140
	2,210
Subtract exports	465
Total value to purchasers of material goods available for consumption, maintenance of capital or saving	1,745
Subtract maintenance of plant, etc. (£175 mn.) and of consumers' stock (£15 mn.)	190
Remainder, available for consumption or saving	1,555
Add value of personal services and occupation of houses ...	375
Add new investments abroad	100
Total income ...	2,030

Consumption and Saving, 1907

	£mn.
Personal consumption: Material goods	1,325
Services and houses	375
	1,700
Additions to capital and stock at home	230
Additions to investments abroad	100
Total	2,030

See also Chapter III, passim.

22. Advertisement is treated as a cost.

23. Depreciation of goods is deducted from 'gross total national income' to arrive at 'actual' national income (see No. 29). Deduction for wear and tear amounted in 1926/27

1 Quoted from *The Division of the Product of Industry*, 1919, by A. L. Bowley (Appendix, p. 59). The figures were rearranged from the Final Report on the Census of Production, 1907.

to 5·3 per cent of total gross income, and 10·4 per cent in 1937/38 of total gross income from profits, pensions and professions, etc. (Schedule D).

Flux estimated and subtracted in the Report of Census of Production for 1937 for maintenance of plant, £175 mn., and of consumers' stock £15 mn., in all £190 mn. That is roughly 11 per cent of the total value to purchasers of material goods available for consumption, maintenance of capital or savings of £1,745 mn.

The income tax authorities have to make allowances for the wear and tear of plant and machinery used in trade and industries. In most cases the allowance is made in the form of a certain percentage of the value of plant and machinery employed in business. Any costs of repairs incurred will generally be allowed as an expense of the firm.

The usual method followed is the annual allowance of wear and tear, but there are cases in which allowance is given in a lump sum. Such a renewal allowance is granted in certain cases, when old plant is scrapped and replaced by new. (Renewal allowances are given for certain plants and machinery used by the railway companies.) Where such an allowance is given by way of renewals it does not appear in the wear and tear figures of the Census and it is a deduction in computing the profits.

See also Nos. 21 and 22.

24. Government expenditure can be divided into expenditure on goods and services and transfer expenditure. The division of Government expenditure on goods and services into services rendered to entrepreneurs and consumers has not been made.

25. Incomes of societies and other bodies are included, but co-operative trading income is excluded. The incomes of charities and friendly societies, schools, colleges and hospitals are included in gross income, but deducted so as to arrive at taxable income.

There are some charities in receipt of profits from trading activities (e.g. schools) which would be normally assessed under Schedule D. Such profits would, however, not be assessed if the statutory conditions as to exemption were fulfilled.

H. Campion points out in *Public and Private Property in Great Britain*, 1938 (Chapter: Public Property not assessed for income tax): 'Government securities held by charities and Government departments can be readily valued, and real property and certain kinds of trading undertakings can be capitalized on approximately the same bases as if under private ownership. There are, however, no satisfactory methods of valuing certain kinds of the property of state and local authorities not yielding money income. While, it is true, as Sir Robert Giffen stated, "there is no property which ought more properly" to be taken into account, it is difficult to find an adequate basis of valuation, and we have been compelled to omit roads and armaments from our estimates of public property on that account.'

Lord Stamp has estimated the value of the property of the State and local authorities not covered by assessments for income tax at £900–1,500 mn. in 1928 and £1,050–1,650 mn. in 1930 for Great Britain and Northern Ireland.

In regard to charities H. Campion points out (p. 100): 'The total number of endowed charities in England and Wales under the supervision of the charity commissioners and the Board of Education is estimated at approximately 90,000.[1] While this number includes educational charities and the charities of the London livery companies, it does not include the Ecclesiastical Commissioners or Universities which are recognized for income-tax purposes. Endowed charities are those entitled to property, real or personal, the capital of which is settled upon permanent trusts and the income only from such capital applicable for charitable purposes....'

No details are available of the aggregate investment of Universities, but according to the Reports of the Universities Grants Committee, the income of Universities (excluding the colleges of Oxford and Cambridge) from Government and other securities has amounted to nearly £1 mn. per annum in recent years.

26. No attempt has been made by British authorities to sum up expenditure on particular commodities to derive a figure for national income.

27. No comparison of inventory and aggregate method has been made by the authorities.

29. There is complete division as far as surtax is concerned. Earlier information gives account of exemption and abatement.

1 Annual Reports of the Charity Commissioners for England and Wales and Report of the Home Office Departmental Committee on the Supervision of Charities (Cmd. 2823, 1927).

In the 36th Report of the Commissioner of H.M. Inland Revenue, for the year ended 31 March 1920, it is pointed out: 'At the request of the Royal Commission on the Income Tax an estimate was prepared, showing for the year 1918/19 the approximate distribution for the estimated amounts of taxable incomes, allowances, etc., among tax-payers, classified according to the amounts of their total incomes in each class.'

The income dealt with is income as computed for purposes of income tax and is, therefore, in part computed by reference to the income of the year and in part by reference to the income of the preceding year or of an average of preceding years. The income dealt with does not therefore correspond with the actual income of tax-payers for the year. A table follows with income classes of £130–160, £160 and over, £200 and over and £300 and over, etc. This table excludes non-personal income and income accruing to non-residents, estimated at £230 mn.

30. According to the Report of the Commissioner of Inland Revenue four definitions are applied:

1. Gross income means income before adjustments are made in respect to lands, houses, etc., empty property, wear and tear of machinery, overcharges in assessment, etc. It includes certain income belonging to individuals whose total income is below the effective exemption limit.

2. Actual income means the statutory income of the tax-payer, estimated in accordance with the provisions of the income-tax Acts, after deduction of the income of the individuals below the effective exemption limit and of the adjustments referred to under the definition of gross income.

3. Assessable income is the actual income less the earned income allowance or, in the case of a person aged 65 years and upwards, the age allowance granted by section 15 of the Finance Act, 1925.

4. Taxable income represents that part of assessable income upon which income tax is actually calculated. It is thus the assessable income less the personal allowances and deductions.

The Census of Production (Final Report, 1935, part 3) gives the following explanation:

Valuation of gross output equals selling value of all goods manufactured in the year, whether sold or not.

Net output results from the deduction of the aggregate costs of materials and fuel used and the amount paid for work given out from the total value of the gross output, minus allowance of depreciation of plant and machinery.

Net value was defined as the actual amount charged to customers after deduction of discounts and payments to railway companies and other transport undertakings for carriage outwards.

The White Paper entitled 'An Analysis of the Sources of War Finance and Estimate of the National Income and Expenditure in 1938 and 1940 (Cmd. 6261), April 1941' gives for the first time an official estimate of National Income from the Income (as contrasted with the Production) aspect.

In the great majority of cases the answers to the questionnaire based on this paper would be the same as in the preceding pages, but the classification is different from that of the Inland Revenue Reports and is brought into line with that of Table IX, Chapter II below. The exact relationship between these two accounts is discussed on p. 84.

Besides estimates of income the White Paper analyses expenditure and saving.

The essential statistics can be arranged as follows:

National Income, 1938, *£mn.*

1. Rents	352	Total I	4,415
2. Profits and interest	1,178	Add:	
3. Salaries	980	7. National Debt interest, Old Age Pensions, Insurance Benefits	490
4. Wages	1,820	Deduct:	
5. Other Income	85	8. Direct tax liabilities	−492
6. Total I	4,415	9. Undistributed profits, Investment income of charities, miscellaneous Government income	−265
		10. Total II	4,148

No. 2 includes National Defence Contributions and Excess Profits Tax, but excludes income due to foreigners and National Debt interest. The former are subtracted under No. 8, the last is added in No. 7.

Total I is then comparable with Total B, Table IX, p. 81 below.

Total II is then the aggregate of personal incomes (after deduction of direct tax liabilities), and is available for personal expenditure and savings.

The expenditure table is in two parts, corresponding to Totals II and I.

Expenditure in 1938, *£mn.*

Food, drink, tobacco	1,648
Rents, rates, fuel, light, domestic services, household goods	959
Clothing and laundry	469
Private motors	118
Other travel	169
Other goods and services	634
Total personal expenditure at market prices	3,997
Balance: gross personal savings	151
Total II	4,148

Personal expenditure	3,997
Central and Local Government expenditure	849
Deduct indirect taxes, rates, etc.	−643
Balance, net investment at home and abroad	212
Total I	4,415

Depreciation and repairs are allowed for in lines 1 and 2 of the first table.

Indirect taxes are not counted as income in Total I in the first table, but since they are part of personal expenditure they are deductive from Total II in the second table to obtain Total I.

Notes are given in the White Paper which explain the contents of the various items more in detail.

A similar White Paper (Cmd. 6347) was issued in April 1942. The table on p. 52 (opposite) was modified by distributing item 5 among other items and by a new treatment of allowance for change in value of stock (see p. 121 below); with other minor unexplained revisions the Total I becomes £4,595 mn. instead of £4,415 mn.

Addendum

U.S.A. Kuznets, *National Income and its composition*, 1919–38 (National Bureau of Economic Research, 1941).

The same definitions are used as in 1937 (see pp. 28, 29 above), but, owing to a revised treatment of 'net savings' and other revisions due to additional data, the totals are modified. In Volume II there are detailed comparisons, both of definition and of estimates, with the Department of Commerce's and W. I. King's accounts (pp. 36, 44 above).

Chapter II[1]

SOME CONSTITUENTS OF THE NATIONAL INCOME

1. *MONEY INCOME*, 1924 TO 1938

THE NUMBER OF 'PERSONS GAINFULLY OCCUPIED'

The Population Censuses of Great Britain show in considerable detail the numbers of persons classed as gainfully occupied at the Census dates. For intermediate years it is necessary to estimate them by interpolation and hypothesis.

The procedure adopted is to take the Registrar-Generals' estimates of numbers of all persons and their age and sex distribution each year, and apply to each grade the percentage of occupied to all recorded for the year 1931. In Table I it is seen that there have been significant changes in some of these percentages in recent decades, and it is interesting to speculate on their causes. For boys under 18 years, and especially under 16 years, the percentage has diminished, it may be hoped for the reason that more continue their education or training after 16 years. On the other hand, for girls and young women in the grades up to 25 years the percentages occupied have increased, presumably a transfer from 'helping mother' to paid work. In other age-groups below 65 years for males and 55 years for females there has been little change. In the higher age-groups for females the reduction (at least between 1911 and 1921) is due to lower employment of married women and widows. For males the reduction is only since 1921; this is possibly due to old age pensions, possibly to greater reluctance to employ elderly men, possibly to changes in age-grouping within the grades. These changes apply to the relatively less important age-groups, while in the central grades, which include the bulk of the occupied population, the changes have been small, and

1 This chapter is a reprint of an Address to the Royal Statistical Society, 18 June 1940, with some minor additions and corrections which incorporate more recent information.

smaller for the numerically more important males than for females.

The age-grouping in respect of occupation is not the same under 25 years as that in the Registrars' Annual Estimates, and adjusted percentages have been used as shown in the lower part of Table I.

The Census of Northern Ireland has not been taken at the same dates or in the same detail as that of Great Britain, but some estimate is available every year. The numbers computed as occupied in Great Britain have been raised year by year by a fraction, falling from 1·0288 in 1924 to 1·0277 in 1931 and rising a little after 1931.

Table I

Occupied Persons as Percentage of all Persons

Great Britain

Age	Males				Females			
	1911	1921	1921	1931	1911	1921	1921	1931
14–	72·8	64·8	64·8	63·2	47·8	44·7	44·7	50·6
16–	92·0	91·5	91·5	89·8	69·4	71·2	71·2	75·6
18–	96·8	96·8	96·8	96·6	65·4	66·5	66·5	70·9
25–	98·5	97·9	97·9	98·4	29·3	28·4	33·6	36·5
35–			97·8	98·2			22·8	24·4
45–	94·1	94·9	96·8	96·7	21·6	20·1	20·8	21·0
55–			90·8	91·2			19·2	17·7
65–	56·9	59·0	79·8	65·4	11·5	10·0	15·2	12·2
70–			40·2	33·4			6·5	5·5
Aggregate 14–	92·7	91·8	91·8	90·5	35·4	33·7	33·7	34·2

Computed from the 22nd *Abs. of Lab. Stat.* pp. 2–3.

Percentages Applied to Annual Estimates of Population to Approximate to Number Occupied

Age-group	Males	Females
14–	51·6	40·0
15–	92·3	70·6
25–	98·4	36·5
35–	98·2	24·4
45–	96·7	21·0
55–	91·2	17·7
65–	47·9	8·2

TABLE II

	Estimated Numbers of Occupied Persons (0000's *omitted*) Great Britain and Northern Ireland			*Estimated Numbers of Wage-Earners* (0000's *omitted*) Great Britain and Northern Ireland		
Year	Males	Females	Total	Males	Females	Total
1921	1,401	583	1,984	1,068	401	1,469
1924	1,413	627	2,040	1,060	429	1,489
1925	1,426	630	2,056	1,068	431	1,499
1926	1,438	632	2,070	1,075	431	1,506
1927	1,456	635	2,091	1,086	434	1,520
1928	1,467	637	2,104	1,092	434	1,526
1929	1,481	641	2,122	1,100	437	1,537
1930	1,495	642	2,137	1,109	437	1,546
1931	1,519	643	2,162	1,124	437	1,561
1932	1,537	642	2,179	1,135	436	1,571
1933	1,543	638	2,181	1,137	432	1,569
1934	1,549	633	2,182	1,139	429	1,568
1935	1,569	639	2,208	1,152	433	1,585
1936	1,587	645	2,232	1,163	436	1,599
1937	1,595	647	2,242	1,166	437	1,603
1938	1,613	653	2,266	1,177	441	1,618

Estimated Distribution by Age of Occupied Persons

Great Britain and Northern Ireland

Age-group	Males			Females		
	1924	1931	1938	1924	1931	1938
14–21	164	151	141	299	286	274
21–55	683	681	679	626	626	626
55–65	112	122	127	54	63	71
65–	41	46	53	21	25	29
	1,000	1,000	1,000	1,000	1,000	1,000

The numbers of occupied persons in the United Kingdom exhibited in Table II have been computed by the methods described in the preceding paragraphs.[1]

1 Dr Frankel, in an unpublished memorandum, estimates that there were changes between 1931 and 1939 in the proportion of persons occupied at various age-groups, namely increases both for males and females under 16 years, a slight rise for males aged 16–65 and a fall for males over 65, and slight increases for females aged over 16. The total for males of all ages is unaffected, while that for females is increased by 4 per cent. The whole occupied population in Great Britain is thus computed as 22·9 mn. in 1939, while, Table II above, the whole occupied population in the United Kingdom was 22·7 mn. in 1938. The effect on the National Wage Bill might be an increase of 1 per cent. Dr Frankel's estimates are based on a close study of the statistics published in connection with National Health and Unemployment Insurance and the Registrar-Generals' Reports.

CHANGE IN AGE DISTRIBUTION

The well-known changes in the age and sex distribution of the population are naturally reflected in the ages of the occupied. The result is summarized in the lower part of Table II.

For both sexes the proportions under 21 years have diminished, those for the central group 21 to 55 years have changed little, and those in the higher age grades have increased.

Since gainful occupation diminishes rapidly among women after the age 25, the effect of this change is shown in a slow rate of increase in the total occupied in the whole period 1924 to 1938, and an actual fall from 1932 to 1935, when the low birth-rates of 1916–29 were effective.

NUMBER OF WAGE-EARNERS. EARNING STRENGTH

It is important to emphasize that for purposes of estimating the National Income by the method of aggregating individual incomes it does not matter much whether a person is counted as a wage-earner or as salaried and in the intermediate group so long as the number concerned is small, since the income in marginal cases is much the same in the two groups. But for purposes of estimating the wage bill we must have some hypothesis on which to base the change in the number of wage-earners, and obtain factors to apply to a better-founded estimate at one date, in this case at 1931.

In my *Wages and Income in the United Kingdom since* 1860, Appendix E, I classify the occupational groups in the Censuses as Wage-Earning and Others, and obtain

Percentage of Wage-Earners to All Occupied

	Males	Females
1921	75·5	68·7
1931	74·0	68·0

Here shop-assistants are excluded from wage-earners.

I have assumed that the fall in the percentages here shown has continued uniformly from 1924 to 1938; e.g. the percentage for males is taken as 75·05 in 1924 and 72·96 in 1938. These percentages are applied in Table II to the numbers occupied to obtain estimates of the numbers of wage-earners in each year.

Allowance is now to be made for the numbers of unemployed wage-earners. For this purpose the usual percentages of insured persons unemployed are averaged annually for males and

TABLE III

Year	Unemployed per cent		Employed wage-earners (0000's)			Index-numbers						Aggregate annual wages (exc. shop-assistants) (£mn.)
						Earning strength	Wage rates		Wage bill			
	M	F	M	F	Total		A_1	B_1	A_2	B_2	D	
1924	11·0	8·6	943	392	1,335	1,000	1,000	1,000	1,000	1,000	1,000	**1,495**
1925	12·2	8·6	938	394	1,332	999	1,014	1,016	1,013	1,015	1,015	**1,520**
1926	(13·5)	(9·9)	(930)	(388)	(1,318)	(990)	1,016	1,012	(1,006)	(1,002)	993	**1,485**
1927	11·0	6·2	967	407	1,374	1,034	1,015	1,006	1,049	1,040	1,040	**1,555**
1928	12·3	7·0	958	404	1,362	1,026	1,007	991	1,033	1,016	1,016	**1,520**
1929	11·6	7·3	972	405	1,377	1,039	1,001	982	1,040	1,020	1,020	**1,525**
1930	16·5	14·8	926	376	1,302	983	992	984	975	968	968	**1,450**
1931	22·6	17·9	870	359	1,229	929	979	965	910	897	897	**1,340**
1932	25·2	13·7	849	377	1,226	928	962	947	893	879	879	**1,315**
1933	23·1	11·4	874	383	1,257	953	949	940	904	896	896	**1,340**
1934	19·3	10·0	917	386	1,303	989	949	944	939	934	950	**1,420**
1935	17·6	9·8	949	391	1,340	1,019	960	955	978	973	1,000	**1,495**
1936	14·8	8·6	991	398	1,389	1,058	985	982	1,042	1,039	1,060	**1,585**
1937	12·15*	7·7*	1,024	403	1,427	1,088	1,020	1,019	1,110	1,109	1,120	**1,675**
1938	13·85*	11·6*	1,014	390	1,404	1,072	1,056	1,059	1,132	1,135	1,130	**1,690**

* Adjusted from the published figures to allow for the change in the method of enumeration and for the inclusion of additional occupations.

females separately, with some adjustment in 1937 and 1938 to eliminate the effects of change in the method of enumeration and the inclusion of additional occupations (Table III).

The numbers of wage-earners thus discounted are shown as 'Employed wage-earners' in Table III. The numbers for the year 1926 were placed in brackets and are subject to modification in the sequel, for the percentage unemployed that year, excluding as it does the men actually involved in the coal-stoppage, does not measure the whole reduction in employment; nor is it probable that it allows sufficiently for reduction of work in other industries.

It is noticeable that with the increase in female unemployment since 1936, the number at work is lower in 1938 than in 1924.

The index-numbers of wage rates used as one factor in estimating the National Wage Bill make no allowance for change in distribution of the labour force by sex or age or between industries.

From details given on p. 68 below it appears that the average wage of males under 21 years is about 45 per cent of adult wages. It may be taken for granted that the average earnings of men over 65 is lower than that of men aged 21 to 65, but it does not seem possible to judge how much lower. In the following table the effect on average wages of the change in age distribution of males over the whole period 1924 to 1938 is shown on various hypotheses.[1] By adult wage rates is meant the average for men aged 21 to 65; by 'elderly' is meant over 65 years, by 'juveniles' under 21.

Effect of Changes of Age Distribution of Males on Average Wages (1924 to 1938)

Percentage elderly to adult wages	Percentage of juvenile to adult wages		
	40	45	50
50	1·009	1·007	1·006
75	1·012	1·011	1·009
80	1·013	1·011	1·010
85	1·013	1·012	1·012
100	1·015	1·014	1·012

1 For example, the central entry is computed from the lower part of Table II, thus:

$$\frac{141 \times 0{\cdot}45 + 806 \times 1 + 53 \times 0{\cdot}80}{164 \times 0{\cdot}45 + 795 \times 1 + 41 \times 0{\cdot}80} = 1{\cdot}0113.$$

The effect of the relative diminution of the young is therefore an increase of about 1·1 per cent spread over 14 years.

For females the average wage over 21 years is about 64 per cent of average adult wages. If the average wage over 55 years was also 64 per cent of average adult wages, no correction would be needed between 1924 and 1938. If we assume that the average under 21 is 64 per cent of the average 21 to 65, while over 65 the average is half that for 21 to 65, the correcting factor is 1·0057, that is, about half that for males. The correction is in any case so small that it is unnecessary to aim at greater precision.

The effect of the increase in the number of male earners relative to female is of more importance.

Write kw for the average wage of females, where w is that of males.

Write I for the index-number of wages, allowing for no change in age or sex distribution.

Use the figures for employed wage-earners in 1924 and 1938.

Then a little consideration will show that when changes in sex and age distribution are taken into account, we should have for the change of the National Wage Bill from 1924 to 1938:

$$\frac{1{,}014 \times 1{\cdot}011 + 390 \times 1{\cdot}006k}{943 + 392k} I$$

instead of

$$\frac{1{,}014 + 390}{943 + 392} I.$$

k is known to be in the neighbourhood of 0·5, and the ratio of these two fractions hardly changes as k varies from 0·45 to 0·55.

The first fraction is nearly 2 per cent greater than the second, and this is the whole increase to be applied over the period to allow for increased earning strength.

To obtain an index of earning strength we have therefore to increase the total numbers of employed wage-earners (Table III) progressively about 0·14 per cent per annum, and it is not worth while to try to adjust this regular progression. This having been done the column is transferred to the base 1,000 in 1924 to give the index of earning strength in Table III.[1]

THE INDEX OF WAGE RATES

In Table III are given two index-numbers of wage rates: A_1 that computed monthly for the London and Cambridge

[1] For example: the figure for 1938 is 1,000 × 1,404 × 1·019 ÷ 1,335 = 1,072.

Economic Service and explained in detail in Memorandum 28 of that Service; B_1 that published by the Ministry of Labour, and discussed by Mr Ramsbottom in the paper to the Royal Statistical Society (1935, Part IV) and brought up to later dates in the *Journal*, 1938, p. 202, and 1939, p. 289. The structure of these numbers is well known. B_1 depends on a wider range of industries than does A_1 and it is adopted in the sequel. It is remarkable that they march closely together and are nearly identical in 1937 (compared with 1924).

Both index-numbers are on the basis of unchanged numbers and age and sex distribution and should therefore be applied to the index of earning strength to obtain an index of the National Wage Bill, not to the unadjusted numbers of earners.

They also neglect any change in the relative importance of industries. I have examined this effect in my *Wages and Income*, pp. 107–10. From 1924 to 1931 it is negligible, and from 1931 to 1935 the computed effect is an increase of under 1 per cent in the industries covered by the Census of Production. But when mining and agriculture are included there may be some modification. I have combined this change with the more important adjustment that I proceed to discuss.

It is clear that index-numbers which depend primarily on changes of time and piece rates do not necessarily give an exact measurement of earnings. For apart from complete unemployment, for which allowance has already been made, there are facilities for increased earnings on piece and for overtime and less broken time, when industry is prosperous. Further, it is well known that an arranged change in piece rates is not necessarily proportional to the corresponding change in earnings. These relationships can be tested by the general returns of earnings published by the Ministry of Labour for 1924, 1928 and 1931, supplemented by information regarding coal-mines, railways and agriculture. On the basis of these data I estimated average earnings for males and females separately in my *Wages and Income*, p. 51. It remains to combine these by the help of the numbers of occupied wage-earners.

Here the index-numbers first given are proportional to average earnings; B_1 is that from Table III, and B_3 is B_1 adjusted for the greater change in 'earning strength' than in numbers occupied, a change which has already had its effect on the estimates of average earnings.

Average Earnings

Year	Males		Females		All wage-earners			
	Numbers (000's)	Average	Numbers (000's)	Average	Average		Index-numbers	
							B_1	B_3
1924	943	54·4*s*.	392	27·5*s*.	46·5*s*. =	100·0	100·0	100·0
1931	870	53·7*s*.	359	26·9*s*.	45·9*s*.	98·7	96·5	97·0
1935	949	54·7*s*.	391	27·3*s*.	46·7*s*.	100·5	95·5	96·3

We find then that earnings of employed wage-earners had decreased rather less than rates between 1924 and 1931, and increased between 1931 and 1935, when rates dropped.

We can make a rough test of the relation between wage rates and earnings by comparing the details of Mr Ramsbottom's index with records of earnings in eight industries, viz. Cotton, Wool, Boots, Bricks, Pottery, Coal, Railways and Iron and Steel Production. The first five depend on the statistics of numbers employed and earnings, given monthly in the *Ministry of Labour Gazette*. For this purpose the average earnings shown each November, as compared with those a year before, have been computed for comparison with Mr Ramsbottom's December figures. For Coal the average earnings per shift in the fourth quarter of each year are taken; for Railways the annual report on earnings for March or April each year; for Iron and Steel Production the annual earnings as computed by the Iron and Steel Institute. There are many minor and some more important difficulties in making the comparison, and it does not seem to be worth while to do more than give rough averages (see Table IV).

The series of general averages agree so closely till 1932 that it seems best not to modify the original index-numbers in Table III prior to 1934; but in the years of improving trade adjustment seems to be justified. The industries selected probably contain on the whole a larger element of piece rates or greater opportunities of overtime (in the case of Railways) than do industries in general, and a smaller increase than that suggested by the figures here is probably justified.[1] The following paragraphs throw some light on the problem.

1 In Table IV it is noticeable that from 1935 to 1936 the general averages earnings increased less than rates. It appears from more detailed records that rates were raised at a later stage in the period of improving trade than the increase of earnings, as indeed we might expect.

TABLE IV

Index-numbers of Approximate Earnings (E) compared with Constituents of Wage Rates Numbers B for December

Year	Cotton		Wool		Boots		Bricks		Pottery		Coal		Railways		Iron and steel		General average	
	E	B	E	B	E	B	E	B	E	B	E	B	E	B	E	B	E	B
1924	100	100	(103)	100	100	100	100	100	100	100	100	100	100	100	100	100	100	100
1926	90	100	100	100	101	103	98	101	110	100	—	99	103	100	—	95	100	100
1928	99	100	102	100	93	98	95	101	103	100	87	87	102	96	96	90	97	96½
1929	94	94	103	99	100	98	96	101	103	100	87	87	102	96	98	90	98	96
1930	85	94	95	91	98	98	96	101	96	91	88	85	100	98	92	90	94	93½
1932	86	86	92	84	94	93	85	100	89	91	87	84	95	94	87	86	89	90
1934	86	86	95	82	95	93	94	100	95	91	87	84	95	95	98	89	93	90
1935	89	84	99	82	98	91	96	101	96	95	88	84	97	95	111	92	97	90½
1936	91	87	100	89	97	92	99	104	99	98	95	91	99	96	108	96	98½	94
1937	98	92	95	89	97	96	103	104	99	100	103	97	102	99	118	110	102	98½
1938	96	92	103	89	101	99	100	104	97	100	106	97	105	99	120	116	103	99½

THE WAGE BILL AND INCOME TAX, SCHEDULE D

There is a close relationship between the computed index-numbers of the Wage Bill and 'Actual Income' under the Income Tax, Schedule D. The data for the years 1924 to 1935 are given in Table V and in the accompanying diagram. 1926 is omitted from the computation, since the average number of occupied wage-earners in that year is doubtful.

TABLE V

Wage-Bill Index and Schedule D

X, Schedule D. Actual Income £mn. ×——× 1925/26 placed under 1924, etc.
Y, Index of National Wage Bill. 1924 = 1,000. o——o.
$Y' = 436 + 0{\cdot}57X + 4{\cdot}6t$, where t is number of years after 1930. -----

Schedule D		Wage-Bill index estimates computed from formula			
Year	Actual income (£X mn.)	Year	Y	Y'	Y'_1
1925/26	1,033	1924	1,000	995	1,004
1926/27	1,064	1925	1,015	1,017	1,021
1927/28	1,013	1926	—	993	996
1928/29	1,065	1927	1,040	1,027	1,024
1929/30	1,078	1928	1,016	1,039	1,032
1930/31	1,032	1929	1,020	1,018	1,010
1931/32	922	1930	968	959	956
1932/33	802	1931	897	896	896
1933/34	756	1932	879	874	874
1934/35	829	1933	896	920	912
1935/36	858	1934	949	941	928
1936/37	944	1935	1,005	995	973

By the usual method of partial correlation, in which the effect of the time element is separated, we obtain the equation

$$Y' = 434 + 0{\cdot}57X + 4{\cdot}6t, \pm 12,$$

where Y' is the wage-bill index, £X mn. is the actual income in Schedule D* and t is the number of years measured from 1930.

The mean square deviation of Y' as computed from Y the given index is approximately 12, or 1·2 per cent.

The fit of the computed line (Y') to the given line is very close from 1929 to 1934.

Y' is computed from values of Y raised in 1934 and 1935 on a priori evidence that earnings increased more than rates.

* The assessment of each year, e.g. 1925/26, is compared with the Wage Bill of the previous year (e.g. 1924).

Wage-Bill Index and Schedule D

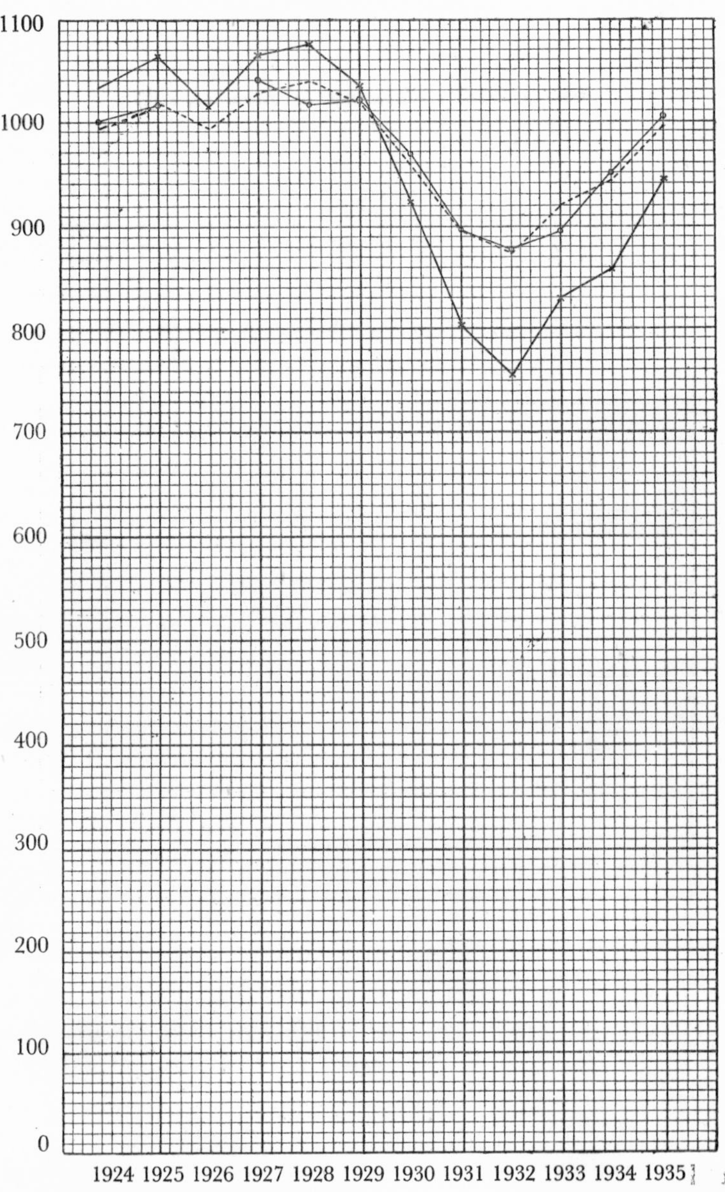

X, Schedule D. Actual Income £mn. ×——× 1925/26 placed under 1924, etc.
Y, Index of National Wage Bill. 1924=1000. o——o.
$Y' = 436 + 3{\cdot}57X + 4{\cdot}6t$, where t is number of years after 1930. -----

See p. 64

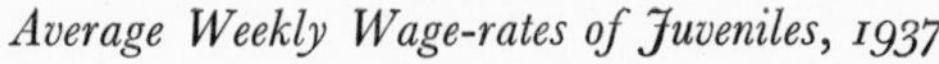

Average Weekly Wage-rates of Juveniles, 1937

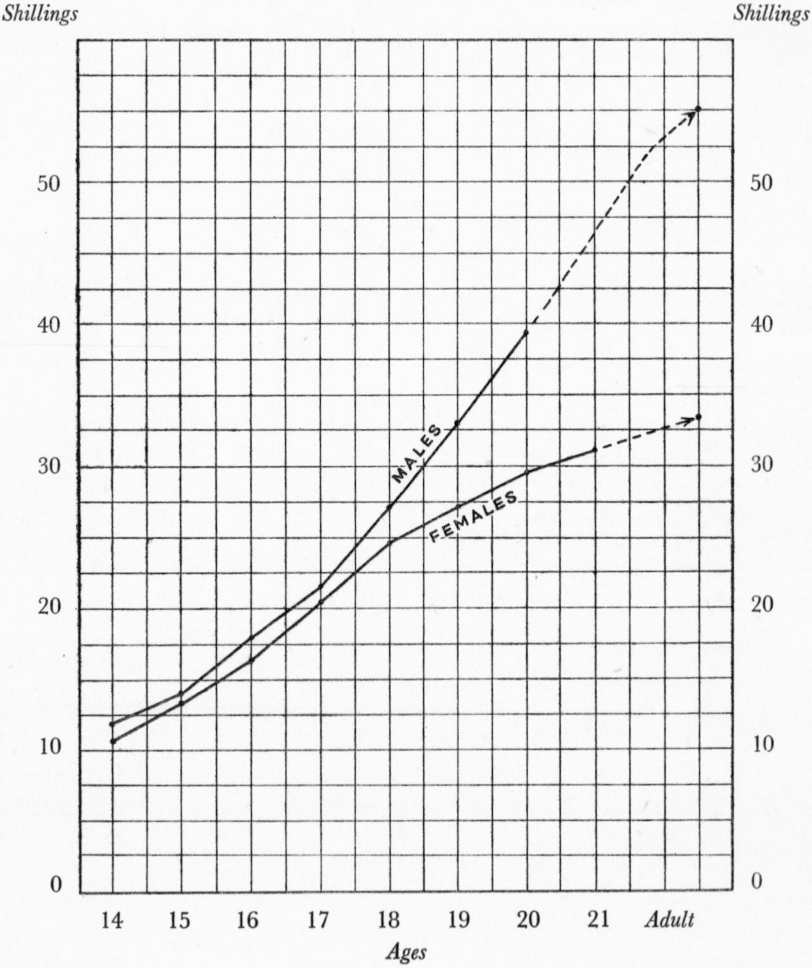

Shillings
Shillings
50
40
30
20
10
0
50
40
30
20
10
0
MALES
FEMALES
14
15
16
17
18
19
20
21
Adult
Ages

See p. 67

If, however, we use the original values of B_2 in these years, we obtain a modified equation

$$Y'_1 = 490 + 0{\cdot}505X + 1{\cdot}29t.$$

Neither equation should be regarded as representing a permanent relationship between the Wage Bill and Schedule D. Different periods of years yield different coefficients. But a close relationship between the movements is demonstrated, and explanations may be sought in years where the divergence is at all considerable.

On the evidence of these figures I propose to adopt the number 993 as the Wage-Bill index for 1926.

For the years 1934 to 1938 the evidence is somewhat conflicting.

Using a provisional estimate for Schedule D for the year 1939–40, we have alternative estimates as follows:

Estimates of Wage-Bill Index

Year	A_2	B_2	Y'	Y'_1	Adopted
1934	939	934 × 1·016 = 949	941	928	950
1935	978	973 × 1·030 = 1,002	995	973	1,000
1936	1,042	1,039 × 1·024 = 1,064	1,048	1,019	1,060
1937	1,110	1,109 × 1·016 = 1,127	1,082	1,044	1,120
1938	1,132	1,135 × 1·016 = 1,153	1,087	1,045	1,130

Here the multiplier applied to B_2 is obtained by assuming that the general excess of the movement of earnings over rates is half that indicated by Table IV. For 1935 the excess is in the same proportion as that indicated by the Wage Census (p. 62 above).

During the time of expanding employment, 1935 to 1937, the wage index-numbers show a stronger movement than does Schedule D, and are I think to be preferred.

In 1938 there was a reaction in industry and employment, and it would be anticipated that the factor to be applied to B_2 would be less than unity, but the tendency to increased wage rates was continued.

From these considerations I adopt the figures shown in the last column with considerable hesitation.

The results are shown under D in Table III.

For completeness at this stage the Wage-Bill index is applied to the estimate of earnings in 1931 discussed below and the results are shown in the last column of Table III. So far the earnings of shop-assistants are excluded.

It is interesting to compare the estimate for 1924, here £1,495 mn., with that made in *The National Income*, 1924 (Bowley and Stamp), which (excluding shop-assistants) was £1,480 mn. The present estimate is based primarily on reports on earnings in 1931, worked back by index numbers of wage rates and earning strength. The earlier estimate was based on the Wage Census of 1906, worked forward by estimates of the occupied and employed population, and wage indices computed partly from the Wage Returns of 1924, but largely from other sources. A possible error of ± 5 per cent was suggested for 1924. It is very remarkable that the two estimates differ by only 1 per cent.

The whole series from 1924 to 1931 is about 1 per cent higher than that given in my *Wages and Income*, p. 77. From 1931 to 1935 it is $1\frac{1}{2}$ per cent higher. The revision of the wage and earnings index and of the number occupied for 1936 makes the new estimate 1 per cent lower than the old in that year.

The paragraphs above are as communicated in June 1940. Since that date the Ministry of Labour has published an account of earnings in October 1938 (*Ministry of Labour Gazette*, 1940, pp. 281 *seq.*, 306–7).

When Groups IV to XVI (excluding Railways) and Local Government (XVIII) are combined from Table VII, below, we get as nearly as possible the industries included in the new account. The average weekly earnings thus computed for 1931 are 48·1*s*. From the Wage Bill (D) and the number of employed wage-earners in the table, the increase in average earnings, 1931 to 1938, is 10·5 per cent. Apply this to the average for 1931 and we have 53·15*s*.

When the Ministry of Labour's figures are weighted by the number of insured workers in the Industries, the average in October 1938 is 53·3*s*.

So close an agreement is partly accidental, since various doubtful factors are involved; but it confirms the general accuracy of the estimates here used.

NOTE ON WAGES OF JUVENILES

There is need for a systematic study of the rates of wages of boys, girls and young persons up to the age at which full adult rates are received, and indeed of the progression of earnings also for younger adults when the maximum is not reached till after some years of experience. I have put together the data relating to the subject in *Standard Time Rates and Hours of Labour*, 1929, a publication which was kindly annotated for me at the Ministry of Labour in connection with another investigation, so that most of the figures used apply to the year 1937.

The table and diagram given should be regarded as the results of only a preliminary and rough investigation, the main purpose of which was to estimate the effect on 'earning strength' of the relative falling-off of young earners. On any reasonable hypothesis that effect was found (pp. 60, 61 above) to be trifling.

The averages in Table VI are simple averages based on 262 entries for males (including 49 for Agriculture) and 128 for females. The entries are not distributed in accordance with the importance of industries, but nothing appeared to be gained by any system of weighting; one which I applied did not affect the result.

TABLE VI

Juveniles' Weekly Wage Rates, 1937

(shillings)

Age ...	14	15	16	17	18	19	20	21
			Males					
Bricks, chemicals	13·1	15·8	19·1	23·2	28·9	34·1	39·3	—
Metal, engineering	11·2	13·4	15·9	19·4	25·3	29·8	34·3	—
Textiles	11·3	13·2	16·7	20·9	26·3	31·1	36·2	—
Clothing	11·4	14·5	19·5	24·1	29·0	32·9	35·8	—
Boots (minimum)	12·0	16·0	20·0	25·0	30·0	36·0	44·0	—
Food	12·6	14·7	17·6	21·5	27·5	33·9	42·0	—
Wood, furniture	—	—	15·5	17·1	25·6	34·1	41·5	—
Paper, printing	11·3	15·0	19·2	24·4	30·2	36·4	44·5	—
Building, artisans	9·8	11·3	14·2	17·2	21·5	28·5	40·8	—
,, labourers	14·4	14·4	21·5	21·5	28·7	28·7	43·1	—
Transport	16·0	16·0	20·0	25·0	30·0	35·0	—	—
Distribution	12·1	14·6	18·4	23·0	28·7	36·1	42·5	—
Agriculture*	11·2	13·9	16·8	20·4	23·9	26·6	29·0	—
Miscellaneous	—	15·2	18·0	22·6	28·6	34·2	39·8	—
General average	12·1	14·3	18·0	21·8	27·4	32·7	39·0	—
			Females					
Chemicals	11·8	13·8	16·1	19·4	22·2	24·2	26·0	28·1
Metal, engineering	10·5	12·3	14·6	17·2	22·0	24·6	25·2	25·3
Textiles	10·8	13·4	16·4	20·1	24·0	26·3	27·9	28·5
Clothing	10·1	13·0	17·0	21·1	25·7	28·3	30·6	31·6
Boots	12·0	16·0	20·0	25·0	30·0	30·0	30·0	30·0
Food	11·8	14·7	16·7	20·9	24·5	27·3	29·5	34·1
Furniture	10·7	12·8	16·6	21·9	29·0	33·8	38·6	38·6
Paper, printing	8·9	11·4	15·9	22·3	25·6	27·3	29·0	31·6
Distribution	10·2	12·4	15·1	18·2	23·1	26·9	30·2	32·7
Miscellaneous	—	11·8	14·4	18·1	22·4	25·5	29·0	30·9
General average	10·6	13·2	16·3	20·4	24·9	27·4	29·6	31·1

* In the year 1933.

There is considerable variety in the upward steps in wages year by year in different occupations, and there is often a distinction between apprentices and others. On the whole the statements confirm the general impression that in unskilled male occupations wages start higher, increase at first more rapidly and reach their maximum at an earlier age, than in skilled occupations. In the latter the wage at 20 years is considerably below the standard rate for adults, and it appears that there is a sudden jump at the age 21.

From the table and diagram it is seen that girls start at nearly the same rates as boys, but make slower progress especially after 17 years of age, and by the time they are 21 are usually receiving adult wages. The actual age at which adult rates are payable varies from trade to trade.

The dotted lines in the diagram are intended to indicate progress towards an average adult wage of 55*s*. to 60*s*. for men and 33*s*. to 36*s*. for women.

The general averages for females agree closely with those recorded in the *New Survey of London Life and Labour*, Vol. VI, pp. 82–4. There earnings in factories, workshops, etc. average 13*s*. 6*d*. at 14 to 16 years, 18*s*. 6*d*. at 16 to 18, 25*s*. 6*d*. at 18 to 20, 30*s*. 6*d*. at 20 to 25, and 33*s*. 6*d*. for all ages 20 to 65. It might have been expected that London wages would be higher than provincial, but the figures here assembled do not support this view.

TOTAL WAGES IN 1931

The Population Censuses of England and Wales and of Scotland in 1931 and that of Northern Ireland in 1926, together with some subsidiary information, enable us to classify gainfully occupied persons as follows:

United Kingdom, 1931

(000's)

	Males	Females	Totals
Wage-earners	9,035	3,793	12,828
Shop-assistants, etc.	606	494	1,100
Salaried and employers in Agriculture	215	20	235
Others	2,548	1,211	3,759
Workers on own account	965	361	1,326
Total	13,369	5,879	19,248
Unemployed	2,014	575	2,589
Total	15,383	6,454	21,837

In this total is included an estimate of the number of fishermen and seamen absent on Census night, and some other slight modifications are made which result in a greater number of wage-earners and a greater total than in Table III.

In the present section shop-assistants are distinguished from other wage-earners and subsequently from the rest of the salaried group, since the various sources of information about their earnings do not allow any clear distinction in their case between manual operatives and salaried or administrative.

For weekly earnings we depend primarily on the returns for 'Average Earnings in the Principal Industries in Great Britain and Northern Ireland' in the week 18 to 24 October 1931, summarized in the *Ministry of Labour Gazette*, 1933 (pp. 8, 45, 82). These, when supplemented by the periodic returns of coal-miners' earnings, cover the Industrial Groups III–XIV in Table VII. Other sources are used for agriculture and railway earnings. For domestic servants a small special investigation was carried out, which gave sufficient information to allow of a fairly reliable estimate. For other occupations we depended on known wage rates for particular occupations or for the class of labour employed. Allowance was made for the value of board, lodging and clothing in the cases where it was relevant.

In the main group covered by the Ministry of Labour's returns there were in some cases difficulties in judging the relative importance of firms employing less than ten persons and of larger firms, for which the returns were separately given. In all cases there was a little doubt whether the returns, which were on a voluntary basis, were closely typical of the whole industries.

The total numbers of male and female wage-earners in Table VII are those given above from the Census of 1931 sub-divided into XXII groups, with sub-groups. The annual earnings were obtained by the application of two assumptions. First some reduction must be made from the Census numbers, since persons away from work through sickness or other interruptions, as well as those temporarily stopped, or changing from one employer to another, would not necessarily record themselves as unemployed—a term which they might regard as seeking employment. On p. 103 it is shown that there is a perceptible deficit, attributable to the category 'temporarily stopped', and the usual estimate for absence through sickness is about 3 per cent. On these grounds the numbers of earners are decreased

TABLE VII

Estimate of Earnings and of Salaries under £125 per annum in 1931

United Kingdom

Industrial Groups	Earners: Males: Numbers 000's	Earners: Males: Weekly earnings shillings	Earners: Females: Numbers 000's	Earners: Females: Weekly earnings shillings	Earners: Together: Annual earnings £mn.	Employers,* Managers and Non-manual Operatives: Males: Numbers All 000's	Males: Under £125: Per cent	Males: Under £125: Average salary £	Females: Numbers All 000's	Females: Under £125: Per cent	Females: Under £125: Average salary £	Together: Total salaries under £125 £mn.
I. Fishing	38†	44·0	1	22·0	4	2·5	20	70	0·2	80	80	0·1
II. Agriculture	778	34·0	52	25·0	65	6·1*	20	70	2·0	80	80	0·2
III. Coal mines	920	49·0§	4	24·0	108	20·2	16	70	1·7	75	86	0·3
Other mines, etc.	91	51·3	2	26·5	11	6·3	16	70	0·7	75	86	0·1
Mineral products	44	65·2	2	29·2	7	5·2	16	70	1·2	75	86	0·1
IV. Bricks, pottery, glass	134	51·7	47	22·4	19	11·6	20	62	4·1	85	77	0·4
V. Chemicals, etc.	110	58·8	36	27·5	18	46·5	13	80	17·8	65	80	1·4
VI. Iron and steel production	129	54·7	1	22·4	17	14·1	21	63	2·8	80	72	0·3
Engineering	326	52·4	19	26·8	42	65·3	20	65	19·5	80	75	2·0
Electrical engineering	139	50·6	45	27·4	20	37·2	12	70	17·7	80	77	1·4
Vehicles	256	57·3	23	28·5	37	39·4	13	70	14·5	80	77	1·3
Ships	145	51·8	2	26·9	18	13·1	24	48	2·5	91	68	0·3
Other metal industries	400	52·3	91	22·8	55	60·1	16	66	20·8	75	74	1·8
Precious metals, watches	20	57·8	11	26·2	4	5·6	20	70	3·4	80	75	0·3
VII. Cotton	151	45·3	269	27·2	34	16·0	22	74	4·7	88	72	0·6
Wool	85	49·3	121	27·6	18	10·9	22	74	3·1	88	72	0·4
Other textiles	107	49·3	252	26·5	29	25·2	22	74	16·1	88	72	1·4
Dyeing, bleaching	72	49·3	21	24·3	10	8·6	22	74	3·2	88	72	0·3
VIII. Leather	42	52·7	21	29·9	7	9·4	25	70	3·8	70	85	0·4
IX. Clothing	203	53·6	435	27·6	54	57·9	14	80	37·6	80	73	2·8
X. Food	193	58·2	126	26·3	35	87·3	12	88	57·7	65	80	3·9
Drink	73	56·9	17	23·8	11	24·2	24	80	3·4	64	90	0·7
Tobacco	12	58·8	29	36·7	4	6·9	20	75	3·3	70	80	0·3

XI.	Wood, furniture	184	52·0	25	26·8	24	33·0	20	75	6·6	80	75	0·9
XII.	Paper	38	57·2	12	26·3	6	4·4	15	65	1·9	60	90	0·1
	Stationery	22	56·1	48	26·8	6	8·7	25	60	5·6	80	70	0·4
	Printing	161	77·4	72	29·2	35	61·7	22	63	21·4	82	71	2·1
XIII.	Building, contracting	790	58·2	4	27·0	111	94·7	14	85	9·6	90	85	1·9
XIV.	Rubber	26	57·3	16	27·0	5	8·2	30	60	4·0	66	90	0·4
	Other manufactures	69	52·9	40	28·0	11	24·5	30	60	12·2	66	90	1·2
XV.	Gas, water, electricity	187	62·3	3	26·5	28	33·1	15	75	4·8	75	77	0·7
XVI.	Railway transport‡	458	66·4	6	30·0	74	67·7	10	80	9·7	50	90	1·0
	Road transport	359	62·2	6	32·8	54	46·1	30	70	11·8	90	70	1·7
	Other transport	288†	55·0	6	27·0	38	53·8	20	70	7·5	80	75	1·2
XVII.	Distribution	505	50·0	116	27·0	68	425·4	28	70	140·0	77	66	15·4
	Banking, etc.	42	50·0	19	20·0	6	261·3	15	80	71·9	55	93	6·8
XVIII.	Defence	336†	45·7	3	28·0	37	39·3	8	74	3·3	55	82	0·4
	Central Government	32	58·6	10	39·5	5	235·8	20½	74	79·4	55	82	6·8
	Local Government	408	52·6	68	26·0	56	83·9	15	76	27·8	41	87	2·0
	Police	—	—	—	—	—	67·0	0	0	—	—	—	0·0
XIX.	Teachers	—	—	—	—	—	66·8	1	111	164·0	3½	106	0·7
	Nurses	—	—	—	—	—	—	—	—	151·6	76	80	9·2
	Professions	69	50·0	83	23·0	13	65·0	18	72	51·0	75	77	3·9
	Others	—	—	—	—	—	148·2	0	0	36·8	20	80	0·6
XX.	Entertainments, sport	55	52·0	16	24·0	8	44·7	20	75	30·8	70	85	2·5
XXI.	Personal service	507	36·0	1,604	22·0	124	86·2	25	75	107·3	85	70	8·0
XXII.	Other	32	36·0	8	25·0	4	8·9	30	70	7·8	75	78	0·6
	Total	9,035	51·6	3,793	24·2	1,340	2,548·0	17½	73	1,209·0	62½	77	90·0

* Employers (farmers) are excluded from the agricultural numbers.

† Including fishermen, sailors and soldiers at sea or abroad.

‡ Including railway shop and artisans as does the Population Census here and not in Group VI.

§ In *Wages and Income*, pp. 22, 51, 113, 45·2*s*. is taken as the average for 52 weeks, while here it is 49·0*s*. to be multiplied by 48 for annual earnings.

by 4 per cent before applying them to the weekly earnings. Secondly, statutory and other customary holidays amount to about two weeks per annum, and in 1931 at any rate they were paid in few cases, so that 50 weeks' work is to be attributed to the reduced numbers.

We thus have: Numbers of earners $\times \frac{96}{100} \times 50$ $(=48) \times$ weeks' earnings = annual earnings, so that the actual numeration in the table is the multiplication of numbers, weekly earnings and 48.

This factor 48 is, of course, not to be considered as exact, but the error resulting can hardly exceed 1 per cent for 1931. But in the most recent years the factor should perhaps be increased to $48\frac{1}{2}$, or even 49, since payment for holidays has become wider spread.

The whole of the data were treated independently by Mr Booker and myself. His first estimate of the total was $3\frac{1}{2}$ per cent below mine; of this difference (£47 mn.) £15 mn. was due to coal-miners' earnings, where I found evidence of a higher average number of shifts, £5 mn. to his use of minimum rates (instead of earnings) in agriculture, £13 mn. to an allowance for deficiency in the returns from small building employers, where the earnings were at lower rates than in larger firms, and the remaining £14 mn. came from a number of industries, and principally from the assumption that small firms were insufficiently represented. I have not had the opportunity of collating these estimates with him completely, but I think that we would agree to at least half of my additions, so that we might write the total wage bill at £1,330 ± 10 mn., so far as this variation of estimate is concerned. In this paper, however, I have taken the higher quantity, £1,340 mn., as the principal estimate.

Apart from this difference of interpretation of the data there is the possibility of small errors in every factor and estimate involved. These are independent of each other and tend to cancel out, and would in that case give a margin of some 1 per cent or less in the total.

Another consideration is that the earnings returns are for one week in October, and may not be applicable as the average of the year 1931. Actually changes in wage rates were very small during the year, and the fluctuations in employment were not such as to lead us to expect any important difference in the relation between earnings and rates, when October is compared with the whole year.

There is, however, the further consideration whether the number recorded in the Census as employed in April was equal to the average number employed during the year. Among insured persons the percentage unemployed was 20·4 in April and 21·3 as the average for 1931 (21·9 in October), so that the percentage not unemployed was 79·6 in April and 78·7 for the year. But the insured population increased by 3 per cent during the year, and the number of insured persons employed was very nearly the same in April as the average for 1931. In the occupations outside insurance the relationship may have been different, and on the whole it seems best not to adjust the main estimate, but to realize that here is a further error of less than 1 per cent. It may be added that various systems of weighting the separate returns within the total have been tested, and that they give very nearly the same results.

The White Paper issued by the Financial Secretary to the Treasury in April 1941 ('An Analysis of the Sources of War Finance and an Estimate of the National Income and Expenditure in 1938 and 1940') estimates wages (including payments to armed forces and earnings of shop assistants) at £1,820 mn. in 1938. It is learnt that £54 mn. was attributed to shop-assistants, as on p. 81. Other wages (£1,766 mn.) were computed by taking the numbers employed on the same principle as in Table III, p. 58, deducting 3·5 per cent for sickness and unpaid holidays, thus following the Ministry of Labour's allowance for loss of time through 'sickness and other forms of unrecorded non-employment apart from recognized holidays'. After a trifling allowance for days lost through trade disputes had been made, the remainder was multiplied by average earnings based on the Ministry of Labour's enquiry (as above) supplemented by other information, and modified by minor adjustments. This £1,766 mn. is 4·4 per cent higher than the £1,690 mn. in Table III, which is intended to cover precisely the same ground.

Since the average earnings corresponding to Table III of all employed has been shown above to correspond very closely with that based on the same data as are used in the White Paper, the difference must be sought in estimates of the number occupied and the number of weeks worked per annum. While 5 per cent is allowed in the White Paper for absence from all causes, so that 49·4 weeks at earnings is allotted per annum, the estimate in Table III allows 4 weeks' absence and 48 weeks' work. This accounts for 2·9 per cent of the difference. The remainder is 1·5 per cent. Part of this may be due to the increase of payment during holidays; if one-third of the wage-earning population was paid during one week's holiday, the addition to the National Wage Bill would be 0·6 per cent. This reduces the unaccounted difference between the estimates to about 1 per cent.

Considering that the earlier estimate was built up from the data of the year 1931 by index-numbers, while the latter is the result of independent work on the 1938 wage returns, the agreement is very satisfactory.

After studying all the factors it seems reasonable to regard the estimates of the total as subject to an error of less than 5 per cent. It is thought that the figure for 1931 is more likely to be over- than under-estimated, while that already given for 1938 is a central result.

Thus the Total National Wage Bill, excluding shop-assistants, may be written as between £1,280 and £1,370 mn. in 1931 and between £1,630 and £1,750 mn. in 1938.

SALARIES BELOW THE INCOME-TAX EXEMPTION LIMIT

As in the years 1911 and 1924, a direct investigation was made into salaries by questionnaires issued to employers. We were successful in obtaining a great deal of information, and at least for the purpose of Table VII, which is to obtain the total of earned incomes other than wages below the exemption limit of £125, the returns were sufficient.

In the computation which leads to the total (£90 mn.) there are a very large number of independent estimates of percentages and averages, and so far as these are concerned the majority of the entries are unlikely to be more than 10 per cent in error and the total should be correct within 5 per cent. But there is some doubt about the numbers to which these percentages should be applied. The columns headed 'Numbers All' include the entries in the Population Census under Employers and Managers (except in Agriculture), as well as estimates of the numbers of non-manual operatives, and it is doubtful how far the returns to the questionnaires included the superior group. Also in some cases there were included rather arbitrary estimates for quite small employers. Taking all these uncertainties into consideration, we may with some confidence write the total as between £80 and £100 mn., keeping £90 mn. as the most probable estimate. This margin includes an allowance for the small variation of salaries (p. 92) between 1931 and 1938. Since salaries were rather lower in 1931 than in 1938 (the year of computation), £90 mn. may be a little too high.

Of course we have not in this table the material for computing average salaries of all employed, but only the average of the lower 17 per cent of the men and the lower 62 per cent of the women. Since the men include beginners preponderantly, while the women include many who have reached their maximum, it is not surprising that the average in these sections is greater for women than for men.

The numbers of those with small salaries are not stated in the table, to save space. The last line may be written:

Under £125 per annum

	Numbers (000's)	Average salary (£)	Aggregate of salaries (£ mn.)
Males	448	73	33
Females	746	77	57
Total	1,194	75	90

SHOP-ASSISTANTS

It will be seen in the sequel that when the aggregate number of incomes is to be estimated, it is necessary to know what employees are classed as 'weekly wage-earners, employed by way of Manual Labour' and are assessed on a half-yearly basis. Unfortunately neither the instructions nor the practice are clear, as regards employees in shops. Shop-managers, shop-walkers, window-dressers, are given as examples of occupations 'not regarded as manual', while working dressmakers are 'regarded as manual'. Counter-hands are not named. The covering definition is: '"Manual Labour" includes all occupations which depend mainly on the exercise of physical exertion, even though a considerable amount of dexterity and training may be involved.'

We have found on enquiry that some distributors include all shop-assistants in their general return to the income-tax authorities, merging them with clerks, etc., while others include them in the special return relating to manual labour.

As a compromise it has been decided for the present purpose to assume that the number of shop-assistants receiving less than £125 per annum—approximately 50*s*. weekly—is equal to the number returned as manual labourers, and that the remainder are included among the number assessed on an annual basis for income tax.

We have received reports that cover 125,000 shop-assistants—that is, about 12 per cent of the number so classed in the Census of 1931—and the numbers and average salaries of those receiving less than £125 per annum in 1938.

Salaries of Shop-assistants in 1938

	Males	Females
Percentage under £125 p.a.	39	89
Average salary:		
Under £125	£61·4	£78·3
£125 or more	£189	£162
All	£139	£87

It is quite possible that the returns, which came from large distributors, do not contain a sufficient proportion of quite low rates for young girls, and that the average (about 35*s.* weekly) for all females is too high. I have reduced the average under £125 somewhat arbitrarily by about 10 per cent in the estimates that follow.

Our returns indicate that salary rates were nearly stationary from 1924 to 1936, that they rose 2½ per cent in 1938 and a further 1 per cent in 1939.[1]

From this information we have to deduce the proportions and average salaries under £125 in 1931 and subsequent years, and under £150 from 1924 to 1930.

As regards the numbers concerned, we have from the Population Census:

Salesmen and Shop-assistants

(000's)

	Males	Females
Great Britain, 1921	352	411
1931	511	484
Northern Ireland, 1926	11	9

The statistics of insured persons under the heading 'Distribution' have a wider content, especially of males, many of whom are presumably drivers and porters.

Insured Persons: Distribution

(000's)

Great Britain and Northern Ireland	Males	Females
1924	808	544
1931	1,137	738
1939	1,282	814

1 See Mr Campion's paper, p. 92 below.

The increase here is much more rapid than that shown by the Census. In the sequel I have taken the Census figures with a uniform rate of growth from 1924 and 1931, and assumed an annual increase of 1 per cent from 1931 to 1938 and no change in 1939, since the Insurance statistics indicate stationariness.

The change in the income-tax exemptions limit, the movement in rates of salary and the correction for the presumed over-estimate of women's salaries affect the proportion and average rates below and above the exemption limit. After trying various hypotheses I have provisionally adopted the estimates in the following table.

TABLE VIII A

Shop-assistants

Estimates of factors involved

	Limit £150			Limit £125			
Year ...	1924	1930	1931	1936	1937	1938	1939
Males							
Total number (000's)	409	505	521	546	551	558	538
Below limit:							
Percentage	50	50	42	42	39	39	39
Number (000's)	204	252	219	229	215	218	218
Average salary (£)	80	80	62	62	61·4	61·4	61·4
Females							
Total number (000's)	443	485	493	498	503	508	508
Below limit:							
Percentage	95	95	91	91	89	89	89
Number (000's)	421	462	449	453	447	452	452
Average salary (£)	75	75	72	72	70·7	70·7	70·7

Between 1924 and 1930 and again between 1931 and 1936 uniform progression in numbers is assumed. Allowing for the change in salaries after 1936 and as the result of some troublesome approximations, the estimates shown in Table VIII B are obtained.

These estimates should be regarded as subject to margin of error of ± 10 per cent throughout.[1] In particular some modification is probably needed to allow for the changing stress of unemployment.

1 In *Wages and Income*, p. 77, the estimate for shop-assistants was £120 mn. in 1924, £100 mn. in 1931, and £120 mn. in 1936. These figures include some distributors who were not shop-assistants, and assumed (in the absence of evidence to the contrary) that the movement in salaries and unemployment was parallel to that in wage-rates.

Table VIII B

Shop-assistants, Numbers and Aggregate Salaries

Male and Female

Year	Number (000's)			Aggregate salaries (£ mn.)			Add roundsmen wages to small salaries (£ mn.)
	Under £150	£150 and over	Total	Under £150	£150 and over	Total	
1924	625	227	852	48	43	91	*57*
1925	640	235	875	50	44	94	*59*
1926	655	243	898	51	45	96	*60*
1927	670	251	921	52	47	99	*61*
1928	684	260	944	53	48	101	*62*
1929	699	268	967	54	50	104	*63*
1930	714	276	990	55	52	107	*64*
	Under £125	£125 and over		Under £125	£125 and over		
1931	668	346	1,014	46	64	110	*55*
1932	671	349	1,020	46	65	111	*55*
1933	674	352	1,026	46	66	112	*55*
1934	677	355	1,032	46	67	113	*55*
1935	680	358	1,038	47	67	114	*56*
1936	682	362	1,044	47	67	114	*56*
1937	662	392	1,054	45	73	118	*54*
1938	670	396	1,066	45	75	120	*54*
1939	670	396	1,066	45	76	121	*54*

In the table on p. 68 the number classified as shop-assistants is 1,100,000; the excess of 86,000 over the number 1,014,000 in Table VIII A and B is due to the inclusion of 'Roundsmen and Van Salesmen', whose annual earnings are about £9 mn. This sum is added to obtain the last column in VIII B, and is used in Table IX.

INCOME IN THE YEAR 1931

In consequence of the reduction of the income-tax exemption limit for earned income from £162 to £125 in the year 1931–32, a considerable additional number of incomes, estimated at 1,100,000, were assessed as taxable, though many were not taxed owing to additional allowances. The greater part of this number was presumably drawn from the 'Intermediate Class', that is, recipients of earned incomes less than £162 arising from non-manual work. The number in this class was estimated at 1,990,000 in 1924 (when the exemption limit was £150) with an aggregate income of £190 mn.

United Kingdom, 1931[1]

	Total (00,000's)	Occupied Persons		Aggregate income under £125 or manual (£ mn.)
		Under £125 or manual (00,000's)	£125 and over non-manual (00,000's)	
Employers, Managers, Salaried	40	12	28	90
On own account	13	6 *18*	7	50 *140*
Shop-assistants	11	7	4	55
Wage-earners	128	128	0	1,340
Total	192	153	39	1,535
Unemployed at Census date	26	—	—	—
Total	218	—	—	—

This table shows 1,800,000 persons in the Intermediate Class (if as in 1924 shop-assistants are counted with wage-earners) with an aggregate income of £140 mn. The average income (under £125) at £78 is to be compared with the £95 (under £150) estimated in 1924.

The number of individuals assessed to tax in 1931–32 was estimated by the Income-Tax Commissioners at about 4,900,000; the exact number is not known, and is less than the number of separate assessments of income, since many persons are assessed under more than one schedule or more than once under one schedule. Among the individuals assessed is a considerable number who are not occupied and derive their income solely from property. A current estimate of this number is 250,000. Thus there are presumed to be about 4,650,000 individuals with incomes £125 or more, partly or wholly derived from gainful occupation. This is 750,000 in excess of the number of occupied persons (as shown in the table above), whose income from occupation is £125 or over. The gap is serious, both as regards number and aggregate income.

One possible way of filling the gap can thus be found:

(*a*) Among the wage-earners may be included some, especially in Industrial Orders XVII to XX, who are not regarded as manual and assessed half-yearly (including here some of the shop-assistants with less than £125 per annum).

1 The Totals columns in the table and the table on p. 68 are equivalent.

(*b*) Among the salaries some will have additional income from property or supplementary work which bring their incomes from under to over £125.

(*c*) Among the salaried there are many married women, whose incomes are merged with their husbands' in assessment, and then the couple counts only as an individual.

(*d*) There is at present no basis for deciding how many of those working on their own account are assessed to tax.

On the assumptions that these classes account for 750,000 persons, and that their aggregate earned income is £60 mn. (i.e. £80 per head, men or women), the gap is closed. Part of this £80 mn. is included in the wage-earners aggregate, part in salaried. The Intermediate Class in the Income Total is replaced by a 'residual class' that includes those incomes which are not assessed to tax or included under wages. The amount to be included is £80 mn., viz. the £140 mn. in the tables less £60 mn.

Income from property that brings individual incomes above £125 is already included in the Income-Tax Total. Any earned income from occasional or supplementary sources should be added, but the amount is not known and can hardly be great enough to affect the total perceptibly.

The estimate for the total of the constituents of national income so far considered in 1931–32 is then:

Assessed to income tax ('actual income')	£2,065 mn.
Shop-assistants under £125	55 ± 5
Wage-earners	1,340 ± 40
Residual class	80 ± 20
Total of these constituents	£3,540 ± 50

The income-tax assessment for Schedules A, B, C is that for the year 1931–32, that for D and E for 1932–33, which is assessed on the previous year's earnings. Income from wages is excluded from E.

The margins of uncertainty indicated are in part complementary, so that less than their sum is suggested for the total. It is possible, however, that on further investigation the £80 mn. for the residual class may need to be modified.

TOTAL NATIONAL INCOME, 1924–38

There is still a number of relatively small constituents to be brought into account in any statement of Total Income. In Table IX these are included, whether they are definitely

Preliminary Estimates of National Income

(£ mn.)

Year ...	1924	1925	1926	1927	1928	1929	1930	1931	1932	1933	1934	1935	1936	1937	1938
Actual Income:															
1. Schedules A, B, C	390	387	403	418	435	442	452	479	482	478	482	487	489	507	_515_*
2. Schedules D, E	1,686	1,738	1,713	1,775	1,800	1,776	1,726	1,585	1,523	1,616	1,682	1,801	1,939	2,030	_2037_*
3. Adjustment for date	118	—	—	—	—	—	—	—	—	—	—	—	—	—	—
Total	2,194	2,125	2,116	2,193	2,235	2,218	2,178	2,064	2,005	2,094	2,164	2,288	2,428	2,537	_2,552_*
Wages and earnings:†															
4. Shop-assistants }	1,600	59	60	61	62	63	64	55	55	55	55	56	56	54	54
5. Wage-earners }		1,518	1,486	1,554	1,520	1,525	1,448	1,342	1,315	1,340	1,421	1,496	1,586	1,676	1,691
6. Residual class	_190_	_190_	_190_	_190_	_190_	_190_	_190_	_80_	_80_	_80_	_90_	_100_	_100_	_100_	_85_
Unearned Income:															
7. Small property	_77_	_77_	_77_	_77_	_77_	_77_	_77_	_45_	_46_	_48_	_50_	_52_	_56_	60	_60_
8. Charities	_42_	_47_	_48_	_50_	_51_	_52_	_53_	_54_	_53_	_54_	_54_	_57_	_61_	62	_65_
9. Savings certificates	_16_	_16_	_17_	_17_	_16_	_16_	_16_	_16_	_16_	_17_	_18_	_18_	_18_	_19_	_20_
Sundries:															
10. Pensions	93	92	92	94	90	86	82	84	82	78	77	75	74	73	72
11. Employers' contributions	35	32	_30_	29	28	29	29	30	32	33	35	36	36	37	_37_
12. Others	_26_	_16_	_26_	_26_	_41_	_51_	_47_	_37_	_2_	_26_	_38_	_31_	_25_	_26_	_18_
A. Total	4,273	4,172	4,142	4,291	4,310	4,307	4,184	3,807	3,686	3,825	4,002	4,209	4,440	4,644	4,654*
Transfers:															
13. Income due to Foreigners	_25_	_25_	_25_	_25_	_25_	_25_	_25_	_25_	_26_	_27_	_28_	_30_	_30_	_35_	_35_
14. National Debt interest	_268_	_261_	_272_	_275_	_272_	_270_	_265_	_260_	_251_	_187_	_184_	_185_	_185_	_185_	_185_
B. Total: A less 10, 13, 14	3,887	3,794	3,753	3,897	3,923	3,926	3,812	3,438	3,327	3,533	3,713	3,919	4,151	4,351	_4,362_ *
B. In round numbers	**3,900**	**3,800**	**3,750**	**3,900**	**3,925**	**3,925**	**3,800**	**3,450**	**3,325**	**3,550**	**3,700**	**3,900**	**4,150**	**4,350**	**4,350** *

The items printed in italics are specially subject to revision. * Amended from original paper.

† Under £150 or £125 per annum.

ascertained or are the subject of rough estimates, subject to considerable revision, if possible, after further investigation.

The separate lines of the table may be briefly explained:

1. The assessments for Schedules A, B, C for each Fiscal Year, such as 1925–26, are taken as applicable to the corresponding Calendar Year, 1925.

2. The assessments for Schedules D and E are antedated one year, so that the assessment for 1926–27 is taken as applicable to 1925[1].

3. Owing to the change in the method of assessment of profits from a three-year average to one year an addition is necessary in 1924.

4 and 5 have already been explained (pp. 68 seq., 75 seq. above).

6. It has been assumed that the 1924 estimate is still valid till 1930, and then reduced at the time of the lowering of the exemption limit. Since 1931 some variation is assumed in parallelism with other entries.

7. Income from property accruing to persons whose total income is under the exemption limit is in some cases assessed under Gross Income and subtracted to arrive at Actual Income; in other cases there is no record. The whole sum was estimated from rough data at £77 mn. in 1924, and again at £45 mn. in 1931, with subsequent adjustments to 1938. In the absence of information the estimate for 1924 has been repeated till 1930, and then reduced as in line 6.

8. Besides the income of Charities, etc., assessed under Gross Income and subtracted to obtain Actual Income, it is known that a sum (estimated at £12 mn., rising to £15 mn.) is unassessed. This estimate has been included.

9. It is assumed that interest at 1*s*. per annum is payable on outstanding certificates less the number purchased in the same year.

10. Pensions here include war pensions to men and dependents and medical treatment, non-contributory Old Age Pensions and the Government grant to Contributory Pensions.

11. Employers' contributions to the National Unemployment and Health Funds, which are not included in Actual Income under Schedules D and E, are here included, on the assumption

1 The entries for 1938 have been modified in accordance with the figures given in the White Paper: An Analysis of the Sources of War Finance and an Estimate of National Income and Expenditure in 1938 and 1940 (Cmd. 6261).

that they are additive to the income of wage-earners which has been computed as including only those actually at work. It is arguable that the Government's contribution should be included. Or we might take the total amount of benefits less the workers' contributions, in which case we should substitute:

Benefits less Workers' Contributions (£mn.)

(Health and Unemployment)

1924	39	1931	115
1925	41	1932	105
1926	49	1933	78
1927	44	1934	83
1928	49	1935	81
1929	53	1936	80
1930	97		

In Table IX, however, the procedure followed in 1924 has been adopted. If the new figures were used, there would have to be an adjustment under 'transfers'.

12. This includes an allowance for evasion less over-assessment in 1924, which has been dropped in subsequent years; an adjustment for income from real property rising £1 mn. per annum between the years of re-assessment, when it is put at zero; a rough estimate of income accruing to Government from property or trading at home, and an addition (or subtraction) for excess of overseas Government receipts over payments.

13. This is largely conjectural.

14. Rough estimates are made of the interest payable to foreigners on the National Debt and are subtracted from the total interest paid.

The Total A corresponds to Aggregate Income in the 1924 study (Bowley and Stamp), while the Total B was termed Social Income. The figures here differ from the earlier owing to an adjustment in line 3 (using final instead of provisional assessments), additions in lines 8 and 9, and a modification and addition in line 12. Since probably there is some duplication of shop-assistants salaries in 1924 in lines 2 and 4, in the final line the total is reduced.

The official White Paper, referred to above (p. 82 n.) gives an estimate of the Net National Income in 1938. The total is £4,415 mn. as compared with £4,362 mn. in the last line of Table IX. By the courtesy of the Central Statistical Office I am able to analyse the differences.

The largest difference is in wages, and is due, as explained above (pp. 73–4), to a larger factor for number of weeks paid for in the year in the later estimate.

In line 1 it is held that Schedule B is under-stated, for which allowance was made in Table IX in line 6, and that Schedule A is under-assessed, for which line 12 possibly includes an item.

	Table IX	White Paper	Excess of Table	Defect of Table
Line 1	515	527		12
Lines 2, 3, 4	2,091	2,091		
Line 5	1,691	1,766		75
Lines 6, 7, 8	210	210		
Line 9	20	11	9	
Line 11	37	0	37	
Line 12	18	}		
Government net income	0	50 }		12
Subtract business losses	0	−20 }		
Total	4,582	4,635		53
Subtract:				
Income due to foreigners	35	35		
National Debt interest	185	185		
Total	4,362	4,415		53

Line 9 is probably estimated in the White Paper with more knowledge of the facts; but the possibility of increasing the £11 mn. to £16 mn. is admitted.

For line 11 employers' contributions are regarded as a tax, not as anyone's income, in the White Paper. The treatment of this sum is to be decided by considering what definition of Income is appropriate for the purpose in hand.

The treatment of Government Income is again a matter of definition.

Estimated business losses can be balanced against under-assessment.

Thus the difference in the totals (1·2 per cent) is partly due to definition, partly to different judgments where the data are incomplete.

2. *CHANGES IN SALARIES IN GREAT BRITAIN*, 1924 TO 1939[1]

By Joan G. Marley and H. Campion

This paper gives a summary of the preliminary results of two enquiries made by the Economics Research Section of the

1 Reprinted with slight modifications from the *Journal of the Royal Statistical Society*, Part IV, 1940, by kind permission of the Council.

University of Manchester relating to changes in salaries in Great Britain from 1924 to 1939. The first was a sample enquiry of salaries paid in 1938 to 700,000 persons, and was undertaken in collaboration with the National Institute of Economic and Social Research. The second was the collection by the Economics Research Section of details of changes in salary rates made by private firms and public bodies between 1924 and 1939. The analysis of the results of the two enquiries has been suspended because of the war, but it is possible to give here details of salaries paid to different classes of salaried persons in 1938 and also index-numbers of changes in salary rates from 1924 to 1939.

A. NUMBER OF SALARIED PERSONS

For the purposes of both enquiries all persons employed in non-manual occupations in private industry and in public administration (excluding employers, persons 'on their own account', the armed forces, and persons paid wholly or mainly by commission) were taken as salaried persons. This basis of classification was chosen to conform with the classifications of salaried persons used by the Board of Trade for the Census of Production, by the Board of Inland Revenue for assessments under Schedule E for income tax and by the Ministry of Labour for purposes of unemployment insurance. Thus our estimates of the number of salaried persons in Great Britain include (*a*) the technical, administrative and clerical staff—to use the description adopted in the Census of Production—employed in manufacturing industries, and (*b*) other persons not in manufacturing industries, who are assessed annually for income-tax purposes under Schedule E (excluding weekly wage-earners in manual occupations and shop-assistants) or are non-manual workers as defined for purposes of unemployment insurance.

No claim can, of course, be made to absolute accuracy in the estimates of the numbers of salaried persons used in this paper. The line of demarcation between manual and non-manual occupations has never been clearly drawn and is less distinct than it was. Other investigators might wish to exclude some persons whom we have included or to make additions to our totals. Their alternative estimates, if shop-assistants are excluded, are not, however, likely to differ much from those given in this paper. Shop-assistants have been excluded throughout from our figures of salaried persons, even though their work may be considered non-manual. Details of earnings of shop-assistants and changes in their rates of earnings since 1924 are given separately in Section D of this paper.

Salaried persons have been classified into nine categories according to the branches of industry in which they were engaged. (In each branch of industry there may be persons engaged in similar occupations. More than half of the salaried class in 1931 were in clerical occupations.) The method of arriving at the estimates in Table I was first to separate persons

TABLE I

Estimated Number of Salaried Persons (excluding shop-assistants) in Great Britain in 1931 and 1911

(thousands)

Branch of industry in which employed	1931			1911		
	Total	Males	Females	Total	Males	Females
TOTAL	2,900	1,775	1,125	1,532	954	578
A. *Private Industry*						
Manufacturing industry and agriculture	726	481	245	279	228	51
Distribution	488	281	207	178	117	61
Finance	324	252	72	57	50	7
Transport	159	130	29	38	36	2
Personal service	122	50	72	49	18	31
Professions	394	213	181	442	224	218
B. *Public Administration*						
Central Government	210	133	77	123	87	36
Local Government administration and industry	248	169	79	169	140	29
Teachers	229	66	163	197	54	143

employed in public administration from persons employed in private industry. Persons employed by the State and local authorities were then divided into salaried officials and wage-earners, and the salaried officials in turn sub-divided into the three categories (*a*) non-manual civil servants employed by the State, (*b*) administrative and clerical staff employed by local authorities and (*c*) teachers employed by local authorities. Salaried persons employed in private industry had to be separated on the one hand from wage-earners and from employers and workers 'on their own account' on the other. They were then sub-divided into the six categories of (*a*) technical, administrative and clerical staff employed in manufacturing industries and agriculture, (*b*) the salaried staff (excluding shop-assistants) of firms engaged in wholesale and retail distribution, (*c*) officials of banks, insurance and finance companies, (*d*) the non-manual workers of railway, road and transport undertakings, (*e*) the salaried staff (excluding domestic servants) of individuals, clubs and businesses engaged in providing personal services and (*f*) the professional, clerical and administrative staff of all individuals and firms providing professional services.

In 1931 the number of salaried persons in Great Britain is estimated to have been 2·9 mn. and to have increased further to 3·2 mn. in 1938—one in seven of all occupied persons in the country. The number of salaried persons has been increasing since before the last war both in total and also relatively as a proportion of the total occupied population. The number increased from 1·5 to 2·9 mn. between 1911 and 1931, and this represented an increase from 8·3 per cent of the total occupied population in 1911 to 13·8 per cent in 1931. The increase in the number of females employed in non-manual occupations has been greater than for males. Females in salaried occupations were 18·0 per cent of the total number of occupied females in 1931. The percentage of occupied males in salaried occupations was only 12·0.

Although the total of all persons occupied in public administration has increased by a greater rate than those occupied in private industry since 1911, the number of salaried persons employed in private industry has risen more than the number of salaried officials of the State and local authorities. There has been a marked expansion of non-manual workers in manufacturing industry, distribution, finance and transport. The number of salaried persons employed by businesses providing professional services has decreased mainly because many industrial concerns and public bodies now employ a larger number of officials with professional qualifications than they did before the last war. The slower rate of increase in salaried persons in public administration is, however, partly explained by the relatively slow growth in the number of teachers employed by local authorities. Civil servants, Local Government officials and school-teachers form still the three largest homogeneous groups within the salaried class, but in 1931 they were less than one-quarter of all salaried persons. 79 per cent of all salaried males in 1931 and 72 per cent of all salaried females were employed in private industry.

B. EARNINGS OF SALARIED PERSONS IN 1938

The first enquiry undertaken by the Economic Research Section was to collect details of the average earnings of persons in each of the nine categories into which we had divided the salaried class in 1938. It was possible to obtain information directly covering the majority of civil servants and teachers, but for the remaining seven categories it was necessary to ask a large number of firms and institutions if they would give details of salaries paid to their technical, administrative and clerical staff in the Calendar Year 1938. They were asked to state:

(*a*) The numbers of males 21 and over, males under 21, females 21 and over and females under 21, receiving salaries classified according to the amounts of salaries they were paid in the last financial year.

(*b*) The total salaries paid (without deductions for superannuation or for unemployment and health insurance contributions) in the last financial year to males and females in each salary group.

TABLE II

Percentage Distribution of Numbers of Salaried Persons (excluding teachers and civil servants) in Great Britain in 1938 *according to salaries received*

(percentages)

Range of annual salaries	Weighted			Unweighted		
	Total	Males	Females	Total	Males	Females
Total	100·0	100·0	100·0	100·0	100·0	100·0
Up to £40	2·2	1·3	4·7	1·5	1·0	3·0
£40–59	4·6	2·9	9·5	3·5	2·4	6·4
£60–89	9·3	5·7	19·1	8·4	5·8	15·8
£90–125	11·4	5·0	28·1	10·8	5·2	26·4
£126–162	10·0	6·6	18·3	9·6	6·4	18·8
£163–250	21·8	22·9	16·2	22·3	21·8	23·6
Over £250	40·8	55·5	4·1	43·9	57·4	6·1

Excluding the information obtained for civil servants and teachers, returns were received from firms and public bodies which employed 308,000 salaried persons and paid £80 mn. in salaries in 1938. Most of the returns received related to the 12 months ending 31 December 1938. The returns covered approximately 11 per cent of the total number of salaried persons (excluding civil servants and teachers) in Great Britain in that year.

TABLE III

Percentage Distribution of Numbers of Salaried Persons classified by amount of salaries received in 1938

(percentages)*

Sex and age of salaried persons	Range of annual salaries	Private industry: Manufacturing industry	Private industry: Distribution	Private industry: Finance	Private industry: Transport	Private industry: Professions	Public administration: Local authorities
	Total	100·0	100·0	100·0	100·0	100·0	100·0
Males, 21 and over	Up to £40	—	—	—	—	—	0·3
	£40–59	0·1	0·1	—	0·1	—	0·3
	£60–89	0·4	0·8	0·5	0·2	1·2	0·8
	£90–125	3·2	8·5	2·4	1·3	7·5	3·1
	£126–162	9·0	20·0	3·7	5·5	18·4	8·9
	£163–250	33·1	30·5	11·7	29·5	34·5	34·4
	Over £250	54·2	40·2	81·7	63·6	38·5	52·3
	Total	100·0	100·0	100·0	100·0	100·0	100·0
Males, under 21	Up to £40	16·1	19·4	2·8	15·4	22·2	5·6
	£40–59	31·3	27·2	10·7	19·7	27·8	21·0
	£60–89	37·7	37·1	53·3	24·5	33·3	45·6
	£90–125	12·3	13·8	29·9	39·9	16·7	25·2
	£126–162	1·3	2·5	3·4	—	—	2·5
	£163–250	0·6	—	—	0·5	—	0·2
	Over £250	0·7	—	—	—	—	—
	Total	100·0	100·0	100·0	100·0	100·0	100·0
Females, 21 and over	Up to £40	0·1	2·0	—	—	1·3	0·7
	£40–59	0·6	1·8	—	0·3	—	1·0
	£60–89	9·4	9·0	2·3	1·4	5·3	3·8
	£90–125	43·5	32·6	18·6	20·3	21·7	21·4
	£126–162	29·3	27·2	23·8	22·0	29·0	25·4
	£163–250	14·5	20·0	45·0	54·2	32·2	35·8
	Over £250	2·7	7·5	10·3	1·8	10·5	11·9
	Total	100·0	100·0	100·0	100·0	100·0	100·0
Females, under 21	Up to £40	15·8	15·4	0·7	5·6	17·0	8·0
	£40–59	31·9	26·0	4·5	11·1	23·4	21·8
	£60–89	43·0	39·3	42·3	30·6	27·7	48·2
	£90–125	9·0	18·9	51·5	52·8	23·4	21·3
	£126–162	0·3	0·4	0·9	—	8·5	0·7
	£163–250	—	—	0·2	—	—	—
	Over £250	—	—	—	—	—	—

* The percentages are given in each case to the nearest figure in the decimal.

The unweighted percentages given in Table II were calculated from the totals of all the returns received. Since, however, the number of persons covered by the returns was not the same proportion for each class of salaried persons, the percentages for each category were combined by weighting the number of persons in each category. The percentage distribution of salaries as weighted in this way is not very different from the unweighted distribution. Table III does, however, show some noticeable differences in the ranges of salaries paid in different branches of industry.

The details of salaries paid to teachers and to civil servants were not received in a form which allowed them to be incorporated in Tables II or III. 85 per cent of male school-teachers employed by local authorities received salaries in 1938 of more than £250 a year, 13½ per cent received between £200 and £250, and 1½ per cent less than £200. Corresponding percentages for female teachers were 54½ per cent more than £250, 30 per cent between £200 and £250, 15½ per cent less than £200. The inclusion of both these classes in Table II would have raised substantially the number of males and females in the higher salary groups. Although detailed figures are not available, it may be estimated that about 30 per cent of salaried male civil servants received salaries of more than £250 a year in 1938, 60 per cent between £125 and £250, and 10 per cent less than £125. For females in non-manual occupations in Government employment the corresponding figures were about 8 per cent more than £250, 53 per cent between £125 and £250 and 42 per cent less than £125.

C. CHANGES IN RATES OF SALARIES, 1924–39

The second enquiry was undertaken to see how far rates of salaries had changed between 1924 and 1939 and to provide the information needed for compiling an index-number of changes in salary rates. All the firms, institutions and local authorities covered by the first enquiry were again approached and most of them were kind enough to give information. In addition, other firms who had not been asked to assist in the first enquiry gave details of changes in their rates of salaries since 1924. Altogether information was received covering 550,000 persons or 17 per cent of the salaried class in 1938. Details of changes in the salary rates of civil servants and of teachers were obtained mainly from official sources.[1]

1 Reports of the Royal Commission on the Civil Service, 1929–31 (Cmd. 3989) and of the Committee on National Expenditure (Cmd. 3920).

Employers were asked to give details not of special increases or decreases made in salaries of individuals, but only of general changes in salary rates which affected all or sections of their salaried staffs. Since, however, many small firms employ only a few salaried persons and since even large firms may have no organized scale of salaries, any index-number of changes in salary rates is necessarily less trustworthy than an index-number of changes in wage rates.

For the returns received, the changes in salary rates for each firm were calculated from 1924 to 1939, expressed as percentages of salary rates paid at December 1924. The percentage changes in rates for different firms were then combined by weighting by the salary bills of the firms in 1938. Separate index-numbers were thus obtained of the changes in salary rates for each category of salaried persons and they are shown in Appendix I; the general index-numbers were reached by weighting the percentages for each category by the estimated total salaries paid to all persons in each category in 1938.

D. EARNINGS OF SHOP-ASSISTANTS

In 1931 the number of shop-assistants in Great Britain was 975,000, of whom slightly more than half were males; the

TABLE IV

Percentage Distribution of Numbers of Shop-assistants in Great Britain according to earnings received in 1938

(percentages)

Range of earnings	Total	Males		Females	
		21 and over	Under 21	21 and over	Under 21
Total	100·0	100·0	100·0	100·0	100·0
Up to £40	10·4	0·1	31·4	0·3	21·9
£40–59	12·6	0·1	31·7	0·9	36·0
£60–89	17·9	0·3	24·1	29·5	37·4
£90–125	18·3	5·8	11·0	55·5	4·5
£126–162	12·2	23·7	1·6	10·2	0·1
£163–250	25·4	62·1	0·1	3·1	—
Over £250	3·3	8·0	—	0·6	—

number is estimated to have increased to at least 1,050,000 in 1938. It was decided to collect figures of the earnings of this important group of operatives and of changes in their rates of earnings since 1924 at the same time as the two enquiries described above, since figures for shop-assistants were not collected for the wage enquiries of the Ministry of Labour. The returns received covered 125,000 shop-assistants who were paid £14¾ mn. in 1938.

E. A GENERAL INDEX OF RATES OF WAGES AND SALARIES

The information given in this paper gives the opportunity for the first time of compiling a general index-number of changes in rates of wages and salaries for Great Britain since 1924.

TABLE V

Index-numbers of Changes in Rates of Wages and Salaries in Great Britain

(percentages)

	Total	Wage rates (excluding shop-assistants)	Wage rates of shop-assistants	Salary rates
1924 Dec.	100·0	100·0	100·0	100·0
1925 Dec.	100·4	100·6	100·0	100·0
1926 Dec.	100·7	101·2	100·0	99·7
1927 Dec.	100·3	100·5	100·0	99·8
1928 Dec.	99·5	99·4	100·0	99·6
1929 Dec.	99·1	98·8	100·0	99·7
1930 Dec.	98·5	98·2	100·0	99·0
1931 June	97·4	97·1	100·0	98·2
Dec.	96·2	96·5	99·7	95·6
1932 June	95·4	95·4	99·7	95·4
Dec.	94·9	94·6	99·7	95·5
1933 June	94·5	94·0	99·7	95·6
Dec.	94·6	94·0	99·7	95·8
1934 June	94·7	94·0	99·7	96·0
Dec.	95·1	94·3	99·7	96·8
1935 Dec.	96·3	95·7	99·7	97·6
1936 Dec.	98·1	98·1	100·3	98·1
1937 Dec.	101·7	103·1	102·8	98·7
1938 Dec.	102·9	104·7	102·8	98·9
1939 June	103·5	105·5	103·7	99·0

Professor Bowley has prepared index-numbers of wage rates from 1924, and it was possible to combine his figures with the index-numbers of changes of salaries and of rates of wages of shop-assistants given in this paper to obtain a general index. The three constituent series of the general index were combined by weighting according to the estimated totals of wages and of salaries paid in 1938. The general index of rates of wages and salaries given in Table V thus covers all occupied persons,

APPENDIX I

Index-numbers of Changes in Rates of Salaries in Great Britain, 1924–39

		Total	Private industry						Public administration		
			Manufacturing industry	Distribution	Finance	Transport	Personal service	Professions	Civil servants	Local authorities	Teachers
1924	Dec.	100·0	100·0	100·0	100·0	100·0	100·0	100·0	100·0	100·0	100·0
1925	Dec.	100·0	100·0	100·0	100·0	100·0	100·0	100·0	100·0	100·0	100·0
1926	Dec.	99·7	99·9	100·0	99·9	100·0	100·0	100·0	98·1	98·9	100·0
1927	Dec.	99·8	99·9	100·0	100·5	100·0	100·0	100·0	98·1	99·0	100·0
1928	Dec.	99·6	99·8	100·1	100·4	100·0	100·0	100·0	96·1	98·3	100·0
1929	Dec.	99·7	99·8	100·2	100·4	100·1	100·0	100·0	98·1	98·4	100·0
1930	Dec.	99·0	99·5	100·2	97·6	100·1	100·0	100·0	96·1	97·7	100·0
1931	June	98·2	98·9	100·2	96·5	99·5	96·9	100·0	92·2	97·7	100·0
	Dec.	95·6	95·5	98·7	95·3	99·5	96·9	98·4	90·3	95·6	90·0
1932	June	95·4	95·1	98·7	95·2	99·1	96·9	98·4	90·3	95·8	90·0
	Dec.	95·5	95·0	98·7	95·0	99·1	100·0	98·4	90·3	95·1	90·0
1933	June	95·6	95·1	98·7	95·3	99·1	100·0	98·4	90·3	95·3	90·0
	Dec.	95·8	95·2	99·0	95·3	99·1	100·0	98·4	90·3	96·8	90·0
1934	June	96·0	96·0	99·0	95·3	99·5	100·0	98·4	90·3	97·3	90·0
	Dec.	96·8	96·9	99·1	95·3	99·6	100·0	98·4	91·2	97·5	95·0
1935	Dec.	97·6	97·9	99·1	95·3	99·7	100·0	100·0	92·2	98·0	100·0
1936	Dec.	98·1	98·6	99·9	95·4	99·9	100·0	100·0	92·2	98·1	100·0
1937	Dec.	98·7	99·9	101·1	95·6	100·2	100·0	100·0	92·2	98·8	100·0
1938	Dec.	98·9	100·1	101·6	95·8	100·2	100·0	100·0	92·2	98·9	100·0
1939	June	99·0	100·3	102·1	95·9	100·2	100·0	100·0	92·2	99·0	100·0

excluding employers, persons working 'on their own account', commercial travellers or persons working mainly on commission and members of the armed forces.

F. CONCLUSIONS

The preliminary results obtained from the two enquiries described in this paper may be conveniently summarized:

(*a*) The salaried class has been growing during the last 30 years. In 1938 one out of every seven occupied persons in Great Britain was engaged in non-manual occupations.

(*b*) About 55½ per cent of males and 4 per cent of females in salaried occupations (excluding teachers and civil servants) received salaries more than £250 a year. 15 per cent of the males and 61½ per cent of the females in salaried occupations received less than £125 a year. Total salaries paid amounted to between one-sixth and one-fifth of the total personal incomes in Great Britain in 1938.

(*c*) Rates of salaries did not fall so much as rates of wages in the depression of 1929–33. Since salaries of important groups of non-manual workers changed between 1924 and 1939 according to the movements of the Ministry of Labour Cost of Living index-number, there was a greater decline in the salary rates between 1924 and 1928 and a slower recovery in salary rates than in wage rates between 1934 and 1939.

NOTE BY A. L. BOWLEY

Since Mr Campion's Paper and my Address are part of the same larger investigation and to some extent cover the same ground, it will be convenient to readers to have their relation to each other explained. While Mr Campion is solely concerned with salaries, I was concerned on the one hand with the whole of 'Intermediate' or 'Residual' Income, but on the other only with that part of the salary aggregate which was below the exemption limit.

Consequently the statistics in my Table VII do not correspond very closely with any given by Mr Campion and Miss Marley. The range of mine is somewhat greater, because some estimates were included for industrial groups for which there were no returns in the questionnaires, and in some cases (other than agriculture) there were small additions to the aggregate income under £125 for small employers. But the main difference is that Mr Booker (whose detailed work I incorporated) took, as the totals to which the computed percentages were applied, the entries in the Population Census that included employers, while Mr Campion's totals excluded them. Thus the total number of salaried males in April 1931 is given by him as 1,775,000 for Great Britain (p. 86), while in Table VII (which includes Northern Ireland) the total of employers, managers and non-manual operatives for the same industrial groups is 2,430,000, of whom 1,578,000 are operatives and 852,000 employers or managers. For females, on the other hand, Mr Campion's total is 1,125,000 for Great Britain, while in Table VII the corresponding total is 1,046,000 for the United Kingdom, including 136,000 employers and managers. These discrepancies are due to some differences of definition and to some doubt about the interpretation of the questionnaire on the part of those who filled it up.

In the industrial groups included in both estimates, Mr Campion's total for salaries below £125 p.a. would be about £70 mn., while mine for all occupied non-manually (except persons working on their own account) is £77 mn., of which £2 mn. is attributable to Northern Ireland. So that the final discrepancy in the aggregate of these incomes is relatively small.

3. *INCOME FROM AGRICULTURE*

Estimates of Income from Agriculture come from two sources. First we have Income Tax Reports, which should include the income of landowners, farmers and others gaining their living from the land, and estimates of wages from general and special wage statistics. Secondly, the Ministry of Agriculture gives annual statistics of the Gross Value of Agricultural Produce. In connection with the 1924 Census of Production an estimate was also made of Net Value, but in other years special and hazardous computations must be made to estimate the cost of feeding stuffs, fertilizers, etc. bought from manufacturers or imported.

The latter method gives the higher estimate, and since there are reasons for holding that farmers' income is understated in the Income Tax Reports, it is to be preferred, with allowance of a considerable margin for doubtful items.

I. ESTIMATES FROM INCOME STATISTICS

From the income side, we have the figures published in the Inland Revenue Reports, under Schedules A and B, but these do not give us exactly what we want. Incomes derived from the ownership of land are assessed under Schedule A. Farmers' incomes can be assessed under either Schedule B or D, but, since very few farmers keep accounts, most of them are assessed under Schedule B, where the tax is based not on actual income but on the annual value of the land. These figures are necessarily approximate, and the total of farmers' incomes, shown under Schedule B, is almost certainly an under-estimate. For although it includes the incomes of some people (e.g. innkeepers) occupying land but not primarily engaged in agriculture,[1] it excludes agricultural incomes assessed under Schedule D, and incomes of managers assessed under Schedule E (neither of these being separately shown), as well as any subsidiary incomes which agricultural households may obtain, e.g. from retail distribution or from paying guests, though the last is probably a small item. The fact that most farmers prefer to be assessed under Schedule B also suggests that the figure is an under-estimate.

From the figures of *Gross Income*, under Schedules A and B, we have to subtract Repairs and Other Reductions and Discharges, in order to arrive at *Net Income*.

Employment figures are based on the Population Censuses (Industry tables) showing the number of operatives employed in agriculture in 1931 (Great Britain) and 1926 and 1937 (Northern Ireland); for other years they are interpolated.

For the course of wages we have monthly statistics of the minimum rates of ordinary labourers ordained for each county. Average earnings are greater than the average of these minimum rates owing to additional payments for special work, overtime, piece-work and other factors, and fairly accurate estimates are available for these from time to time. The aggregates of annual earnings are probably not subject to an error greater than £5 mn.

The totals so obtained for 1931 are:

Schedule A	£35 mn.
B	40
Wages	64
Total	£139

1 That the number of such people may be considerable is illustrated by the fact that, in 1931, the number of agricultural holdings in Great Britain of more than one acre is stated (in *Agricultural Statistics*) as 468,000, a figure considerably in excess of the 365,000 recorded in the Census of that year as employers, managers and workers on their own account engaged in agriculture. But the total incomes derived from the occupation of land of these people is not likely to be very large.

To this we must add a small sum for farmers assessed under Schedule D, about £1 mn. for non-manual salaries, and £5 mn. or more for the net income of firms which undertake tractor, ploughing and reaping; the numbers thus employed are included under Agriculture in the Census of Population, but the value of their services is not included in the Census of Production. We thus arrive at £145 to £150 mn. for the income arising from Agriculture in 1931, and similarly £140 to £150 mn. in 1938.

II. ESTIMATES FROM PRODUCTION STATISTICS

For 1938 Mr M. G. Kendall (*Journal of the Royal Statistical Society*, 1941) estimates the Income and Expenditure of Great Britain and Ireland treated as one 'National Farm', 'inter-farm transactions such as the transfer of livestock or sales of crops grown for animal feeding on farms being ignored'.

Estimated Income and Expenditure Account of the National Farm (United Kingdom)

(Average 1937–39)

Income	£mn.	Expenditure	£mn.
Sales of products	—	Labour	65
Livestock and livestock products	200	Rent and mortgage payments	33
Farm crops	84	Feeding stuffs	65
Miscellaneous (seeds for export, etc.)	1	Fertilizers and seeds	9
		Taxes, rates, etc.	4
		Interest on loans, etc.	7
		Miscellaneous expenses (machinery, etc.)	20
		Balance	82
	285		285

For the purpose of computing Net Output as in the Census of Production we must ignore the expenditure on feeding stuffs, fertilizers and seeds. The miscellaneous expenses are as regards about £10 mn. for repairs, replacements, etc. and may reasonably be subtracted on the same ground that allowances are made in the Income Tax Returns and in most treatments of the Census of Production statistics. The remaining £10 mn. may be regarded as out payments to tractor and other companies, of which £5 mn. may be taken as their net income.

The balance in the table is the farmers' income. We therefore have as a very rough approximation:

Rents, interests	£40 mn.
Taxes, rates	4
Farmers' income	82
Subsidiary income	5
Labour	65
Total	£196 mn.

Part of taxes, rates, etc. are necessary payments for drainage, etc., but on the whole this small item is somebody's income, though not evidently agricultural.

The production estimate thus exceeds the income estimate by about £50 mn.

In *The National Income*, 1924 (Bowley and Stamp), p. 25, the relation of Schedule B to farmers' income was analysed, by considering the numbers of holdings of different sizes in relation to apparent income. As a working hypothesis it was taken 'that farmers with holdings of 100 acres or more were assessed as having incomes over £150'. By comparison of the number of farmers in the Population Census and the number of holdings, it was deduced that holdings of under 10 acres were equal to land occupied by non-farmers. Then there were left 260,000 holdings of from 10 to 100 acres not accounted for. 'The average holding in this group is about 36 acres and a house, and if we assume that the income from this group is £100 (per holding), the whole contribution to Intermediate Income is £26 millions.'

There is no need to make any additional entry in the table on p. 81. For these small farmers are included in the 'Residual Class', which contains all earners not accounted for in lines 1 to 5.

Table A shows the sequence of figures for the estimate from Incomes. Table B gives details of the estimates of those classes of expenditure which are deductive on the Census of Production method. Also the estimated value of Gross Output is entered year by year and hence the Net Output.[1] This Net Output is divisible among landlords, farmers, agricultural wage-earners and others, and for repairs, etc. as discussed above. Mr Kendall, however, estimates £74 mn. for feeding stuffs, etc. in 1938, whereas in the table the estimate is £82 mn. The difference is mainly due to an allowance for transport and selling costs.

1 For 1924 and 1930 the Net Output is very nearly the same as those given some time ago in connection with the Census of Production, small holdings and forestry excluded.

These estimates are not easily reconcilable with each other, and there remains a considerable margin in the total which should be attributed to income as tabulated in Table IX (p. 81) from the agricultural community as a whole. The following table, which contains rough and uncertain estimates, shows the nature of the problem rather than giving definite results:

Constituents of Agricultural Income

(£000,000's)

	1924	1930	1938
Rents, tithes and mortgage interest	38	36	31
Farmers' income:			
Schedule B	41	41	42
Addition	26	26	26
Schedules D and E:			
Interest on loans	7	7	7
Salaries	2	2	2
Tractor, etc. companies	5	5	5
Wages	67	67	62
Total income	186	184	175
Feeding stuffs, fertilizers, etc.	85	58	82
Balance	24	18	28
Gross output	295	260	285

The line termed Balance is obtained by subtraction. Its main element is the upkeep of buildings, tools and machinery, fences, etc. The figure for 1938 is higher than Mr Kendall's estimate and there is no evident reason, except a general lowness of prices, why it should be so much lower in 1930.

NOTES ON TABLE B

Home-produced feeding stuffs are estimated for 1924 and 1930 from Census of Production. For other years we assume that the proportion of their cost to total gross output can be linearly interpolated and that the same proportion holds from 1930 onwards. Imported feeding stuffs include the following items from Trade Returns: maize, maize products, oats, oat products (other sorts), cereal by-products, oil-seed cake and meal. Expenditure on fertilizers is roughly estimated from value of imports and home production (available for Census years), the figures being increased by 15 per cent for distribution costs and reduced by value of exports.

Gross Output figures:

1. England and Wales. 1924/25 and 1930/31 from Agricultural Censuses (Cmd. 4605, p. 39); 1931/32 to 1937/38, estimates

Table A

Agricultural Incomes in the United Kingdom

(£ mn.)

	1924	1925	1926	1927	1928	1929	1930	1931	1932	1933	1934	1935	1936	1937	1938
Net income, Schedule A	38	39	38	37	37	36	36	35	33	32	32	32	32	31	31
Net income, Schedule B	41	41	41	41	41	41	41	40	40	41	42	43	42	42	42
No. of labourers employed (thousands)	973	968	954	935	928	927	882	839	820	846	831	825	803	802	745
Average annual wages (£)	68·7	75·4	76·2	76·2	76·2	76·2	76·2	76·3	75·4	74·3	74·6	76·6	77·7	80·0	83·5
Total wage bill	67	73	73	71	71	71	67	64	62	63	62	63	62	64	62
Total agricultural income	146	153	152	149	149	148	144	139	135	136	136	138	135	137	135

Table B

Agricultural Costs, Gross Output and Net Output

(£ mn.)

	1924	1925	1926	1927	1928	1929	1930	1931	1932	1933	1934	1935	1936	1937	1938
Feeding stuffs:															
Home produced	33·9	33·0	30·7	29·9	29·3	27·9	24·8	22·9	23·6	24·9	26·3	26·8	28·4	29·1	29·5
Imported	29·8	26·1	22·1	26·0	27·5	27·5	18·2	17·3	20·1	17·6	21·5	21·5	25·5	34·0	29·8
Seeds and plants:															
Imported	2·4	2·5	3·0	3·2	3·1	2·7	3·1	2·6	2·2	2·1	3·2	3·2	3·4	3·2	3·8
15 per cent for transport, etc.	9·9	9·2	8·4	8·9	9·0	8·7	6·9	6·4	6·9	6·7	7·7	7·7	8·6	10·0	9·5
Fertilizers	9·4	8·8	9·8	9·9	8·3	6·7	5·1	7·8	7·6	7·2	8·6	8·8	9·3	8·9	8·9
Total expenditure	85·4	79·6	74·0	77·9	77·2	73·5	58·1	57·0	60·4	58·5	67·3	68·0	75·2	85·2	81·5
Gross output	295	295	282	285	287	282	260	239	227	239	253	258	273	280	285
Net output	210	215	208	207	210	208	202	182	166	180	185	190	198	195	203

by Ministry of Agriculture published in *Agricultural Statistics*, 1938, Part 1; 1925/26 to 1929/30 = Ministry of Agriculture estimates + 3·3 per cent for each year since original estimates for Census years were deficient by this amount, on average, compared with final estimates; 1923/24 by linear interpolation of Census figures for 1908 and 1925.

2. Scotland. 1924/25, 1930/31, 1935/36 from Censuses. Other years after 1930/31, estimates of Department of Agriculture for Scotland. For years between 1924/25 and 1930/31 by linear interpolation of the proportion of output of Scotland to rest of Great Britain. 1923/24, same proportion assumed as in 1924/25.

3. Northern Ireland. 1925/26 from Census. Other years from official figures, increased by 3 per cent for fruit and vegetables (1926/27 to 1928/29, 1930/31, 1932/33, 1935/36); estimated for remaining years by interpolating the proportions of Northern Ireland output to that of England and Wales.

An Index of Agricultural Production (quantity) is given on p. 194 below.

4. *NUMBERS OF EARNERS*

The only complete statistics of the numbers of earners and other occupied persons are to be found in the Census of Population (Great Britain 1931, Northern Ireland 1926). The Unemployment Insurance Scheme covered about 75 per cent of the earners before its extension to Agriculture and some smaller groups. The Censuses of Production include only about half of the employed population. National Health Insurance accounts for over 80 per cent of the occupied population. When the differences of definition and scope are analysed, it is found that these four sets of statistics are broadly consistent with each other.

The Census of Population of 1931 shows in considerable detail the numbers, ages and sex of persons occupied in the aggregate and in each of a great number of industries. A distinction is drawn between employers, managers, persons working on their own account, and the main body of salaried and wage-earners. Also the number who stated that they were out of work is recorded.

The Unemployment Insurance Scheme in 1931 excluded non-manual employees earning more than £250 per annum, all persons under 16 or over 65 years, and agriculture and domestic service. Also employees in the service of Railways,

Public Utility Works and Government (Central or Local) were excluded when they were provided for under other schemes.

In Table A the statistics of the Population Census and the Insurance Scheme are compared. For each industry the Census figures are adjusted as in the following example:

Males, Cotton Industry

(000's)

Enumerated in Great Britain		217
Northern Ireland		0
		217
Subtract:		
Employers, managers and persons working on own account	6	
Those under 16 and over 65	15	
		21
Hence insurable		196

Such figures are shown in the A columns of the table.

In the B columns are given the numbers insured in April 1931, estimated by interpolation from those recorded in July 1930 and July 1931.

For the comparison of A and B the Census figures are grouped as closely as possible in the same industrial groups as those listed monthly in the *Ministry of Labour Gazette*. There is always difficulty in sub-classification of the great metals group, which includes all branches of engineering, motors, ships, metal production and a great variety of trades working mainly in metals.

In the Industries down to the first sub-total the agreement between columns A and B is fairly close. A should run higher than B because it includes persons with salaries over £250. It also probably includes under Food and Wood (furniture) a number who are both makers and dealers, and are classified under Commerce for insurance purposes.

In the latter entries, insured transport workers exclude a great number insured under the special railway schemes. In Government Employment, Commerce, Professions and Entertainments a considerable proportion of the men and some of the women have salaries over £250.

In the second part of Table A the numbers stated at the Census to be out of work (D) are compared with insured persons wholly unemployed (E) and those 'temporarily stopped' (F), that is, persons who expect to return to their occupation in a short time when there is work, and meanwhile do not seek other employment; coal-mining and the textile industries account for a large proportion of this group. It is generally the case among the males that the numbers under D are greater than those under E, but do not exceed them by as much as those under F. Thus it appears that men who were temporarily stopped did not in many cases regard themselves as out of work on Census day. The reason for the excess of E over D among females is not evident; probably many married women who had not worked at their occupation for some time registered at the Labour Exchanges in the hope of benefit, but recorded themselves as engaged in household duties at the Census. Other differences are explicable on the same grounds as in the first part of the table. It should be added that sick persons are not counted as unemployed for insurance purposes, and that columns D should be discounted, possibly up to 4 per cent of columns A, to allow for illness or accident as a cause of being out of work, before comparison is made with columns E and F.[1]

In Tables B the statistics of employment shown in the Censuses of Production are compared with the relevant insurance returns. The classification of industries is expanded a little in succeeding years. In B 1, Earth products includes mining products, cement, bricks, earthenware and glass; Metals, vehicles include all metal production, engineering and metal industries; Food, etc. includes drink and tobacco. In each table Wood includes furniture, and Gas, etc. includes electricity and water. In B 2, Engineering includes electrical cables. Building includes public works contracting, etc. In general the classification follows the lines of the Insurance statistics in the *Ministry of Labour Gazette*.

In the Censuses of Production, Manual or Operatives exclude employees (clerks, etc.) in the administrative offices; but these are included under 'All'. The first two columns relate to firms employing more than ten persons; to the second are added estimates for employees in small firms on the assumption that the division by sex is the same in them as in larger firms in each industrial group.

For the Insurance figures the average number unemployed in the year (taking March, June, September and December in 1924 and every month in 1930 and 1935) is subtracted from the number insured in July. In 1930 and 1935 the subtraction is done in two steps, first taking off those wholly unemployed and

1 It is, of course, only a coincidence that for males the grand totals of E and F together very nearly equals that of A.

Table A

United Kingdom. Census of Population 1931, *and Unemployment Insurance Statistics*

(000's)

	Numbers of persons of insurable age				Unemployed					
	Males		Females		Males			Females		
	A	B	A	B	D	E	F	D	E	F
Coal	1,084	1,046	6	6	216	181	97	1	1	0
Other mining	109	105	3	2	20	18	5	0	0	0
Mining products	56	46	3	3	11	9	2	0	0	0
Bricks, earthenware, glass	152	153	56	59	24	21	11	9	10	9
Chemicals	164	156	52	58	25	23	3	4	5	1
Engineering	629	687	104	113						
Vehicles	316	291	39	30						
Ships	276	249	5	4	485	405	166	37	47	15
Metals and metal trades	721	620	137	160						
Cotton	196	192	354	361	50	42	28	100	96	49
Wool	94	96	132	144	13	12	11	16	21	18
Other textiles	221	210	313	320	35	35	30	41	56	34
Leather	49	42	26	24	8	6	2	4	4	1
Clothing	228	194	437	408	31	21	10	29	27	12
Food	265	201	176	173	35	25	2	23	25	4
Drink	95	86	23	26	11	9	1	2	4	0
Tobacco	19	16	32	32	1	1	0	1	3	1
Wood	224	191	31	34	42	32	4	3	4	1
Paper	71	69	64	62	6	5	3	5	6	2
Printing	203	180	90	97	19	15	1	8	10	1
Miscellaneous	129	99	72	59	22	15	4	8	8	2
Building	963	1,096	13	11	196	212	8	1	1	0
Gas, etc.	229	165	7	7	20	14	1	0	0	0
Sub-total	6,493	6,190	2,175	2,193	1,270	1,101	390	292	330	151

Transport	1,304	827	48	35	154	176	5	3	3	0
Commerce	1,580	1,282	809	806	173	144	6	62	69	4
Fishing	44	29	2	1	10	5	0	0	0	0
Government	1,188	403	402	43	103	51	3	8	2	0
Professions	227	75	266	56	11	5	0	13	2	0
Entertainments	112	59	54	31	24	12	0	10	6	0
Other	136	105	43	37	96	42	1	28	4	1
Sub-total	4,591	2,780	1,624	1,009	571	435	15	124	86	5
Agriculture	635	—	58	—	62	—	—	3	—	—
Personal service	524	165	1,649	360	64	26	0	137	50	3
Grand Total	12,243	9,135	5,506	3,562	1,967	1,562	406	557	466	159

A. Enumerated in Census, including those out of work, less managers, etc. and persons under 16 or over 65 years. An estimate for Northern Ireland is included.

B. Numbers insured.

D. Numbers recorded in the Census as out of work, including managers, etc.

E. Insured persons wholly unemployed.

F. Insured persons temporarily unemployed.

In each entry the number is given to the nearest thousand.

Table B 1

Employees: Census of Production and Insured, 1924

(000's)

	Males			Females			Insured less unemployed (000's)	
	Manual	All	+ Small firms	Manual	All	+ Small firms	Males	Females
Coal-mining	1,172	1,192	1,196	5	6	6	1,181	7
Other mining	78	83	88	1	1	1	94	2
Earth products	148	161	171	45	48	49	176	46
Chemicals	108	133	140	35	45	48	147	48
Metals, vehicles	1,255	1,389	1,510	162	211	230	1,611	224
Textiles	461	511	517	738	752	760	454	715
Leather	31	35	41	12	13	15	44	19
Clothing	133	158	211	298	318	424	180	346
Food, etc.	220	283	348	140	157	193	275	188
Wood	103	115	155	19	23	31	151	25
Paper, printing	175	212	230	115	131	142	208	128
Miscellaneous	97	110	118	50	56	60	78	43
Building	386	413	553	1	5	6	752	9
Gas, etc.	156	183	190	1	4	4	154	5
Total	4,524	4,978	5,468	1,622	1,768	1,969	5,505	1,805
Transport	246	258	258	2	4	4	—	—
Local Authorities	186	192	195	0	1	1	—	—
Government Departments	86	95	95	2	3	3	—	—
Grand Total	5,042	5,523	6,016	1,626	1,776	1,977	—	—

Employees: Census of Production and Insured, 1930

(000's)

	Males			Females			Insured persons (000's)			
							Males Insured less unemployed		Females Insured less unemployed	
	Operative	All	+ Small firms	Operative	All	+ Small firms	Wholly	All	Wholly	All
Coal-mining	912	928	930	3	4	4	921	845	5	5
Other mining	83	86	94	0	0	0	93	88	2	2
Cement, pottery, glass, bricks	135	147	163	45	48	48	167	157	54	46
Chemicals	104	133	142	33	45	48	146	143	52	51
Metals and products	447	492	538	95	111	118	529	462	141	134
Engineering, vehicles	821	939	1,035	92	135	149	1,095	1,040	137	134
Textiles	387	435	442	611	628	640	447	368	710	577
Clothing	126	152	195	318	340	438	174	164	371	353
Leather	29	33	39	12	14	16	39	37	21	20
Food	143	177	231	124	146	191	181	179	151	147
Drink	67	84	93	18	21	24	78	78	22	22
Tobacco	10	14	14	28	30	31	15	15	29	29
Wood	123	137	195	27	32	46	166	163	30	29
Paper, printing	194	235	256	126	145	157	229	227	147	144
Miscellaneous	98	116	126	50	58	63	102	99	51	49
Building and materials	444	475	642	1	9	9	832	824	11	11
Gas, etc.	180	216	223	2	7	7	149	148	6	6
Total	4,303	4,799	5,358	1,585	1,773	1,989	5,363	5,037	1,940	1,759
Transport	224	237	237	2	3	3	—	—	—	—
Local Authorities	223	236	236	1	2	2	—	—	—	—
Government Departments	79	92	92	2	3	3	—	—	—	—
Grand Total	4,829	5,364	5,923	1,590	1,781	1,997	—	—	—	—

TABLE B 3

Employees: Census of Production and Insured, 1935

(000's)

	Males and Females			Insured less unemployed	
	Operative	All	+ Small firms	Wholly	All
Coal-mining*	745	762	764	761	698
Other mining*	73	78	86	88	83
Mining products	48	55	55	47	45
Bricks	86	91	94	91	89
Pottery	63	68	69	66	58
Glass	41	46	48	42	40
Chemicals	143	194	206	197	195
Metals, products, vehicles	1,516	1,766	1,916	1,899	1,832
Textiles	989	1,055	1,069	1,065	979
Leather	45	51	58	65	63
Clothing	483	536	644	561	536
Food	299	377	477	360	354
Drink	79	101	113	99	98
Tobacco	36	43	43	39	39
Wood*	149	167	236	205	201
Paper, printing*	329	401	434	392	388
Miscellaneous	155	183	196	136	142
Building*	399	434	703	974	966
Gas, etc.*	198	252	259	181	180
Total	5,876	6,660	7,470	7,278	6,986
Transport	204	217	217	—	—
Local Authorities	199	212	216	—	—
Government Departments	91	102	102	—	—
Grand Total	6,370	7,191	8,005	—	—

* Statistics mainly from Preliminary Reports.

then also those temporarily stopped; some of the latter may be counted as employed in the Census of Production account.

For the comparison the Census of Production should be discounted, especially for men, for those whose salaries are over £250, and also the numbers in small firms should be reduced to exclude working managers. On the other side the insured should be discounted by about 4 per cent for sickness, raised in each year by about 4 per cent for boys and girls under 16 years, and raised also by 4 per cent in 1930 and 1935 for employees over 65 years who were not insurable after 1927. With these possible adjustments the numbers in most cases have the expected relations to each other, but there is some difficulty in engineering, building and gas, etc. The Census of Production gives figures (see p. 125) for the production by Central and Local Authorities, and by Railway Companies. The last named includes locomotive and other engineering and construction work, which for insurance purposes may be under engineering, vehicles, contracting or transport.[1] The Central Government also includes shipbuilding and other industries. Since Local Governments undertake directly or indirectly a lot of work that might be insured under building and contracting, the number insured in this category exceeds that in private firms. We cannot separate in the Insurance figures Government employees who are doing administrative work from those engaged in production, though probably the latter form only a small proportion. It is also possible that persons engaged in gas, electricity or water works are included under Local Government for insurance purposes.

Outworkers, whose status in insurance is doubtful, are excluded from these tables. They numbered 42,000 in 1924, 31,000 in 1930, and 26,000 in 1935. The bulk of them were in textile and clothing industries.

A summary comparison between the Censuses of Production and the Insurance statistics may be given as follows:

Census of Production

(000's)

	Large and small firms operative, administrative and outworkers	Operatives in large firms only	Insured (over 16) at work in July in Census of Production industries
1924	8,055	6,670	7,360
1929	—	—	7,520
1930	7,950	6,420	7,020
1931	—	—	6,480
1934	—	—	7,040
1935	8,030	6,370	7,170

In the last column the figures have been raised in the later years to allow for persons over 65 years, and it is assumed that the number absent through illness is balanced by uninsured boys and girls. They exclude Fishing, Transport, Distribu-

1 In March 1930 the Railway Companies employed 657,000 persons; of the men 96,000 were office staff or supervisory, 62,000 on permanent way, 132,000 shop and artisan, 310,000 in traffic or other departments, and 33,000 in ancillary businesses. There were also 24,000 women. In 1935 the total number of employees was 581,000.

tion, Commerce, Government, Professional and Personal and Miscellaneous Services[1].

The Censuses of Production do not relate exactly to the Calendar years (Chapter III), and in view of the changes in unemployment in 1929–31, 1934–35 additional figures are given for those years.

It will be seen that the figures in the last column are in each year very near the average of the two previous columns, so that we may conclude that the relationship between the Census and the Insurance accounts has, in the aggregate, changed very little in the eleven years.

The National Health Insurance Scheme includes all persons who come under the Unemployment Insurance Scheme, together with domestic service and agriculture. Besides this main body there is a number who, though their income is over £250, join the scheme voluntarily, and some other small groups. From the gross total of women we have to exclude women who have retired from occupation on marriage, but are still insured, when we are making comparative estimates of the number of persons occupied. There are thus several definitions and corresponding totals which we can use, and it would need a close study of the Insurance Acts and their administration before we could be confident that our definition covered the same classes over a period of years, and to make explicit the differences between the insured population and the whole occupied population.

In Table C are set out for males and females separately the changes from 1924 to 1938 (i) in the estimated number occupied based on the Population Census of 1931 and carried backward and forward on the assumption that the proportion of occupied to all in each age-group had not varied significantly from year to year (see p. 56); (ii) in the numbers entitled to benefit under the National Health Insurance Acts, excluding unoccupied married women, and showing separately the numbers under 65 years; (iii) in the numbers insured against unemployment and the numbers not recorded as unemployed.

The statistics relating to males are fairly consistent in the three records. The first two columns are closely parallel till 1935 or 1936, allowance being made for slight differences in date (the

1 The totals here differ from those in Table B, since here only July unemployment records are used and allowance is made for persons over 65 years.

Table C

United Kingdom. Index-Numbers of Occupations

Year	Males					Females				
	Population Census all ages	Health insurance		Employment insurance 16–65		Population Census all ages	Health insurance		Employment insurance 16–65	
		All ages	16–65	Insured	Employed		All ages	16–65	Insured	Employed
1924	100	100	100	100	100	100	100	100	100	100
1925	101	101	101½	101½	99½	100½	102	102	103½	103½
1926	102	104	104	103	98	101	105	104½	104	100
1927	103	105½	106	103½	105	101	107	106½	105	109
1928	104	104½	105	104	103	101½	111	108	106½	109
1929	105	105½	106	106	106	102	113½	110	109	112
1930	106	107½	108½	108	102½	102½	115½	111½	114½	106
1931	107½	108½	109½	111	97	102½	116	112	117	106
1932	109	109	110½	112½	94½	102½	116	111	115	109
1933	109	108	110	113	98	102	115	110	115½	113½
1934	109½	108	110½	114	104	101	115½	110	115½	115
1935	111	109	112	115	107	102	116	111	115½	115
1936	112	114	117	117½	113	103	121	115	118½	119
1937	113	116	119	120	120½	103	123½	117	123	126
1938	114	119½	122	122	119	104	127	121	125	121

Insurance figures are for December, the Census for mid-year). The third and fourth columns, that relate to the numbers of males aged 16 to 65 insured for health and unemployment respectively, show nearly similar movements throughout, except that the latter increase more rapidly in the years 1930–35. But after 1935 there is so rapid an increase in the number insured in both schemes, that it cannot be explained by any known change in scope or administration. It implies a drift from uninsured to insured groups, of the order of 100,000 per annum. Possible sources are a reduction in salaries which brought more men under the £250 limit, and a transfer from persons working on their own account to the position of employees. There is, however, a difficulty, when one compares the Census with the Insurance figures, that the former include earners under 16 years, whose numbers have varied greatly in reflection of the varying number of births from 1908 to 1924, and it would be a tedious process to make the series strictly comparable, and the correction for the number of juniors would be quite small.

As regards the females the differences between the statistics of the two insurance schemes are of a minor character and can be no doubt sufficiently explained by close analysis of their contents. The Unemployment Insurance are the more satisfactory and it will be sufficient to examine their relation to the Census figures. In more detail we have:

Females. Numbers employed as indicated by the Population Census

	(000's)			(percentage)		
Ages	1924	1931	1938	1924	1931	1938
14–	1,880	1,840	1,790	100	98	95
21–	3,920	4,020	4,090	100	102	104
55–	340	410	460	100	120	135
65–	130	160	190	100	125	145
Total	6,270	6,430	6,530	100	102½	104
21–55	4,260	4,430	4,550	100	104	107

Females. Insured for Unemployment

	(000's)			(percentage)		
	1924	1931	1938	1924	1931	1938
Distribution and transport	561	773	855	100	140	150
Commerce	37	75	93	100	200	250
Government	50	44	112	100	90	225
Professions, etc.	69	89	168	100	130	250
Hotels, laundries	281	366	446	100	130	160
Together	998	1,347	1,674	100	135	168
Industry	2,033	2,236	2,313	100	110	114
Total	3,031	3,583	3,987	100	118	132

The Insurance figures need adjustment to eliminate persons over 65 in 1924 and certain new classes of personal service newly insured in 1938; when this is done the percentages of the total become 117 in 1931 and 125 in 1938.

The main cause of the discrepancy is thus to be found in services, as contrasted with industry, especially in distribution (shops, etc.) and hotel and restaurant service. In the fourteen years the insured population gained on the Census estimate by nearly 700,000 persons. But in 1924 less than one-half of the occupied women were insured, and it is not impossible that 50,000 per annum who would have been working on their own account (e.g. as dressmakers), or only partly employed, or in domestic service or other uninsured occupations, may have turned (or rather their successors may have turned) to insured occupations. Also women who have in fact given up paid occupation may continue to register as unemployed insured.

But we cannot ignore the possibility that larger proportions of women at various ages were occupied in 1938 than in 1924, and in computing the wage bill we should keep as a margin the earnings of an addition of about 60,000 persons per annum, or over the 14 years an addition of about £30 mn.

NOTE ON THE DISTRIBUTION OF INCOMES AMONG PERSONS

The purpose of this note is to examine the statistics that relate to distribution, and the conclusion is unfortunately that no trustworthy results can be obtained. The problem contains three parts:

A. Income assessed for income-tax purposes.

B. Income, other than wages, below the income-tax exemption limit.

C. Wages.

The only complete official estimate relates to 1918–19 and is given in the Report of the Inland Revenue Commissioners for 1919–20. Since many of the incomes included were the averages of three or more earlier years during which time there were very rapid changes, its utility was never great, and in any case is completely out of date.

A. In recent years the only statements relating to distribution of income are of the numbers and incomes of those assessed to surtax. When, as was the case till 1920, the tax payable was regulated by a system of abatements for incomes under £700, the data were sufficient for estimating the numbers of incomes all up the scale by the use of Pareto's Law, though there were some abnormalities which were not readily explicable. Now (apart from the surtax figures) we have only estimates of the total number of payers of tax and total 'actual income', with separation of those assessed half-yearly (wage-earners) from others. In these numbers the income of a wife is merged with that of her husband.

B. The number and amount of small salaries are discussed above (pp. 88, 89). While there is some information about the distribution of these amounts, there is none about the distribution of other small incomes or profits. Also, since the salaried may have other sources of income, and husband's and wife's salaries are merged, the numbers under this heading overlap into A.

C. There has been no general account of the distribution of wages or earnings by their amounts since the Wage Census of 1906. Local estimates, such as that of London in *London Life and Labour*, 1934, Vol. VI, pp. 78 seq., cannot be generalized; they can only be used as indicating the probable algebraic or graphical shape of the distribution about the average.

There is a mass of data about rates of pay for different occupations, and also of average earnings in industries which include a multitude of occupations, but there are no means of relating them to each other. Attempts to build up a table by applying wage rates to the numbers in occupations, as given in the Census of Population, break down because the Census does not give sufficient detail for this purpose. For example, apart from division by age, sex and district, all 'hewers and getters' in coal-mines are merged together, all 'dippers and glazers' in pottery, all cotton weavers, and so on. These include a variety of occupations; where there is payment by piece there is great variety in earnings and even on time rates uniformity is far from complete. We can therefore draw only very broad conclusions by this method, and in particular we cannot tell what proportion of workers pass the income-tax exemption limit[1] and thus overlap with A.

An additional path of research is found in Insurance figures, since besides all manual workers, all salaried persons (over 16

1 The numbers available of persons receiving more than the exemption limit of £125 exclude a considerable proportion of the very numerous married men for whom the exemption limit was £225 (in 1936–38).

and under 65 years old) whose income does not exceed £250 per annum are included. The total, less wage-earners, should then give the number of salaried with incomes under £250, and this can be checked against the special study of salaries. But little reliance can be placed on this figure, since it is the difference between two large numbers, that arise from different sources with many slight variations in detail, and the difference is only some 10 per cent of the total. Thus an unknown but possibly large proportion of the difference may be due to variety of definition. In any case, when we come to weld this number with those based on A and C, we have again the difficulty that incomes in A include those from property as well as earnings, and merge husband's and wife's income. Also A includes incomes derived solely from property.

For these reasons no attempt is made to re-work in detail Mr Colin Clark's estimates.[1] They depend on bold hypotheses whose adequacy can only be partially checked, and for the reasons discussed above it is impossible that the picture can have anything approaching the accuracy suggested by the neat tables given to decimals of percentages. Work over the same ground shows that, when the uncertainties are allowed for, the picture is so blurred as to be only suggestive of broad results.

ESTIMATES BY PARETO'S LAW

Pareto's so-called Law of Income Distribution can be written

$$N = Ax^{-a},$$

where N is the number of incomes over £x, and A and a are constants. The total amount of income over £x is then $x^{1-a}.Aa/(a-1)$ and the average income above x is $xa/(a-1)$.

The number of incomes between x_1 and x_2 is $A\,(x_1{}^{-a} - x_2{}^{-a}) = X$ and their aggregate is $A\,(x_1{}^{1-a} - x_2{}^{1-a})\; a/(a-1) = Y$.

Hence if we know X and Y we can eliminate A and determine a.

It has been found that Pareto's formula fits the British super-tax statistics in many years except that there is some deficiency in the highest incomes; but for the year 1931–32, with which we are here concerned, the deficiency is found for incomes above £10,000 or £15,000.

It is reasonable to suppose that the formula which covers incomes from £2,000 (the lower limit of super-tax) to £10,000

1 *National Income and Outlay*, 1937, Chap. v.

can be used for the upper part of the range below £2,000. To project it downwards all the way to £250 is known by experience[1] to be very hazardous, but since it is the only kind of hypothesis available it is worth examining whether the results are consistent with what is known of the total number of incomes and the number under £250.

In the equations given above, with $x_1 = 2{,}000$ and $x_2 = 10{,}000$ we know from the super-tax statistics that

$$X = 87{,}028, \quad Y = 320{,}192{,}000 \ (£).$$

Solution by approximation gives $a = 1{\cdot}50$. In order to show how the numbers are affected by varying a, the results are given also for $a = 1{\cdot}55$.

Incomes Estimated from Super-tax Statistics, 1931–32

Income range	Actual		$a = 1{\cdot}50$		$a = 1{\cdot}55$	
	Number	Amount	Number	Amount	Number	Amount
£		£ mn.		£ mn.		£ mn.
250–2,000	—	—	2,066,400	1,346	2,183,000	1,142
2,000–10,000	87,028	320	87,041	318	86,831	331
10,000 or more	7,059	149	8,549	256	7,809	220

Here it is seen that the actual numbers above £10,000 are much lower than those computed. Between £2,000 and £10,000,

Income range £	Number of incomes	
	Actual	$a = 1{\cdot}50$
2,000–2,500	25,572	27,180
2,500–3,000	16,577	16,370
3,000–4,000	18,746	18,250
4,000–5,000	10,149	9,620
5,000–6,000	6,123	5,770
6,000–7,000	3,865	3,800
7,000–8,000	2,655	2,660
8,000–10,000	3,341	3,391
10,000–15,000	3,709	3,787
15,000–20,000	1,364	1,738
20,000–25,000	701	861
25,000–30,000	375	518
30,000–40,000	383	576
40,000–50,000	184	305
50,000–75,000	189	348
75,000–100,000	57	149
100,000 or more	97	167

1 'The British super-tax', *Quarterly Journal of Economics*, 1914, pp. 255 seq.

$a = 1 \cdot 50$ fits the data well, except that there is an excess below £2,500, possibly due to a leakage of incomes liable just above the lower limit.

Our hypothesis thus gives:

	Number		Income (£ mn.)
£250–£2,000	2,066,400	Computed	1,346
£2,000 or more	94,087	Actual	469
Total £250 or more	2,160,500		1,815

With $a = 1 \cdot 55$ the corresponding totals are 2,277,000 and £1,620 mn. These incomes on the one hand include a number arising solely from property, and on the other do not count separately incomes of occupied wives of occupied men. Balancing these, our hypothesis gives in round numbers 2,000,000 incomes of occupied persons with £250 or more per annum.

The number of incomes from occupations below £250 may be roughly estimated thus:

Great Britain, 1931

(000's)

Aged 16–65. Insured for health	15,800
Over 65	500
Under 16	800
	17,100
Add for Northern Ireland	400
U.K. salaried and wage-earners	17,500
Workers on own account	900
	18,400

The Insurance figures include those unemployed at the Census date. Assembling these figures we have:

Number of Incomes from Occupation

Under £250	18,400,000
£250 or more	2,000,000
	20,400,000

The actual number computed from the Census of Population is 21,800,000, and considering all the hazards of the estimate this difference of 7 per cent is not surprising.

But if we proceed in the opposite direction and subtract the number, 18,400,000, of lower incomes from the total 21,800,000, we find 3,400,000 above £250, which is very different from the 2,000,000 found by extrapolation by Pareto's formula.

In these circumstances there is nothing to be gained by endeavouring to classify incomes (below £2,000) according to their amount, and a good deal to be lost by publishing with spurious accuracy statistics based largely on guess-work.

In the higher ranges of income, say over £400 per annum, it is not unreasonable to regard the income recipients as forming a fairly homogeneous group of responsible adults, most of whom have dependants with no incomes. But the analysis now rejected as insufficient relates to such a heterogeneous population as to have little meaning when applied to all the 20,000,000 separate incomes. How heterogeneous the group is may be judged from the following example:

England and Wales, 1931
Persons occupied
(000's)

Ages	Males		Females	
	Single or widowed	Married	Single	Married or widowed
Under 21	1,989	15	1,667	14
21 to 25	1,102	224	858	83
25 or over	2,239	7,678	1,795	1,188
Total	5,330	7,917	4,320	1,285

Total:		
	Males	13,247
	Females	5,605
	All	18,852

There seems to be no utility in merging in one group the wages of a girl of 14 years and the income of a married man with dependants.

The method used by Sir John Orr,[1] of estimating the numbers of families in a graduation where the income is divided by the number of persons in a family, has a definite purpose and meaning, and the statistics he gives (pp. 59–60) in round numbers are probably broadly correct. But they are suggestive rather than factual, for the Census (on a sample from which he depended) does not for the reasons given above permit of anything but rough guesses at income for a large proportion of the families. When the estimate was re-worked on a new sample, unpublished tables show that a quite considerable margin must be allowed for the proportions in each group.

1 *Food, Health and Income*, 1936, Appendix V.

If such an analysis is intended to show the relation of incomes to needs, a more refined method than that of assuming that needs are the same for every individual is wanted. Necessary expense for a young child is less than that for an adult working man. Re-working of the analysis on the basis of assigning relative needs by age and sex, and treating a family as consisting of so many equivalent male adults, modified the table very significantly, reducing the proportions in apparent poverty or insufficiency, and while establishing more definitely the existence in 1931 and probably in 1937 of at least a considerable number whose incomes were on any modern standard insufficient, showed also that the proportion whose income was adequate for health, if spent with reasonable prudence, was greater than that suggested (but not definitely affirmed) by Sir John Orr's analysis.

NOTE ON THE VALUATION OF STOCKS AND PARTLY FINISHED GOODS

The profits of a company, after allowance for depreciation of plant, may be in part undistributed and used as a reserve, or employed in increasing the physical capital or stocks of goods. Undistributed profits are normally included in aggregate income, and for consistency they should be adjusted for any change in the values of stocks of materials or of partly finished products. When prices of materials are changing at all rapidly, there is an ambiguity, which may be important, in the value to be attributed to them.

In the table on p. 81, in the amounts included under Schedule D of the Income Tax (and also in Chapter III on the Census of Production Returns), a manufacturer is entitled to reckon stocks either at their cost price or at the change in their value from the beginning to the end of the year. Since he will probably take the lower of the two estimates, in times of changing prices the resulting income is lower than it should be, on some definitions of income and higher on others. Since importance has been attached to this inconsistency by Mr Colin Clark,[1] Mr Kuznets[2] and others, it is well to define and examine the problem.

Write p_0, p_1 for the prices per unit of a material in stock at the beginning and at the end of a year, and q_0, q_1 for the quantities. The analysis is easily adjusted to the usual case when there is more than one kind of material.

1 *National Income and Outlay*, 1937. 2 See ref. in Addendum p. 53 above.

The most straightforward method is to write

$$X = p_1 q_1 - p_0 q_0$$

for the addition to (or subtraction from) income during the year due to the change in the value of stocks.

To estimate the difference between X and the income-tax method some assumptions are necessary. Suppose that purchases and production are distributed uniformly through the year. Write q for the amount of material used in a year, $sq = q_0$ for the initial stock, and bq for the amount purchased. Then

$$q_1 = q(s + b - 1).$$

Assume that the materials are used m years after they are purchased, where m is a fraction ($\frac{1}{3}$ if the interval is 4 months).

Assume that prices change uniformly during the year and that

$$p_1 = p_0(1 + r).$$

Then the increase (or decrease) in the value at cost price is

$$Y = [sqp_0 + bq(p_0 + \tfrac{1}{2}rp_0) - qp_0(1 + r/2 - mr)] - sqp_0.$$

Here the second term in the square bracket relates to the purchases at their average cost and the third term to the consumption at its average cost at the time of purchase.

Mr Clark[1] takes as the objective, by arbitrary definition, the net increase in value of stocks reckoned at current prices, which he interprets as

$$Z = p\,(q_1 - q_0),$$

where p is the average price in the year, $= p_0(1 + r/2)$ on our assumption.

The differences between these reckonings may be written

$$X - Y = \{s + \tfrac{1}{2}(b - 1) - m\}\, r \,.\, qp_0,$$
$$X - Z = \{s + \tfrac{1}{2}(b - 1)\}\, r \,.\, qp_0,$$
$$Y - Z = mr \,.\, qp_0.$$

Thus Mr Clark virtually assumes that $m = 0$.

The magnitude of the differences may be judged by the following illustrative table. In it s, the multiple of a year's consumption in stock at the beginning, is taken as from $\frac{1}{4}$ to $\frac{3}{4}$; m, the interval between purchase and use, as $\frac{1}{4}$ or $\frac{1}{2}$; and b, the multiple of a year's consumption that is purchased in the year, as from $\frac{3}{4}$ to $1\frac{1}{4}$.

The values are given, as percentages of the value of a year's consumption at the initial price, in the cases of a price rise of

1 *Loc. cit.* p. 293. Mr Kuznets takes the same definition.

10 % and of a fall of 10 %. Since each column's entries contain r as a factor, the signs are reversed in the right-hand part of the table. 10 % is an unusually rapid change. The effect of other percentages can be obtained proportionately.

Percentage of annual consumption, valued at initial price

			Prices rising 10% p.a.		Prices falling 10% p.a.		
s	m	b	$X-Y$	$X-Z$	$X-Y$	$X-Z$	
$\frac{1}{4}$	$\frac{1}{4}$	$\frac{3}{4}$	−1·25*	+1·25	+1·25†	−1·25	(*d*)
		1	0	+2·5	0	−2·5	
		$1\frac{1}{4}$	+1·25†	+3·75	−1·25*	−3·75	
$\frac{1}{2}$	$\frac{1}{4}$	$\frac{3}{4}$	+1·25†	+3·75	−1·25*	−3·75	
		1	+2·5†	+5·0	−2·5*	−5·0	
		$1\frac{1}{4}$	+3·75†	+6·25	−3·75*	−6·25	
$\frac{1}{2}$	$\frac{1}{2}$	$\frac{3}{4}$	−1·25*	+3·75	+1·25†	−3·75	(*d*)
		1	0	+5·0	0	−5·0	
		$1\frac{1}{4}$	+1·25†	+6·25	−1·25*	−6·25	
$\frac{3}{4}$	$\frac{1}{2}$	$\frac{3}{4}$	+1·25†	+6·25	−1·25*	−6·25	
		1	+2·5†	+7·5	−2·5*	−7·5	
		$1\frac{1}{4}$	+3·75†	+8·75	−3·75*	−8·75	

* X preferred. † Y preferred by manufacturers.
(*d*) Conclusions differ from Mr Clark's.

When X is greater than Y, we may expect the manufacturer to prefer Y, and vice versa. The preferences are marked with * or †.

Mr Clark reaches a different conclusion, viz. that with rising prices Z is preferred, being less than X, and that with falling prices X is preferred. In our notation this is equivalent to taking $s > \frac{1}{2}(1-b)$, which may normally be expected, and $m=0$. But if m is not zero, the condition is $s-m > \frac{1}{2}(1-b)$, and Mr Clark's conclusion is negatived in the lines marked (*d*).

There is no sufficient information to make a general and accurate estimate of the proportion that the value of the stock bears to the profit of manufacture. But on any reasonable assumption it would need a very rapid movement of prices to make the adjustment from Y to X have a significant effect on the estimates of National Income given in this chapter—significant, that is, when the margin of uncertainty of the total is already considerable. The years that might be affected in our period are 1926, 1930, 1931, 1937 and 1938.

In Cmd. 6347, Table I (see p. 53 above) the quantity $Z-X$ is added to the earlier estimate to correct Schedule D. This quantity is evaluated at £135 mn. (See Maizel in *Economica*, 1941, p. 161.)

Chapter III

THE CENSUS OF PRODUCTION

This chapter is divided into four Parts. The first deals with the statistics of Output and Employment, published in the Census Reports for 1924, 1930 and 1935. The second examines the relation between these Census results and total National Income. In the third Quantities, Prices and Efficiency in the Census years are considered. In the fourth an Index of Production for each year 1924 to 1938 is compiled. Details relating to the chapter are to be found in Appendices, pp. 157–79 below.

Since there have been changes in classification and contents in the successive Census publications (see App. 1, p. 157) and unofficial writers have made adjustments for their own requirements, some of the figures quoted in the tables of this chapter appear to show discrepancies. Within each table comparability has been preserved.

1. *THE CENSUS RESULTS*

The Censuses cover Mining and Manufacture, Building and Contracting, including engineering production by Railway Companies, work undertaken by Local Authorities, and production for Defence Services and other Government Departments. Agriculture is excluded. Transport of materials from the mines, ports or other factories to manufacturers is included in Gross Output, but is subtracted with the cost of materials to obtain Net Output. Transport to consumers is excluded.

Gross Output is the aggregate selling value of goods as they leave the mines, factories, or their employees if they undertake delivery. Net Output is obtained by subtracting from Gross Output the value of materials, partly finished goods, coal, etc. These materials (if not imported) are already included in the returns of other factories or mines, or are to be accounted for in agriculture. Net Output is sometimes termed 'the value added by manufacture'. This value is the total for the firms of rents, royalties, interests, rates, salaries, wages, advertisement, allowances for depreciations, and profits, including undistributed profits. These are all constituents of national income, except that depreciation and rates may be subtracted or treated differently under different definitions.

Government Production includes no profits, except possibly those from some services rendered by Local Authorities.

In the accompanying tables the values stated exclude payments to the Government in the form of excise or customs, since they do not become personal income, but they include subsidies, since these are divisible among the owners or employees. In the table on pp. 166–7 material is assembled which makes it possible to treat these sums so as to correspond with other purposes or definitions.

The Censuses of 1930 and 1935 were confined to firms employing more than ten persons. In the table the figures for 1924 have been made comparable by excluding any such firms as were covered at that date. But in each Census material is available by which estimates can be made for the output of and employment in these small firms.[1] The details are discussed below (pp. 174–9), while the results are included in the accompanying table. This table deals only with large industrial groups, the contents of which are shown on pp. 157–161. The order and arrangement of groups is that adopted in the Census publications with some additional sub-divisions.

The numbers employed include here all manual workers (or operatives) and salaried persons (or administrative).

The results may be summarized thus:

	Value £ mn.	Number employed (000's)	Value per head £	Percentage changes		
				Value	Number employed	Value per head
1924	1,668	8,036	208	100	100	100
1930	1,640	7,952	206	98·3	99	99
1935	1,759	8,019	219	105·5	99·8	106

How these figures are affected by the change of prices is discussed in Part III (p. 136 seq.).

The Table B, p. 126, indicates the relative importance of each group in the total of industrial production. There have been significant relative increases in Building, Timber, Chemicals, the Metal Groups, Food, Paper, and Group XVIII, and decreases in Coal-mining, Textiles. The remaining groups show little variation.

1 Since there is special uncertainty about the numbers in small building firms, a margin of error is assigned to Group III.

Table A

Census of Production. Net Output and Numbers Employed in 1924, 1930, 1935

Industrial group		Net output (£ mn.)			Numbers employed (000's)*			
		Large firms†	Small firms†	Total	Large firms†	Small firms†	Out-workers	Total
1		2	3	4	5	6	7	8
I. Coal-mining	1924	209·7	0·6	210·3	1,197	5	0	1,202
	1930	138·6	0·3	138·9	932	2	0	934
	1935	120·9	0·2	121·1	762	1	0	764
II. Other mines and quarries	1924	16·6	1·1	17·7	84	5	—	89
	1930	16·6	1·5	18·1	87	8	—	95
	1935	15·3	1·6	16·9	78	8	—	87
III. Clay, building materials and building	1924	124·2	24·8 (±3·2)	149·0 (±3·2)	628	151	—	779
	1930	139·2	32·0 (±1·5)	171·2 (±1·5)	678	183	—	861
	1935	140·0	50·3 (±4·6)	190·3 (±4·6)	680	275	—	955
IV. Chemicals, paints, oils	1924	65·8	3·2	69·0	178	11	—	189
	1930	72·9	3·8	76·7	178	12	—	190
	1935	88·7	4·7	93·4	194	12	—	206
V. Iron and steel	1924	98·7	5·1	103·8	499	39	1	539
	1930	91·7	6·6	98·3	494	38	1	533
	1935	116·5	5·7	122·2	539	32	1	572
VI. Engineering, shipbuilding and vehicles	1924	198·4	13·8	212·2	986	87	—	1,073
	1930	230·0	15·2	245·2	1,075	110	—	1,185
	1935	249·3	18·4	267·7	1,104	106	—	1,210
VII. Non-ferrous metals, jewellery, etc.	1924	25·2	2·1	27·3	115	14	1	130
	1930	23·5	3·1	26·6	110	16	1	127
	1935	29·9	2·6	32·5	122	12	—	135
VIII. Textiles	1924	221·8	3·8	225·6	1,262	15	11	1,288
	1930	147·4	2·8	150·2	1,061	19	6	1,086
	1935	157·5	2·5	160·0	1,055	14	5	1,074
IX. Leather	1924	11·6	1·1	12·7	48	8	—	56
	1930	10·2	1·3	11·5	46	8	—	54
	1935	10·7	1·2	11·9	51	7	—	58
X. Clothing	1924	75·7	23·9	99·6	474	161	26	661
	1930	78·2	22·4	100·6	493	141	20	653

	1935	106·6	22·9	129·5	377	101	—	477
XII. Drink	1924	62·7	2·6	65·3	104	11	—	115
	1930	64·5	4·1	68·6	104	13	—	117
	1935	66·5	4·3	70·8	101	12	—	113
XIII. Tobacco	1924	24·7	0·2	24·9	40	—	—	40
	1930	31·2	0·1	31·3	45	—	—	45
	1935	28·4	0·1	28·5	43	—	—	43
XIV. Timber	1924	27·3	7·9	35·2	138	49	—	187
	1930	31·5	10·8	42·3	168	72	1	240
	1935	32·3	13·5	45·8	167	69	1	237
XV. Paper, printing, stationery	1924	93·9	4·7	98·6	343	29	1	373
	1930	103·3	5·4	108·7	380	33	1	414
	1935	109·7	7·5	117·2	401	33	1	435
XVI. Rubber	1924	11·7	0·2	11·9	47	1	—	48
	1930	14·5	0·3	14·8	52	1	—	53
	1935	14·3	0·3	14·6	56	1	—	57
XVII. Miscellaneous	1924	29·7	1·8	31·5	118	11	1	131
	1930	28·3	2·9	31·2	122	14	1	137
	1935	29·4	2·2	31·6	127	13	1	141
XVIII. Gas, electricity, water	1924	69·3	3·4	72·7	187	7	—	194
	1930	94·5	3·2	97·7	223	7	—	230
	1935	109·7	3·5	113·2	252	7	—	259
XIX. Transport and communication‡	1924	45·1	—	45·1	261	—	—	261
	1930	40·9	—	40·9	241	—	—	241
	1935	37·5	—	37·5	217	—	—	217
XX. Local Authorities	1924	31·6	0·4	32·0	196	4	—	200
	1930	36·8	0·6	37·4	238	4	—	242
	1935	33·4	0·7	34·1	212	4	—	216
XXI. Government Departments	1924	19·7	—	19·7	96	—	—	96
	1930	18·8	—	18·8	92	—	—	92
	1935	21·8	—	21·8	103	—	—	103
Totals	1924	1,548	120 (±4)	1,668 (±4)	7,298	696	42	8,036
	1930	1,505	135 (±2)	1,640 (±2)	7,141	780	31	7,952
	1935	1,600	159 (±5)	1,759 (±5)	7,177	816	26	8,019

* Nearest £100,000 or nearest 1,000 persons. † Large firms, more than ten employees; small firms, ten or fewer.

‡ Production by Transport Undertakings (Engineering and Construction), not cost of or persons concerned in actual movements of persons or goods.

Table B

Contribution of the various Groups to the Total Net Output and Employment. Industries included

(All firms)

Industrial group	Net output			Employment		
	1924 Per cent	1930 Per cent	1935 Per cent	1924 Per cent	1930 Per cent	1935 Per cent
I. Coal-mining	12·6	8·5	6·9	15·0	11·8	9·5
II. Other mines and quarries	1·1	1·1	1·0	1·1	1·2	1·1
III. Clay, building materials and building	8·9	10·4	10·8	9·7	10·8	11·9
IV. Chemicals, paints, oils	4·1	4·7	5·3	2·3	2·4	2·6
V. Iron and steel	6·2	6·0	6·9	6·7	6·7	7·1
VI. Engineering, etc.	12·7	14·9	15·2	13·3	14·9	15·1
VII. Non-ferrous metals, etc.	1·6	1·6	1·8	1·6	1·6	1·7
VIII. Textiles	13·5	9·2	9·1	16·0	13·7	13·4
IX. Leather	0·8	0·7	0·7	0·7	0·7	0·7
X. Clothing	6·0	6·1	5·6	8·2	8·2	8·3
XI. Food	6·3	6·8	7·4	4·8	5·3	6·0
XII. Drink	3·9	4·2	4·0	1·4	1·5	1·4
XIII. Tobacco	1·5	1·9	1·6	0·5	0·6	0·5
XIV. Timber	2·1	2·6	2·6	2·3	3·0	2·9
XV. Paper, printing, etc.	5·9	6·6	6·7	4·6	5·2	5·4
XVI. Rubber	0·7	0·9	0·8	0·6	0·7	0·7
XVII. Miscellaneous	1·9	1·8	1·8	1·6	1·7	1·8
XVIII. Gas, electricity, water	4·4	6·0	6·4	2·4	2·9	3·2
XIX. Transport	2·7	2·5	2·1	3·2	3·0	2·7
XX. Local Authorities	1·9	2·3	1·9	2·5	3·0	2·7
XXI. Government Departments	1·2	1·1	1·2	1·2	1·2	1·3
All trades	100·0	100·0	100·0	100·0	100·0	100·0

2. *THE CENSUSES OF PRODUCTION AND TOTAL INCOME*

The Census of Production of 1930 accounted for rather less than half either of the income of the United Kingdom or of the total number of occupied persons. It relates to physical productions of goods up to the stage where they leave the mines, factories or the farms. To obtain the selling values of the goods to the final consumers we have to add the cost of transport before and after manufacture and the incomes of merchants, distributors and dealers. Total income includes also that arising from personal, professional and other services, and from the direct use of houses and other property. Another item that must be included at some stage is the income of some 1,300,000 persons who were in 1931 working on their own account directly for customers.

There are official or semi-official estimates which account for part of the gap between the Censuses of Production of 1924 and 1930 and total income, and for 1924 (as for 1907) Sir A. Flux made an estimate which accounted for the residue of income. No corresponding estimate is available for 1935.

I. NET OUTPUT

	£ mn. 1924	£ mn. 1930
Net output of industry:		
Larger firms*	1,549	1,505
Smaller firms	121	134
Agriculture, forestry, fishing	248	226
Waste products re-worked	16	12
Total home Net Output	1,934	1,877

* Employing more than ten persons.

The procedure for estimating the Net Output of Agriculture, etc. here included is as follows:

	£ mn. 1924	£ mn. 1930
Gross Output: Agriculture*	297	254
Small holdings†	18	15½
Forestry	2	1½
Fishing	20	19
Total	337	290
Less: Imported materials	34	25
Materials from industry	55	39
Net Output	248	226

* Holdings of an acre or more.
† Including allotments and gardens.

The materials obtained from Industry (fertilizers, feeding stuffs, etc.) are already accounted for in the net output of Industry. Industry also obtained materials from Agriculture, etc. (estimated at £98 mn. in 1924 and £80 mn. in 1930), the value of which is included in the net output of Agriculture, and subtracted from the gross output of Industry.

II. SELLING VALUE

Industry and Agriculture

	£ mn. 1924	£ mn. 1930
Net Output	1,934	1,877
Imported materials: for industry	660	483
for agriculture, etc.	34	25
Transport of materials	96	72
Value of home-produced goods	2,724	2,457
Imports: value on arrival	444	449
Customs and excise	227	235
Selling value of goods for home use or export	3,395	3,141
Less exports	743	535
(Wholesale) selling value of goods for home use	2,652	2,606

This selling value is as at the time the goods leave the mines, factories or farms or as imports reach the docks.

The statistics so far given are in nearly every case taken from the Final Report of the Census of Production (1930), Part V, pp. 52–4.[1]

The accounts of imports had been scrutinized so as to yield the following classification:

	£ mn. 1924	£ mn. 1930
Imports: Materials for industry	660	483
Materials for agriculture	34	25
Ready for use	444	449
Total imports	1,138	957

Re-exports are excluded from this table.

To obtain the selling value, customs on imports and excise on production are added.

As regards exports it is desired to obtain the value as at the factories, while the usual statistics give f.o.b. values. It is also

1 Details of the estimates are to be found in the *Journal of the Royal Statistical Society*, 1929, pp. 8 seq., Flux; 1934, pp. 545 seq., Leak. In the latter some of the earlier statistics are amended.

proper to subtract waste products (old iron, wool rags, etc.) which are not additional output of manufacture.

Exports of British Produce

	£ mn.	
	1924	1930
Value at factory	743	535
Waste products	2½	2½
Transport and lading	55½	33½
Value f.o.b.	801	571

Many of the items included in the totals, especially those relating to transport, are rather rough estimates, and the final results given in the Census of Production Report are 1924, £2,652 ± 28 mn.; 1930, £2,606 ± 26 mn.

III. TOTAL INCOME

In his Presidential Address to the Royal Statistical Society (*Journal*, 1929, p. 1) Mr Flux estimated the National Income in 1924.[1]

For the items already discussed he arrived at a total £2,635 mn., instead of £2,652 mn. as amended above. His further estimates can be arranged as follows:

		£ mn.
1924.	Selling value of goods	2,635 ± 35
	Less depreciation of capital	305
	Net	2,330
	Transport, distribution, dealing	945 ± 135
	Houses and services	650 ± 50
	Increase of investments abroad	50
	National Income	3,975 ± 225

The allowance for depreciation, which excludes replacement and maintenance carried out by employees of the establishments concerned, is provisional and should have a margin of error assigned to it.

To obtain the cost of distribution, percentages are assigned to two or more broad classes of goods, and are added to the £2,635 mn. to obtain the value of sales to final consumers. The author considered that the large margin allowed was sufficient to cover the uncertainties of the data.

The basis of the estimate for the annual value of houses and services is not explained in detail. It covers (1) value of dwelling-houses, hotels, schools, etc., £225 mn., (2) domestic

1 The corresponding estimate for 1907 is given on p. 48 above.

and hotel service, £120 mn., (3) passenger transport, less cost included in the Census, (4) postal service, other than that for business, (5) professional and artistic services, excluding professional services rendered to business, and excluding services 'rendered by persons in the employ of the central or local governments'.

The last item in the table is obtained by subtracting from the total of £86 mn. the excess of exports over imports, the value of ships' stores and fuel and certain financial services already included in the value of goods.

No explanation or discussion is given for the exclusion of the value of services rendered by Government employees. It appears to exclude the incomes of the main body of teachers,[1] for example, and not only officials who may be considered to be aiding industry or commerce. For the discussion of this, reference must be made to our earlier chapter on Definitions and the later chapter on Real Income. Since there were considerably more than a million persons employed in Government service, their inclusion or exclusion is of considerable importance.

In the discussion on the paper Stamp considered the possible causes of the not very great difference between this estimate (£3,975 ± 225 mn.) and that more recently published[2] (£3,800 ± 100 mn.) by the method of aggregating incomes. He finds three possible reasons:

(1) In the Census of Production method the value is of goods produced in a year; in the Income method it is nearly the value

1 This part of the Address in 1939 was based on the analysis given on p. 33 of the Final Report of the First Census of Production of the United Kingdom (1907), published in 1912. The relevant passages are:

'The classes of income to be included in the total of remunerated services now to be brought into account include mainly the following:

'vi. Central and local government services, the receipts for which (exclusive of rents, post office, water, gas, electricity, tramways, loans, and sale of property) amounted in 1907/8 to about £216,000,000, about £81,000,000 of this total being loan charges and repayment of loans. Out of the remaining £135,000,000, however, £69,300,000 represents Customs and Excise duties and licences included in the value of goods, and £30,000,000 is covered by value of work included as output for Census of Production purposes.

'vii. The income of the professional and artistic classes, other than doctors, teachers, etc., in the employment of the State or of Local Authorities —that is, the clerical, medical, teaching, literary, scientific, artistic, musical, and dramatic professions; and the engineering, surveying, banking, insurance, and legal classes, except in so far as their services were rendered to manufacture or distribution and have already been taken into account.'

2 *The National Income*, 1924, Bowley and Stamp.

sold to the final consumer. The change in the value of stock between the beginning and end of a year may be important.[1]

(2) The treatment of depreciation for income-tax purposes differs from that in the Census of Production method, especially since in the latter goods used for replacement are not counted as income, while the income-tax assessment is based on the value of the plant, etc., independent of the method of replacement.

(3) In the inclusion of indirect taxation some part of transfers of income (without corresponding services) is counted as income.

It may be added that the near consilience of the totals, which come to a large extent from different sources and which necessitate a great deal of rather arbitrary estimating, and which in minor cases use different conceptions of income, is very satisfactory.

But in spite of this agreement it is necessary to consider whether the two measurements have really the same objective. Let us go back to first principles. 'The labour and capital of a country, acting on its natural resources, raise annually a joint product consisting of a certain net aggregate of commodities, material and immaterial, including services of all kinds. This is the true net annual income of the country.'[2] 'The terms National Income and National Dividend are convertible.' 'The National Dividend is at once the aggregate net product, and the sole source of payment for, all the agents of production within the country; it is divided up into Earnings of Labour, Interest of Capital, and lastly the Producer's Surplus, or Rent of Land and of other differential advantages for production. It constitutes the whole of them and the whole of it is distributed among them....'[3]

We have thus the equation:[4]

National dividend = National income = Earnings, interest and rent = Sum of incomes of individuals.

We may leave aside for the present purpose many of the problems of definition discussed in Chapter 1, such as income accruing abroad, unpaid services and the use of possessions other than houses.

1 That is, stock in the possession of merchants and retailers. Changes in stock in the factories, etc. are allowed for in the Census of Production method.
2 Marshall, *Principles of Economics*, 1907 edition, pp. 76 and 79.
3 Marshall, *Economics of Industry*, 1894, p. 257.
4 Bowley, *Economic Journal*, 1929, p. 2.

Mr Flux undoubtedly aimed at the selling value of the 'net aggregate of commodities, including services'. His estimate may be re-tabulated as follows:

1924	£ mn.
Census of Production: Mining, industries, agriculture	1,917
Consumers' waste products exported	2
Transport and distribution	1,095
Imports less exports	337
Customs and excise	227
Houses	225
Services	425
Selling value of products and services	4,228
Less depreciation	305
	3,923
Income accruing abroad	50
National Income*	3,973 ± 225

* There is no indication that account was taken of the value of the products of persons (such as carpenters, bootmakers, dressmakers) working on their own account without paid employees. There were about 330,000 such persons in 1931 (or 300,000, excluding outworkers who may have classed themselves as working on their own account) and their income was probably between £30 and £50 mn. This is additive to the National Income, unless they are already included in the composite item services.

The equating of the selling value of products, etc. to the total of individual (and corporate) incomes assumes not only that there was no significant change in the value of goods in the possession of merchants and dealers as between the beginning and end of the year (as Stamp pointed out), but that all income is spent during the year or deposited in such a way that it was at once turned into physical capital—in brief, that saving is equivalent to spending. It would need a difficult investigation to find out whether this was approximately true for a single year or whether the lag between saving and its investment was sufficiently regular to allow us to neglect it over a period of years. Similar considerations apply to undistributed profits of companies.

A more important question arises from Mr Flux's treatment of Government service. Included in the Census of Production aggregate are the values of the physical output of the Central Government (dockyards, arsenals, etc.), that is, £19 mn. in 1924, and of Local Authorities (roads, buildings, etc.) amounting to £96 mn. The employees included numbered 96,000 and 200,000 respectively. But under 'services' all other Government employees were excluded. We have no statistics for their numbers in 1924, but an idea of them can be obtained in 1930 or 1931.

	Census of Population Employees (000's) 1931	*Census of Production* Employees in physical output (000's) 1930
Defence	382	—
Central Government	357	91
Local Government	588	242
Police	67	—
Teachers*	231	—
Nurses	152	—
	1,777	333

* Employed by the Central or Local Authorities.

Discounting the numbers of nurses so as to exclude those employed privately, there were in 1930 about 1,650,000 persons in public employment, of whom about 350,000 (allowing for services rendered to industry) would be included in the Census of Production.

None of these was paid directly by private individuals or groups of individuals. Their payments are met out of taxes and rates, and it is not clear why dockyard and arsenal workers and road-makers and builders are treated differently from administrators and Government clerks. Even if it is argued that the army, navy, police and central and local administrators are regarded as an expense properly attributed to industry, the same can hardly be said of teachers and nurses, whose services in any case cannot logically be charged to industry if they are public employees, while if in private employ they are chargeable to individuals. Stamp appeared to take the view that customs and excise (entered in selling value) were implicitly balanced against public services in Mr Flux's reckoning, and indeed the £227 mn. under this head might be of the same order of magnitude as the expense of these services; but if there were this equality it would be accidental, since direct and indirect taxation are merged in the national accounts, and several classes of services are borne partly on rates and partly on taxes. We cannot say that direct taxation and rates on private premises[1] are transfers of income, while indirect taxes are for value received. So far as can be ascertained, Mr Flux did not deal with these questions explicitly in his estimates based on either the 1907 or the 1924 Census, and his line of reasoning must remain obscure.[2]

1 These latter are not brought into Mr Flux's account.

2 At the time of writing Sir A. Flux is in Denmark and beyond the reach of correspondence.

The most direct balance should be found between the total of goods and services that are paid for by individuals and groups of individuals at their selling value, as reckoned by the Census of Production method, and the total income of individuals and groups less taxes and rates.

Then in 1924 the Census of Production method gives £3,973 mn. + £50 mn. (workers on their own account) − £115 mn. (Government products) = £3,900 mn. (± 225) approximately. On the income side we have £4,273 mn. as the aggregate of incomes including pensions (*Statistical Journal*, 1940, p. 517, Total A), less about £600 mn., direct taxation and rates, which gives about £3,700 mn. ± £100 mn. Thus these rather hypothetical rectifications leave the relative position of the two estimates very much as Stamp put it (p. 130 above).

We may usefully compare these estimates with the study of consumption made by Mr Feavearyear in the *Economic Journal*, 1931, pp. 51–60. His final table, abridged, is:

Average Annual National Expenditure, 1924–27

	£ mn.
General expenditure	3,140
Saving	400
Compulsory insurance	85
	3,625
Direct taxation	375
	4,000

The average of the Totals A for these years (*loc. cit.*) is £4,200[1] (± £100) mn. These totals may contain some small items which are excluded from Mr Feavearyear's reckoning, but broadly they should cover the same ground.

Thus the various methods of approach give results which agree within 5 per cent of each other when the appropriate definitions are taken. Each contains considerable elements of approximation, and when reasonable allowance is made for these it may be held that they are mutually consistent.

The statistics already given show that the physical output of the industries included in the Censuses of Production and Agriculture, less the estimate for depreciation, accounted for about £1,600 mn. income in 1924, while transport, distribution, houses and services accounted for about £1,750 mn. In 1930 the totals and proportions were nearly the same. Thus material

1 Subtracting Income due to Foreigners (£25 mn. per annum).

production was valued at less than services and the direct use of property. It is therefore natural to consider the number of occupied persons concerned in direct production and in rendering services. The closest comparison available is between the Census of Population of 1931 and that of Production in 1930.

Approximately on the average through the year 7,952,000 were employed in industry and mining, including small firms and outworkers, according to the Census of Production. From the Census of Population the number occupied (excluding unemployed) in this group was about 8,070,000, to which we should add about 570,000 employed in production for Public Authorities, making 8,640,000. The excess is partly to be explained by the inclusion in the larger total of about 355,000 employers, directors or managers, and no doubt some persons who did not state that they were out of work, though in fact they were in an interval between jobs (see p. 103). On the other hand, in April 1931 about 400,000 more persons were unemployed in these groups than in the average of 1930, and after all allowances the Census of Population gives a slightly higher total than does the Census of Production. Since the difference is not very great, we may use the Census of Population to get a broad view of the relative importance of physical production to services.

United Kingdom, 1931. *Number of Occupied Persons. Estimated from the Census of Population*

(000's)

Industry, mining	8,400	
Agriculture, fishing	1,100	
		9,500
Transport, seamen	1,300	
Commerce, dealing	2,300	
		3,600
Services, neither employers nor employed	1,000	
Government, Central, Local, Defence, Police	1,400	
Teachers, nurses	400	
Banking, finance	400	
Professions, entertainments	600	
Personal and other services	2,300	
		6,100
Total		19,200
Unemployed		2,600
Without occupation		24,300
Total population		46,100

'Unemployed' of course means following some occupation but temporarily without a job. 'Without occupation' includes wives, not working for pay, children and aged, etc.

Thus physical production accounted for about 50 per cent of the occupied population, transport and dealing for about 20 per cent, and administration, defence and services for about 30 per cent.

3. *THE VOLUME OF PRODUCTION*

CENSUS DATES 1924, 1930, 1935

In the Final Report on the Fourth Census of Production of the United Kingdom[1] (1930), Chapters III and IV relate to the Index of and the Volume of Production. We will write Q for the number of units produced of any commodity in 1924, P for the price per unit in the same year, $V=PQ$ for the value. q, p, v stand for the corresponding items in 1930.

Two methods are available. (A) We can re-value the goods in 1930 at the prices of 1924, or (B) we can re-value the goods in 1924 at the prices of 1930. Each method eliminates price-changes.

(A) gives $J_1=\frac{S(Pq)}{S(PQ)}=\frac{S(Vq/Q)}{S(V)}$ for an index of quantity.[2] J_1 is the weighted average of the quantity ratios, the weights being the values at the first date.

The index of prices most closely related to J_1 is

$$I_2=\frac{v}{V}\div J_1=\frac{S(qp)}{S(qP)}=\frac{S(v)}{S(vP/p)}.$$

(B) gives similarly

$$J_2=\frac{S(pq)}{S(pQ)}=\frac{S(v)}{S(vQ/q)},\quad I_1=\frac{S(Vp/P)}{S(V)}.$$

Irving Fisher's 'ideal index-numbers' for quantity and prices are $\sqrt{(J_1J_2)}$ and $\sqrt{(I_1I_2)}$ respectively.

Unfortunately these methods cannot be applied to the data of the Censuses of Production without considerable elements of approximation and hypothesis. Quantities are, necessarily, only stated for a proportion, large or small according to the nature of the goods, of the commodities produced in each industry.

1 Part V, General Report, 1935.

2 J and I are usually multiplied by 100 to give percentage index-numbers.

It is necessary to assume in one form or another that the quantity index computed for the measurable goods in each industry can be applied without serious error to the whole of that industry. Though for some industries this procedure is very risky, it may be expected that the uncertainty will be less when all industries are combined.

The well-known distinction between Gross Output and Net Output has great importance in the computation. Gross Output is reckoned on the basis of the selling value of the goods as at the time they leave each producer. Thus yarn is included at the price at which it is sold to the manufacturer, without deduction of the cost of the raw cotton, and the piece-goods are included at their selling prices without deduction of the cost of the yarn. There is consequently a great deal of re-duplication. To obtain Net Output each producer deducts all his expenses of raw materials and of partly finished articles.

In the General Report for 1930, Appendix II, the basis of calculation is Gross Output, and the method (B) is employed. In each of over 130 industries the value of the Gross Output in 1930 is compared with that of 1924 re-priced 'at 1930 average values'. Each of these index-numbers is the result of a similar process applied to separate products in each industry. Thus for each industry and group of industries we have the value of J_2.

In Chapter II of the Report, however, a different process is followed to obtain a general result applicable to all industries together. Here (p. 43) the basis is Net Output of fourteen large industrial groups in 1924. The net output, for example, of the Iron and Steel group in 1924 was £98·6 mn. The index obtained from Appendix II is $J_2=1{\cdot}026$. The product of these, viz. £101·2 mn., is described as the 'Estimated net output in 1930 on basis of 1924'. The result in its simplest form is

$$S\left(P'Q'\times\frac{pq}{pQ}\right)\Big/S(P'Q'),$$

where P', Q' refer to the net output in 1924. On the assumption that for each industry the index of volume pq/pQ, based on gross output, equals with sufficient approximation $p'q'/p'Q'$, based on net output, this result is

$$S\left(P'Q'\times\frac{p'q'}{p'Q'}\right)\Big/S(P'Q')=S(P'q')/S(P'Q')=J'.$$

All the letters with $'$ refer to net output.

For the tables, pp. 147–150 below, however, a more elaborate method was adopted. Each of the 130 industries was taken separately and it was assumed that for each the change in quantity (as computed for the Report, Appendix II) was the same for gross and for net output, that is, that in each industry the change in the quantity of material equalled the change in the quantity of the product. Since each industry produces a range of products, not necessarily in the same proportions in the two years, the assumption is only approximately true. It holds, however, with greater validity when we combine the separate industries into groups, and the groups into a whole, for this process of averaging tends to eliminate sporadic errors; but if throughout industry on the average there is a tendency to use the materials for finer purposes—to put, for example, more work in making a ton of metal into an elaborate machine—this is uncorrected, and the index for net output is under-estimated. There appears to be no statistical means of allowing for this bias, if it exists.

The process may be shown by an example:

Leather Trades

Gross Output

	1924 Value as returned (£000's) PQ	Valued at 1930 prices (£000's) pQ	1930 Gross Output (£000's) pq	Index of production $J_2 = q/Q$	1930 at 1924 values $PQ \times J_2 = Pq$
Fellmongery	4,718	2,820	3,186	1·13	5,321
Tanning, etc.	32,215	30,140	27,792	0·92	29,638
Saddlery and goods	5,112	5,380	5,002	0·93	4,754
Total	42,045	38,340	35,980	—	39,713

Net Output

	1924 Value as returned (£000's) $P'Q'$	1930 Value as returned $p'q'$	1930 at 1924 values $P'Q' \times q/Q = P'q'$	1924 at 1930 values $p'q' \div q/Q = p'Q'$
Fellmongery	873	516	986	457
Tanning, etc.	8,444	7,355	7,768	7,979
Saddlery and goods	2,312	2,309	2,150	2,483
Total	11,629	10,180	10,904	10,919

For the group of Leather Trades we have:

Gross Output: $W = S(pq) \div S(PQ) = 35{,}980 \div 42{,}045 = 0{\cdot}856$
$J_1 = S(Pq) \div S(PQ) = 39{,}713 \div 42{,}045 = 0{\cdot}945$
$J_2 = S(pq) \div S(pQ) = 35{,}980 \div 38{,}340 = 0{\cdot}938$
$I_1 = S(pQ) \div S(PQ) = 38{,}340 \div 42{,}045 = 0{\cdot}912$
$I_2 = S(pq) \div S(Pq) = 35{,}980 \div 39{,}713 = 0{\cdot}906$
$W = J_1 \times I_2 = J_2 \times I_1 \qquad W' = J_1' \times I_2' = J_2' \times I_1'$

Net Output: $W' = S(p'q') \div S(P'Q') = 10{,}180 \div 11{,}629 = 0{\cdot}875$
$J_1' = S(P'q') \div S(P'Q') = 10{,}904 \div 11{,}629 = 0{\cdot}938$
$J_2' = S(p'q') \div S(p'Q') = 10{,}180 \div 10{,}919 = 0{,}933$
$I_1' = S(p'Q') \div S(P'Q') = 10{,}919 \div 11{,}629 = 0{,}939$
$I_2' = S(p'q') \div S(P'q') = 10{,}180 \div 10{,}904 = 0{\cdot}933$

In the above table the first four columns under Gross Output are the figures given in the Report; the last is deduced by a process which would be exact if there was only one uniform product. It may be noticed that the product of the numbers in the first and third columns equals that of those in the second and fourth.

Under Net Output the first two columns are from the Census. To obtain the third and fourth it is assumed that the quantity change (q/Q) of gross output, as taken in the upper part of the table, is sufficiently near to q'/Q' as is needed for the lower part.

From these figures indices of value, quantity and price are worked out for the Industrial Group and entered as percentages to the nearest unit in the tables, pp. 147–150.

The same process is applied to each of the groups. To obtain the indices of production for industry as a whole the quantities Pq, pQ from each industry must be added, but there is no need to reproduce them. For the totals $J_1 = S(Pq) \div S(PQ)$, and similarly for the other indices.

From the same data we can obtain two index-numbers of prices (p. 136) for each industry, each group and the total. As is well known[1] the Index I_1 (Laspeyrc's) is less than I_2 (Paasche's) if the increase in quantities is negatively associated with the index of price. Such negative correlation is present when persons with little change in real income aim at economy by substituting goods of which the price has risen little for those which are relatively dearer. Whether this takes place depends

1 $I_1 = S(pQ)/S(PQ)$, $I_2 = S(pq)/S(Pq)$. Then

$$I_2 - I_1 = \{S(QP)\,(q/Q - J_1)\,(p/P - I_1)\} \div S(qP),$$

and $I_2 < I_1$ if the differences between q/Q, p/P and their weighted averages are negatively correlative.

on the demand for different goods at different price levels. When applied to wholesale production in the period 1924 to 1930, there is no clear tendency in this direction. Since $J_2 \times I_1 = V = J_1 \times I_2$, then $J_1 > J_2$ if $I_1 < I_2$.

We can obtain an estimate for the changes in price of materials and partly finished manufactures from the same data, for the price of a unit of finished goods is a combination of that of a unit of the corresponding material and the cost (including profit, etc.) of manufacturing a unit. In our notation I_1 or I_2 measures the change in the selling price of the finished goods and I_1' or I_2' the 'value per unit added by manufacture'. Write ${}_rI_1$ and ${}_rI_2$ for the corresponding change in price per unit of materials or semi-manufactured goods. The formula is

$${}_rI_1 = \frac{\text{Cost per unit of materials at second date}}{\text{Cost per unit of materials at first date}}$$

$$= \frac{\text{Whole cost at second date}}{\text{Whole cost at first date}} = \frac{pQ - p'Q'}{PQ - P'Q'}.$$

$$\therefore {}_rI_1 (PQ - P'Q') = pQ - p'Q' = PQ \times I_1 - P'Q' \times I_1',$$

and, similarly,

$${}_rI_2 (Pq - P'q') = Pq \times I_2 - P'Q' \times I_2'.$$

For aggregates each quantity, such as pq, is summed.

For example, in the illustration from the leather trades,

$${}_rI_1 (42{\cdot}0 - 11{\cdot}6) = 42{\cdot}0 \times 0{\cdot}912 - 11{\cdot}6 \times 0{\cdot}939, \quad {}_rI_1 = 0{\cdot}90,$$

$${}_rI_2 (39{\cdot}7 - 10{\cdot}9) = 39{\cdot}7 \times 0{\cdot}906 - 10{\cdot}9 \times 0{\cdot}933, \quad {}_rI_2 = 0{\cdot}895.$$

I_1 is necessarily between I_1' and ${}_rI_1$, unless they are all equal.

In all the industries included in the Census this computation shows a fall of 18 per cent in the price of materials, of 10 per cent in the value per unit added by manufacture and of 14 or 15 per cent in the price of finished goods.

This fall of 18 per cent may be compared with that of the wholesale price of materials from other sources:

Index-Numbers of Materials

	Board of Trade	*Statist*		Board of Trade	*Statist*
1924	100	100	1930	100	100
1929: 1st half	80	83	1934: 1st half	91	88
2nd half	79	78	2nd half	88	87
1930: 1st half	73	71	1935: 1st half	89	90
2nd half	66	62	2nd half	91	94

Since the Census returns were for the most part for the Calendar year 1930, the figures in the period 1924 to 1930 are only consistent if materials were purchased many months before the goods were sold; but in the later period where the ${}_rI_1$ method shows a fall of 10 per cent from 1930 to 1935 the agreement is very close.

The tables on pp. 147–150 also show the relationship between the numbers employed and production in each industrial group. For this purpose the average of the indices of production is divided by the ratio of the numbers of operatives (or manual workers).[1] The result is headed index of efficiency. The index shows an increase of 12 per cent in the six years. If, however, the salaried (administrative, technical and clerical) class is included in the divisors, the measurement of increase in efficiency is reduced to $5\frac{1}{2}$ per cent. The numbers in the salaried class increased during the six years, while the numbers of 'operatives' diminished.

1930 AND 1935

The same process is adopted for analysing the change in production from 1930 to 1935; but, at the time of writing, the Board of Trade's account of the physical output is not complete and where necessary use has been made of Dr Rhodes's computations (London and Cambridge Economic Service, Special Memorandum No. 47).

Dr Rhodes's work brings out the essential ambiguity of the measurement; for, working on the most detailed statements of quantity possible, he finds that the forward and backward measurements (J_1' and J_2') differ perceptibly in many of the hundred (or so) separate industries, markedly in the fourteen industrial groups, and even more considerably when these groups are aggregated. He weights by the net output of each of the hundred industries.

In the accompanying Table A, J_1' and J_2' are as given by Dr Rhodes. J_1 and J_2 are computed by applying his indices in each industry to the gross output of that industry. The Board of Trade gives J_2 for each industry, and in computing J_1', J_2'

1 $$\frac{1}{2}\left\{\frac{S(P'q')}{S(n)} \div \frac{S(P'Q')}{S(N)} + \frac{S(p'q')}{S(n)} \div \frac{S(p'Q')}{S(N)}\right\} = \tfrac{1}{2}(J_1'+J_2') \div \frac{S(n)}{S(N)},$$

where n, N are the numbers employed in 1930 and 1924.

Table A

Measurements of Change in Production, 1930–35

Industry	Devons	Rhodes				Re-worked from Final Reports			
		J_1' Given	J_2' Given	J_1 Computed	J_2 Computed	J_1' Computed	J_2' Computed	J_1 Computed	J_2 Given
Iron and steel	125·0	122·6	115·6	120·6	113·4	128	118	122	114
Engineering, ships, vehicles	126·3	147·8	120·8	149·5	122·8	124½	107	135	182
Non-ferrous metals	119·6	142·6	132·3	144·0	146·7	132	135	147	150
Textiles	132·8	135·5	131·1	133·0	130·4	133	132	134	131
Leather	115·2	95·2	95·0	95·8	95·2	115	98	99	98
Clothing	117·4	115·1	113·8	114·9	113·7	117	119	119½	118
Food, drink, tobacco	110·0	108·9	107·6	110·1	107·3	115	110	112½	111
Chemical products	119·5	116·2	114·0	116·9	114·4	127	115	118½	113
Paper, printing	131·2	143·2	140·4	141·6	138·0	*142*	*140*	*142*	*138*
Timber*	110·0	80·2	76·7	80·2	76·7	*114*	*113*	*114*	*113*
Building and materials	126·2	131·9	109·5	127·0	105·6	*127*	*110*	*127*	*106*
Miscellaneous	110·8	110·8	111·5	112·3	111·8	122	113	113½	113
Mines and quarries	92·7	92·7	92·3	92·9	90·2	*93*	*92*	*93*	*90*
Public Utilities	123·4	123·6	117·6	122·8	122·4	123	118	123	112
All	119·4	123·4	113·8	123·6	114·4	122	114	123	114
* Revision suggests:									
Timber		114·0	113·4	114·0	113·4				
Total		124·0	114·8	124·1	115·5				

Note. Some of the entries for J_1', J_2' differ from those in Table IV, p. 150, since in the latter some modifications were made, which are not relevant to Mr Devons' treatment.

and J_1, it has been assumed that in detail the same factor may be taken for each computation.[1]

1 The following shows the working of the Industrial Group 'Non-Ferrous Metals':

Board of Trade

	Gross Output					Net Output				
	Given*			Computed		Given*			Computed	
	pq 1930	p_1q_1 1935	q/q_1	p_1q	pq_1	$p'q'$ 1930	$p_1'q_1'$ 1935	q_1'	$p_1'q'$	$p'q_1'$
Copper, brass	21·0	21·3	0·69	14·7	30·4	5·8	7·0	0·69	4·8	8·4
Aluminium, lead	26·5	33·2	0·83	27·6	31·9	6·2	9·8	0·83	8·1	7·5
Gold, silver	8·1	31·2	0·34	10·6	23·8	1·1	1·0	0·34	0·3	3·2
Finished brass	10·7	11·5	0·88	10·1	12·2	5·7	6·8	0·88	6·0	6·4
Plate, jewellery	8·7	9·2	0·97	8·9	9·0	4·6	4·6	0·97	4·5	4·7
Watches, clocks	0·9	1·4	0·35	0·5	2·6	0·5	0·7	0·35	0·2	1·4
£ mn.	75·9	107·8		72·4	109·9	23·9	29·9		23·9	31·6

$$J_1=\frac{109·9}{75·9}=1·45;\quad J_2=\frac{107·8}{72·4}=1·49;\quad J_1'=\frac{31·6}{23·9}=1·32;\quad J_2'=\frac{29·9}{23·9}=1·25.$$

(In the tables, pp. 142, 147–150, these J's are multiplied by 100.) Here it is assumed that $q'/q_1'=q/q_1$. In each line this factor is used for the 'computed' entries.

Dr Rhodes

	Net Output						Gross Output			
	Given†				Computed		Given†		Computed	
	$p'q'$	$p_1'q_1'$	J_1	$1/J_2$	$p_1'q'$	$p'q_1'$	pq	p_1q_1	p_1q	pq_1
Copper, etc.	5·8	6·9	1·45	0·69	4·8	8·4	21·0	19·7	13·6	30·5
Aluminium, etc.	6·2	9·8	1·21	0·88	8·6	7·5	26·5	33·1	29·0	32·0
Gold, etc.	1·1	1·0	2·08	0·47	0·5	2·2	8·1	30·7	14·5	16·8
Finished brass‡	5·7	6·6	(1·43)	(0·76)	(5·0)	(8·1)	10·7	11·3	(7·8)	(15·4)
Plate, etc.	4·6	4·4	1·56	0·64	2·8	7·2	8·7	8·8	5·7	13·5
Watches, etc.	0·4	0·6	1·23	0·81	0·5	0·6	0·9	1·1	0·9	1·1
£ mn.	23·9	29·3			22·2	34·0	75·9	104·7	71·5	109·3

$$J_1'=\frac{34·0}{23·9}=1·43;\quad J_2'=\frac{29·3}{22·2}=1·32;\quad J_1=\frac{109·3}{75·9}=1·44;\quad J_2=\frac{104·7}{71·5}=1·46.$$

* From Final Report.
† From Preliminary Report.
‡ The figures in ( ) are interpolated from the values of J_1 and J_2 computed from the remainder. This is equivalent to Dr Rhodes's method. He gives no index for Finished brass.

Mr Devons, in working on the 1930–35 changes, adopts a different hypothesis from that of Dr Rhodes, and a comparison of the two methods brings to light part of the essential difficulty of any computation of the physical volume of production.

Using now capitals for 1930 and small letters for 1935, we can express the data thus:

For each industry we are given V, v, V', v', that is, the values of the gross and net outputs at each date. For some commodities we are given separately Q, q, $P \div p$, but not $P' \div p'$, that is, we have the quantities and change in selling prices for part of each industry. By using a rather rough assumption[1] we can separate the prices for the first part of the industry, for which quantity data are available, so as to have this scheme:

Industry	Value 1930	Value 1935	Quantity 1930	Quantity 1935	Average price 1930	Average price 1935
1st part	V_1	v_1	Q_1	q_1	P_1	p_1
2nd part	V_2	v_2	—	—	—	—

For the second part of the industry, we only have V_2, v_2, V_2', v_2'. The ratio of the values, v_2/V_2, is the product of the ratios of the quantities (q_2/Q_2) and prices (p_2/P_2).

Dr Rhodes and Mr Devons both proceed on the assumption that the results obtained for the first part of the industry are applicable to the whole, but Dr Rhodes interprets this as meaning that the ratio of quantity (q_1/Q_1) is applicable, Mr Devons that the ratio of prices (p_1/P_1) is applicable. Thus Dr Rhodes uses

$$J_1 = \frac{V_1 \times q_1/Q_1 + V_2 \times q_1/Q_1}{V_1 + V_2} = \frac{q_1}{Q_1},^*$$

1 Neither of the authors nor the Board of Trade make clear the method by which Q_1, q_1, P_1, p_1 are obtained from the details. The sequence may be:

$$\left.\begin{array}{ll} Sv \times P/p = SPq, & p_1 \div P_1 = Sv \div SPq \\ \text{or} \quad SV \times p/P = SpQ, & p_1 \div P_1 = SPq \div SV \end{array}\right\} \text{ where the price ratios are known,}$$

$$\left.\begin{array}{ll} \text{or} \quad Sv \times Q/q = SpQ, & q_1 \div Q_1 = Sv \div SpQ \\ \text{or} \quad SV \times q/Q = SPq, & q_1 \div Q_1 = SPq \div SV \end{array}\right\} \text{ where the quantity ratios are known.}$$

It is only the ratios p/P, q/Q that are needed, not the terms separately.

* q_1/Q_1 is already composite as shown in the previous footnote, and different values are generally used in the working of J_2.

while Mr Devons has

$$J_1 = \frac{V_1 \times q_1/Q_1 + v_2 \times P_1/p_1}{V_1 + V_2} = \frac{V_1 \dfrac{q_1}{Q_1}\left(1 + \dfrac{v_2}{v_1}\right)}{V_1 + V_2}.$$

These would be equal if $V_2/v_2 = V_1/v_1$, which is not usually the case. The required measurement is

$$J_1 = \frac{V_1 \times q_1/Q_1 + V_2 \times q_2/Q_2}{V_1 + V_2},$$

and in the Board of Trade's Reports some value is assigned in each industry to pQ and therefore to q/Q, but it is not clear how the difficulty has been overcome.

The numerators of J_1 are added to obtain the numerator for a group of industries, and also the denominators added.

The results of the different methods are shown in the accompanying Table A, p. 142. At the time of writing the Board of Trade's Report on four groups is not available, and Dr Rhodes's figures are given in italics in these cases and used for the combination of all industries.

Mr Devons's numbers agree nearly with those worked from the Final Reports in the Iron and Steel, Engineering, Textiles, Leather, Clothing and Food, etc. groups, but differ for Non-ferrous Metals, Chemical Products and Miscellaneous. Dr Rhodes's numbers show for about half the groups considerable dispersion between J_1 and J_2. In many cases the J_1', J_2' computed for the Final Reports lie within or nearly within Dr Rhodes's margin, but not for Iron and Steel, Leather, Food, etc., Chemical Products and Miscellaneous. Unless for the Final Reports there was more quantitative information than was at Dr Rhodes's disposal, it may be held that information is insufficient to give a precise measurement in these groups.

For a single measurement of the volume of production there seems to be no better course than to average J_1 and J_2. We then have

	J	J'
Devons	—	119·4
Rhodes	119·4	119·8
Final Report	118·3	119·1

for all the Industrial Groups together, and this consistency enables us to state an increase of a little less than 20 per cent in the period 1930 to 1935 with some confidence.

The results of this investigation are set out in the accompanying Tables I, II, III, IV. For all the industries together we have:

Index-numbers relating to Industrial Production

		1924	1930	1935	1930	1935
Value:	Gross Output	100	91	95	100	104
	Net Output	100	97	103	100	106½
Volume:	Gross Output	100	107	126½	100	118½
	Net Output	100	108	129	100	119
	Economic Service*	100	107	130	100	121
Price:	Gross Output	100	85½	75	100	88½
	Net Output	100	90	80½	100	89½
	Materials	100	81½	71	100	87
Operatives:	Number	100	96	95	100	99
Efficiency:	Operatives	100	112	135	100	120
	Operatives and administratives	100	105½	126	100	119½

For this table the averages of the values J_1, J_2, etc. are used.

* Excluding Agriculture.

As regards prices, the fall in wholesale prices of materials according to the Board of Trade was 37½ per cent from 1924 to 1934 and to 1935, by *The Statist*, 42 per cent to 1934, 39½ per cent to 1935, and for imports of materials, roughly estimated, 56 per cent, as compared with 32 per cent in this table.

The tables relate necessarily only to firms employing more than ten persons.

The gross and net values exclude excise and the sugar subsidy, but include implicitly the building subsidy. For the index-numbers of volume, price and efficiency the exclusion or inclusion only affects the system of weighting the average, but it is well to make a rough estimate of the change when we add excise and subtract subsidies[1], thus using as weights more definitely the 'value added by manufacture'.

Net Output (adjusted)

1924 to 1930	$\frac{1}{2}(J_1'+J_2')$	$\frac{1}{2}(I_1'+I_2')$	Efficiency
Food, drink, tobacco	107	88½	102
Building and materials	125	90	116
Total	108	89½	112

1930 to 1935	$\frac{1}{2}(J_1'+J_2')$	$\frac{1}{2}(I_1'+I_2')$	Efficiency
Food, drink, tobacco	109	92	102
Building and materials	121½	83½	121
Total	118	89	120

1 The building subsidy is roughly estimated at £6 mn. in each Census year, that is £100 for each of 60,000 houses.

TABLE I

Censuses of Production, 1924 and 1930

Industrial group	Gross Output: Value of (£ mn.)		Index of value	Index of quantity		Index of price		Materials Index of price*	
	1924	1930	(1930 expressed as percentage of 1924)						
	PQ	pq	$W=pq/PQ$	$J_1=Pq/PQ$	$J_2=pq/pQ$	$I_1=pQ/PQ$	$I_2=pq/Pq$	${}_rI_1$	${}_rI_2$
Iron and steel	295	238	78	97	98	81	82	77	78
Engineering, ships, vehicles	402	461	115	119	116	99	96	98	96
Non-ferrous metals	92	108	117	138	138	86	85	85	85
Textiles	763	432	57	80	80	70	71	66	67
Leather	42	36	86	94	94	91	91	90	90
Clothing	183	180	99	110	109	90	89	87	86
Food, drink, tobacco	654	662	101	114	113	89	89	87	86
Chemical products	194	182	94	107	108	87	87	79	80
Paper, printing	162	177	110	117	117	94	94	92	92
Timber	59	69	116	126	128	91	91	92	92
Building and materials	232	266	115	126	126	91	91	93	93
Miscellaneous	94	92	97	117	119	82	83	80	80
Mines and quarries	273	187	69	93	94	73	73	73	73
Public Utilities / Government Departments†	283	306	108	120	118	92	91	82	84
Total	3,729	3,397	91	107	107	85	86	81	82

* $PQ.I_1=(PQ-P'Q')\,{}_rI_1+P'Q'.I_1'$, and $Pq.I_2=(Pq-P'q')\,{}_rI_2'+P'Q'.I_2'$.

† There is a slight modification from the Census, since the details instead of the total are used in this case.

TABLE II

Censuses of Production, 1924 *and* 1930

Industrial group	Net Output									
	Value of (£ mn.)		Index of value	Index of quantity		Index of price		Operatives (000's)		Index of efficiency
	1924 $P'Q'$	1930 $p'q'$	W'	J_1'	J_2'	I_1'	I_2'	N	n	$\frac{1}{2}(J_1'+J_2') \div n/N$
Iron and steel	99	92	93	103	102	92	91	456	447	103
Engineering, ships, vehicles	198	230	116	120	116	100	97	852	914	110
Non-ferrous metals	25	24	93	109	104	90	85	101	95	113
Textiles	222	147	66	84	83	80	79	1,198	997	100
Leather	12	10	88	94	93	94	93	43	41	98
Clothing	76	78	103	109	110	93	94	430	444	107
Food, drink, tobacco	172	188	109	113	112	97	97	370	389	107
Chemical products	66	73	111	110	110	101	101	143	137	115
Paper, printing	94	103	110	116	116	95	94	290	320	185
Timber	27	31	115	129	129	89	90	123	149	106
Building and materials	124	139	112	125	125	90	90	580	625	116
Miscellaneous	41	43	103	119	122	85	87	146	148	119
Mines and quarries	226	155	69	93	94	73	74	1,255	999	117
Public Utilities, Government Departments	166	191	115	120	119	97	96	678	713	114
Total	1,549	1,505	97	108	108	90	90	6,665	6,418	112

TABLE III

Censuses of Production, 1930 *and* 1935

Industrial group	Gross Output								
	Value of (£ mn.)		Index of value	Index of quantity		Index of price		Materials Index of price	
	1930	1935	(1935 expressed as percentage of 1930)						
	pq	p_1q_1	$W=p_1q_1/pq$	J_1	J_2	I_1	I_2	$_rI_1$	$_rI_2$
Iron and steel	238	280½	118	122	114	103	97	100	94
Engineering, ships, vehicles	461	490½	106	135	102	105	79	108	82
Non-ferrous metals*	76	108	142	147	150	95	97	96	102
Textiles	433	446	103	134	131	79	77	77	76
Leather	36	34	96	99	98	97	97	94	93
Clothing	181	179	99	119½	118	84	83	83	81
Food, drink, tobacco	659	661	100	112½	111	90½	89	88	86
Chemical products	180½	194	107	118½	113	95	91	88	82
Paper, printing	177	181	102	142	138	74	72	72	69
Timber	69	69	100	114	113	88	88	85	85
Building and materials†	266	271	102	127	106	97	80	103	85
Miscellaneous	92	91½	99	113½	113	88	88	86	85
Mines	187	166	88	93	90	98	95	113	98
Public Utilities	283	306	108	123	122	88	88	85	91
Government Departments	29	32	110	(123)	(122)	—	—	—	—
Total	3,367	3,510	104	123	114	92	85	90	84

* Non-ferrous metals. In the earlier reports gold refined on commission was included, in the later it was excluded.
† Including earthenware and glass as well as bricks, cement, etc.

Table IV

Censuses of Production, 1930 *and* 1935

Industrial group	Net Output									
	Value of (£ mn.)		Index of value	Index of quantity		Index of price		Operatives (000's)		Index of efficiency
	1930 $p'q'$	1935 $p_1'q_1'$	W'	J_1'	J_2'	I_1'	I_2'	1930 n	1935 n_1	$\frac{1}{2}(J_1'+J_2')\div n_1/n$
Iron and steel	92	117	127	125	118	108	102	447	487	111
Engineering, ships, vehicles	229½	249	109	142	107	102	76	913	923	123
Non-ferrous metals	24	30	125	146	135	93	85	95	106	126
Textiles	147½	157½	107	137	132	81	78	996	989	135
Leather	10	11	104	98	98	106	106	41	45	89
Clothing	78	81	104	120	119	87	86	445	484	110
Food, drink, tobacco	187	202	108	112	110	98	97	389	414	104
Chemical products	72½	88	122	117	115	106	104	136	143	111
Paper, printing	103	110	106	143	140	76	74	320	329	138
Timber	31½	32	103	114	113	91	90	149	149	114
Building and materials	139	140	101	132	110	92	76	624	623	121
Miscellaneous	43	44	102	112	113	91	91	148	155	107
Mines	155	136	88	93	92	95	95	999	818	113
Public Utilities	171	180 }	106	123	118	90	86	714	691	125
Government Departments	19	22 }								
Total	1,503	1,599	106½	124	114	93½	85½	6,416	6,356	120

4. *INDEX OF PRODUCTION*, 1924 *TO* 1938

ANNUAL MOVEMENT 1924 TO 1938

The published data for annual measurements of production are the Board of Trade index, the London and Cambridge Economic Service index, and the index-numbers suggested by Mr Stone. These have to be collated with the more complete accounts at the Census dates. A supplementary measurement is obtained from the numbers of persons employed in the Industrial Groups covered.

The Board of Trade index did not include building (prior to 1934), clothing (other than boots) nor Local and Central Government activities nor Public Utilities (other than gas and electricity); in consequence it showed a much lower increase than those in the tables above, and is not suitable for interpolation for the aggregate. The Economic Service index agrees very closely with the Censuses, but the intercensal movements show only an intermittent parallelism with the movement of employment, and need reconsideration as in later paragraphs especially for the years 1936, 1937 and 1938.

Mr and Mrs Stone virtually reject the Economic Service index and construct indices based on the Censuses, the results of Import Duties Acts enquiries and the volume of employment (*Economic Journal*, 1939, pp. 476 seq.). In the end they adopt a formula:

$$\text{Output} = a + b \times \text{Employment} + c \times T,$$

where T is the number of years measured for a base year. The values of a, b, c are obtained by the method of least squares from five given index-numbers, viz. Censuses at 1924, 1930 and 1935 and the Import Duties results for 1933 and 1934. The last named are difficult to bring into line with the others, and in any case do not cover the whole field.

There can be little doubt that in times of busy trade production increases more rapidly than the number of insured persons not unemployed at particular dates, owing to more overtime and less part time, while the reverse is true in times of depression, and in particular years other circumstances affect the relationship. The measurements of efficiency given in the tables (pp. 148, 150) show that there was a more rapid increase in the five years 1930–35 than in the previous six years 1924–30; 1930 was a year of increasing depression, 1924 and 1935 years of moderately good trade. We are not justified in assuming, as in Mr Stone's formula, that the increase in efficiency (indicated by the coefficient of T) was uniform throughout the whole period (1924–38) that he takes, and in particular we cannot assume that the same relationship holds in the years 1936, 1937 and 1938.

The connection between employment and production can be best examined by supposing a uniform increase from 1924 to 1930 and another uniform increase from 1930 to 1935. Thus in the period 1924 to 1930 the formula used is

$$\text{Output} = \text{Employment} - ct,$$

where $t=0$ at 1930, and output is taken at 93·5 (as in C) in 1924, so that $c=\frac{1}{6}(104{\cdot}6-93{\cdot}5)=1{\cdot}85$. In the first period 1·85 is subtracted cumulatively each year from the Employment index, column H, in the annexed table—thus 11·1 is subtracted in 1924, 9·3 in 1925, and so on. In the second period 3·84 is added each year cumulatively, so as to obtain the same numbers in 1935. The resulting numbers are shown in the last column of the table.

Index-numbers of Production and Employment

Volume of Production

	Board of Trade		Economic Service		Census of Production		Mr Stone	Insured workers	C combined with H
	A	B	C	D	E	F	G	H	
1924	97·0	—	93·5	94·4	92·5	94	93·8	104·6	93·5
1925	—	—	93·9	94·2	—	—	—	102·4	93·1
1926	—	—	82·0	80·8	—	—	—	99·5	92·1
1927	103·5	—	104·4	102·8	—	—	103·3	107·3	101·7
1928	103·0	—	101·3	101·4	—	—	103·9	104·1	100·4
1929	108·4	—	109·1	108·8	—	—	110·2	107·1	105·3
1930	100·0	100·0	100·0	100·0	100	100	101·7	100·0	100·0
1931	90·5	—	90·5	89·4	—	—	92·3	92·3	96·1
1932	90·1	—	90·9	90·0	—	—	94·5	90·1	97·8
1933	95·3	—	99·7	98·2	—	—	102·4	95·1	106·6
1934	107·2	106·2	113·2	110·6	—	—	112·3	100·2	115·6
1935	—	113·4	121·3	119·0	120	119	118·1	102·1	121·3
1936	—	124·4	132·0	129·5	—	—	129·4	108·1	131·1
1937	—	132·8	139·0	136·9	—	—	142·2	115·7	142·6
1938	—	124·2	125·5	122·9	—	—	140·5	112·0	142·7

A, D and F exclude Building.
B, C and E include Building.
G excludes Building, Public Utilities and Government Departments.

The Board of Trade index is taken from the *Ministry of Labour Gazette*, in which the most recent revisions are included. The index is given separately for each quarter of the year; and these entries are averaged for the year. The earlier numbers have been adjusted proportionately so as to give 100·0 in 1930.

The Economic Service numbers are computed from the *London and Cambridge Economic Service Bulletin*, May 1939. Agriculture has been excluded.

Mr Stone's numbers are from the *Economic Journal*, September 1939, p. 477, column (5). The insured workers employed are obtained by excluding the Industrial Groups Transport, Distribution, Commerce and Miscellaneous Trades and Services, and then subtracting the numbers unemployed in June from the estimated number insured in July. The resulting numbers are expressed as percentages of the number in 1930.

The last column is as explained above. When these are compared with the Economic Service index (column C) it is seen that the employment index under-estimates the fall in 1926 (the year of the coal stoppage) and the rise in 1927 when arrears were made up. Similarly it rises less in 1929 and falls less in 1931, the worst year of the depression. These are precisely the relationships that we should expect. But in 1937 the employment index rises more rapidly than we should expect and does not fall in 1938. Since the Board of Trade index (column B) shows a smaller fall than does that of the Economic Service, the index-numbers for 1937 and 1938 must remain rather uncertain. It may be noticed that the changes in columns B and C are nearly equal for the whole period 1930–38, and also for the sub-period 1934–37.

Reviewing all the evidence, we conclude that the Economic Service index is the most consistent, and that in default of any conclusive evidence to the contrary may be used as a fairly adequate measurement for the field of industrial and mineral production that it covers. It cannot claim any great precision, and it has been shown on pp. 136–141 above that there are inseparable inherent difficulties in defining and measuring physical production, even if we had complete data.[1]

NOTE ON WEEKLY WAGES AND ANNUAL EARNINGS

Information about wages comes from three sources. The Ministry of Labour collects from time to time statements from employers of the numbers of wage-earners employed and the

1 Cf. *Journal of the Royal Statistical Society*, 1939, pp. 6 seq. All the numbers in the table above are weighted by values in the base year, that is, they are based more or less directly on the formula named J_1 in this chapter.

total payments made to them in a selected week. No distinction is made between occupations within the factory. The results are assembled for each of several scores of industries, with detail that has varied from enquiry to enquiry, such as division by sex, distinction between large and small firms, amount of time lost and overtime, hours of work. The returns are not compulsory, and the proportion of the numbers returned to those in the industry as a whole varies considerably between the industries. To obtain a general result problems of weighting occur, but the various methods tried for averaging result in very nearly the same figures, and it is not necessary to describe them in detail. It is, of course, possible that the returns are biased, since firms paying low rates may be less willing than others to report, but it is believed that this influence, if it exists, has negligible effects.

The Ministry of Labour also publishes each month all known changes in wage rates, but has not for many years shown details of the numbers affected, only giving the total numbers for large industrial groups. Each January there is a summary account of changes, and in recent years an estimate of the total effect on wages has occasionally been given. Such data lead to the index-numbers of change of wage rates used in our main computation, pp. 60–66. In computing the movement of total earnings by the use of these index-numbers, naturally care is taken to give full effect to changes not only of the numbers 'occupied', or registered for insurance purposes, in each industry, but also to the numbers unemployed, wholly or temporarily; and some check is also possible from scattered statements of part-time work, and by the relation of hours worked to normal hours in some of the Wage Census Reports. But among those fully employed, especially on piece-work, there is variation from time to time between the relation of a week's earnings to standard rates, earnings increasing in times of industrial activity. In spite of all these uncertainties, it has been found that the changes in average earnings in the periods 1924 to 1931 and 1931 to 1935, as shown by the general returns of average earnings at those dates, are almost exactly the same as those already shown by the index-numbers of rates.[1] It is improbable that this relation changed much in intermediate years.

1 See *Wages and Income in the United Kingdom since* 1860, Appendices A and C, for further discussion of the Census statistics.

The third source of information is found in the Final Reports of the Censuses of Production of 1924 and 1930. (Unfortunately that for 1935 is not available.) Here we have statements of the totals paid in wages by about two-thirds of the firms (employing more than ten persons) that are included in the Censuses. Also we have recorded the numbers employed by these firms in one week in 1924, and in the middle week of each month in 1930.

One would expect that factories were at work for 50 weeks in the year, allowing two weeks for public and trade holidays, and consequently that average weekly earnings would be obtained by dividing total wages by the average number of operatives, and the quotient by 50. The annexed table, however, shows that when we divide average annual earnings thus computed for 1924 and 1930 by average weekly earnings as computed from the wage returns in 1924 and those of 1931 adjusted to 1930, we find 51 and 51·7 for the main group of Factory Trades. The figures for coal-mining depend on difficult estimates of the number of shifts worked, while agreement is not to be expected for building, since the figures are confused by the existence of many small firms which are not included in this extract from the Census Reports.

Census of Production. Great Britain

	Factory trades		Building and contracting		Coal-mines	
	1924	1930	1924	1930	1924	1930
Total wages (£ mn.)	494	490	59	64	162	104
Average number of operatives (000's)	4,219	4,171	379	411	1,175	915
A. Wages per head per annum, £	117·1	117·5	156	158	138	114

Wage Returns. United Kingdom

	1924	Oct. 1931	1924	Oct. 1931	Per shift	
Weekly earnings	45*s.* 11*d.*	44*s.* 6*d.*	60*s.*	58*s.* 3*d.*	10·65*s.*	9·29*s.*
					Shifts per annum	
B. Average 1930*	—	45*s.* 4*d.*	—	59*s.* 7*d.*	—	—
A÷B. No. of weeks or shifts	51	51·8	52	53	260	245

* Deduced from October 1931 by applying index-numbers of wage rates.

No complete explanation has been found for this discrepancy. The exclusion of Northern Ireland from the Census statistics cannot make any significant difference. Possibly, since October 1931 was in a period of severe unemployment, the percentage of insured persons unemployed being 21·6, while the average for 1930 was 15·8, average earnings in 1931 were lowered by short time (not counted as unemployment) more than in 1930. Or the explanation may lie in the different methods of sampling and recording, and the number of approximations in the computations, each of trifling uncertainty but possibly accumulating in one direction. After all, the difference in the main average, 51·7 weeks, and the expected, 50, is less than 4 per cent.

In computing the Total Wage Bill we have to choose between these estimates. As explained on p. 58, our basis is the number of occupied persons recorded in the Population Census as occupied and not out of work in 1931, since the Census of Production does not cover the whole ground. We have assumed that the average number of weeks actually worked by those who described themselves as following an occupation and not out of work was 48, allowing two weeks for holidays and two weeks for absence through sickness or other causes. This 48 is then to be multiplied by average weekly earnings. After weighing all known factors, it is thought that the average computed from the October 1931 wage returns is more appropriate for the basis of the total and change of the National Wage Bill, than the slightly higher figure suggested by the Census of Production.

Thus the principal table on p. 81 gives the number of wage-earners occupied as computed from the Population Census, average earnings as computed from the wage returns of October 1931, supplemented by other information, and for annual earnings the product of these averages by the number of persons and 48, the number of weeks worked on the average in the year.

This question is discussed also on pp. 69, 72, 73 and 74 above.

Appendices to Chapter III

APPENDIX I

SOURCES OF STATISTICS IN PART 1

In this Appendix explanations are given of the statistics in Part 1, further details of classification and such other matters as may be useful for reference. No attempt is made to cover the whole of the ground of the Censuses of Production.

The main Industrial Groups in the table on p. 126 are obtained by separating Coal from other Mines and Quarries, giving Food and Drink separately from Tobacco, isolating Rubber from Miscellaneous Trades, and dividing Public Utility Services and Government Departments into four groups. On the other hand the Census Groups 'Clay and Building Materials' and 'Building and Contracting' are merged. Building by official bodies is, however, kept (as in the Census) in the Government groups. The small unclassified item for Northern Ireland is divided equally between Drink and Tobacco. The numbering consequently differs from that used by the Census. The divisions follow fairly closely those used by the Ministry of Labour.

The sub-groups treated separately in the detailed Census Reports are as follows:

I. Coal Mining.

II. Other Mines and Quarries include:

(1) Metalliferous Mines and Quarries.
(2) Non-Metalliferous Mines and Quarries (including Oil Shale Mines).
(3) Slate Mines and Quarries.
(4) Salt Mines, Brine Pits and Salt Works.

III. Clay, Building Materials and Building:

(1) Brick and Fireclay.
(2) China and Earthenware.
(3) Glass.
(4) Cement.
(5) Building Materials.
(6) Building and Contracting.

IV. Chemicals, Paints, Oils, etc.:

(1) Chemicals, Dyestuffs and Drugs.
(2) Paint, Colour and Varnish.
(3) Seed Crushing.
(4) Oil and Tallow.
(5) Fertilizer, Glue, Sheep Dip and Disinfectant.
(6) Soap, Candle and Perfumery.
(7) Starch and Polishes.
(8) The Metal Trade.
(9) Ink, Gum and Sealing-Wax.
(10) Petroleum.
(11) Explosives and Fireworks.

V. Iron and Steel:

(1) Pig Iron and Ferro-alloys (Blast Furnaces).
(2) Smelting and Rolling.
(3) Foundries.
(4) Tinplate.
(5) Hardware, Hollow Ware, Metal Furniture and Sheet.
(6) Chain, Nail, Screw.
(7) Light Castings in the 1924 Census (which in later Censuses were included in Foundries).
(8) Wrought Iron and Steel Tubes.
(9) Wire Trade.
(10) Tools and Implements.
(11) Cutlery.
(12) Blacksmithing in the 1924 Census (which in later Censuses was included in other groups).
(13) Needle, Pin and Metal Smallwares.
(14) Small Arms (private firms).

VI. Engineering, Shipbuilding, and Vehicles:

(1) Mechanical Engineering.
(2) Electrical Engineering.
(3) Shipbuilding (private firms).
(4) Motor Vehicles and Cycles (Manufacturing).
(5) Motor Vehicles and Cycles (Repairing).
(6) Aircraft.
(7) Railway Carriage and Wagon Building.
(8) Carriage, Cart, Wagon.

VII. Non-Ferrous Metals, Jewellery, Watch and Clock:

(1) Copper and Brass (Smelting, Rolling, etc.).
(2) Aluminium, Lead, Tin, etc. (Smelting, Rolling, etc.).
(3) Gold and Silver Refining.
(4) Finished Brass.
(5) Plate and Jewellery.
(6) Watch and Clock.

VIII. Textiles:

(1) Cotton Spinning and Doubling.
(2) Cotton Weaving.
(3) Woollen and Worsted.
(4) Silk and Artificial Silk.
(5) Linen and Hemp.
(6) Jute.
(7) Hosiery.
(8) Furnishing (Bleaching and Dyeing).
(9) Lace.
(10) Rope, Twine and Net.
(11) Canvas Goods and Sack.
(12) Asbestos Goods and Engine and Boiler Packing.
(13) Flock and Rag.
(14) Elastic Webbing.
(15) Coir Fibre, Horsehair, Feather.
(16) Roofing Felt.
(17) Packing.

IX. Leather:

(1) Fellmongery.
(2) Leather (Tanning and Dressing).
(3) Leather Goods.

X. Clothing:

(1) Tailoring and Millinery.
(2) Artificial Flower in the 1924 Census, which in later Censuses was included in Tailoring.
(3) Boot and Shoe.
(4) Hat and Cap.
(5) Glove.
(6) Fur.
(7) Umbrella.

XI. Food:

(1) Grain Milling.
(2) Bread, Cakes, etc.
(3) Biscuit.
(4) Cocoa and Sugar Confectionery.
(5) Preserved Foods.
(6) Bacon Curing and Sausage.
(7) Butter, Cheese, Condensed Milk and Margarine.
(8) Sugar and Glucose.
(9) Fish Curing.
(10) Cattle, Dog and Poultry Foods.
(11) Ice.

XII. Drink:

(1) Brewing and Malting.
(2) Spirit Distilling.
(3) Spirit Rectifying, Compounding and Methylating.
(4) Aerated Water, Cider, Vinegar and British Wines.
(5) Wholesale Bottling.

XIII. Tobacco.

XIV. Timber:

(1) Sawmilling, etc.
(2) Furniture and Upholstery.
(3) Cane and Wicker Furniture and Basketware.
(4) Crates, Cases, Boxes.
(5) Coopering.

XV. Paper, Printing, Stationery:

(1) Paper.
(2) Wallpaper.
(3) Stationery.
(4) Cardboard Boxes.
(5) Printing, Binding, Stereotyping, Engraving.
(6) Typefounding and Electrotyping in the 1924 Census, which in later Censuses was included in Printing, Binding, etc.
(7) Printing and Publication of Newspapers and Periodicals.
(8) Pens, Pencils, Artists' Materials.

XVI. Rubber.

XVII. Miscellaneous:

(1) Scientific Instruments.
(2) Fancy Articles.
(3) Coke and By-products.
(4) Manufactured Fuel.
(5) Linoleum and Oilcloth.
(6) Musical Instruments.
(7) Brush.
(8) Games and Toys.
(9) Sport Requisites.
(10) Manufactured Abrasives.
(11) Incandescent Mantles.
(12) Cinema Film Printing.

XVIII. Gas, Electricity, Water:

(1) Gas.
(2) Electricity.
(3) Water.

XIX. Transport and Communication (Engineering and Construction):

(1) Railway Companies.
(2) Tramways and Light Railways.
(3) Canal, Dock and Harbour.

XX. Local Authorities (Construction, etc.).

XXI. Government Departments (Production, not Civil Service or Transport):

(1) Admiralty.
(2) General Post Office.
(3) War Office.
(4) Air Ministry.
(5) Other Government Departments.

XXII. Laundry, Cleaning and Dyeing.

Net output of the Laundry, Cleaning and Dyeing Group which is available only for the year 1924 is treated separately as Group XXII.

Regrouping of the Sub-Groups as between the *various Trade Groups* (*Inter-group shifts*)

In order to make the returns of the Trade Groups comparable through all the Censuses of Production we had to make a certain amount of re-allocation of the various Sub-Groups. This applies especially to the 1924 Census, the subject-matter of which was arranged differently from the later Censuses. Thus, *Trade Group I* (Coal Mining) included in the 1924 Census the net output of the Manufactured Fuel Trade, valued £0·4 mn., which in our table is classed with Trade Group XVII (Miscellaneous), following the practice of later Censuses.

Trade Group III in the 1924 Census included the net output valued £0·6 mn. of Manufactured Abrasives (shifted to Miscellaneous, Group XVII); £2·1 mn. of Asbestos Goods and Engine and Boiler Packing, which in our table is classified together with Trade Group VIII (Textiles); £0·4 mn. of Roofing Felt has been alternatively tabulated with Textiles (Trade Group VIII), though we left it in the total of Trade Group III.

Trade Group IV (Chemicals) included in the 1924 Census a net output of £5·1 mn. of Coke and By-products which in our table is presented together with the Miscellaneous Trades (XVII).

Trade Group VI (Engineering) in the 1924 Census did not include the net output of £3·2 mn. of the Carriage, Cart and Wagon Trade which was classed together with the Timber Group.

Trade Group VIII in the 1924 Census included £0·2 mn. of Incandescent Mantles classed together with Linen and Hemp, though in the later Censuses that sub-group was separated and treated together with the Miscellaneous Trades. In our Table B, p. 126, we left them as in the 1924 Census in the Trade

Group VIII, though perhaps it would be better to put them with the Miscellaneous Group XVII. The item is very small.

The net output of £1·9 mn. in 1924 of Canvas Goods, Sacks, etc. Trade is included in Trade Group VIII, though in the 1924 Census it is presented together with the Leather and Rubber (Trade Group IX).

The whole Trade Group IX, viz. Leather Trades, in the 1924 Census is lumped together with the net output of £11·8 mn. of our Trade Group XVI (Rubber), and in addition includes £1·9 mn. of the Canvas Goods and Sack Trade belonging in our table to Trade Group VIII.

Trade Group X (Clothing) in the 1924 Census includes £16·3½ mn. of net output of Laundry, Cleaning and Dyeing which in our table is relegated to a separate Group XXII in order to make the Group X comparable with the Censuses of later years.

In the 1924 Census *Trade Group XIV* (Woodworking) included the net output valued at £1·8 mn. of Brush-making Trade relegated in our table to Trade Group XVII (Miscellaneous).

Trade Group XV (Paper, Printing, etc.) includes the net output valued at £1·3 mn. of Pens, Pencils, Artists' Materials Trades which in the 1924 Census was presented together with Trade Group XVII (Miscellaneous Trades).

Other minor changes had to be made, but they do not affect the unit million figure.

Sources of Information

At the moment of writing this commentary (January 1941) three parts of the Final Report of the Fifth Census of Production have been published. As each of the Censuses of Production gives comparative data for some of the previous Census years, and as it was found that the entries of net output for the same year of the same trade group and trade sub-groups differ, in some cases even considerably, we decided to give comparable information taken from the three Censuses of Production (table, p. 164). Thus for the year 1924 we have drawn our information (first in column A) from the 1924 Census; in the next column (B), from the 1930 Census.

For the Census year 1930 our information has been drawn from two sources: the Final Reports of the 1930 Census, and the Preliminary Reports of the 1935 Census, or for those Trade Groups which are available from the first three published volumes of the Final Report of the 1935 Census. We use the same procedure adopted for arriving at the 1930 total on the basis of the Final Census of Production, 1935, which we suggested for the year 1924 in respect of information derived from the same Census. The figures are given to the nearest million £. If they had been to £100,000, more discrepancies would have come to light.

In the case of the net output figures for the Census year 1935 we have been using two sources of information, viz. the Preliminary Reports of the 1935 Census and the Final Reports of the 1935 Census (column D) for all those trade groups for which information has been already published. In the summary table, pp. 127–8, columns B are used for 1924 and 1930 and column D for 1935.

The differences between A and B under 1924 are, apart from changes of classification already named, due to the inclusion of firms with not more than ten employees. For 1935 the entries under D are greater in some cases than those under C owing to the inclusion of additional returns. It may be expected that some further additions will be made in the Final Reports on the industries for which only the Preliminary Reports are available.

There are other details which affect comparability to a slight extent.

The maintenance, construction and repairs of the London buses are included in Motor and Cycles (Repairs) in the years 1924 and 1930; but in 1935 the same item (now the London Passenger Transport Board) has been transferred to the Local Authorities, Group XX.

The following classes of business were not included in the 1930 and 1935 Censuses: Taxidermy Work; Wig-making; Flax Scutching; Portrait or Trade Photography, other than making of or printing from blocks or metal plates prepared by photographic processes, and the printing of cinematographic films; work done by employees of Parish Councils and Parish Meetings and by inmates of Poor Law Institutions.

Army clothing factory (closed in 1931), Army bakeries and Ordnance electricity undertakings are included in Trade Group XXI (Government Departments).

In some cases the net output figures are returned '*At Cost*' basis, i.e. they exclude profits, though the 'appropriate establishment charges' have been duly met. Thus they are entered

Net Output as reported in the Main Tables in 1924, 1930, 1935

A. From the 1924 Census.
B. From the 1930 Census.
C. From the Preliminary Reports of the 1935 Census.
D. From the Final Reports of the 1935 Census.

Industrial group	1924		1930		1935	
	A	B	C	C or D	C	D
I. Coal Mining	210	210	139	139	121	*
II. Other mines	17	17	17	17	15	*
III. Building and materials	142	124	139	139	140	*
IV. Chemicals	69	66	73	73	87	88
V. Iron and steel	110	99	92	92	115	117
VI. Engineering, ships, vehicles	202	198	230	229	241	249
VII. Non-ferrous metals	26	25	24	24	29	30
VIII. Textiles	223	222	147	148	156	157
IX. Leather	13	12	10	10	10	11
X. Clothing	89	76	78	78	77	81
XI. Food	99	85	92	92	104	107
XII. Drink	64	63	64	65	65	67
XIII. Tobacco	25	25	31	31	28	28
XIV. Timber	33	27	32	32	32	*
XV. Paper, printing	98	94	103	103	110	*
XVI. Rubber	12	12	14	14	14	14
XVII. Miscellaneous	29	30	28	28	29	29
XVIII. Gas, electricity, water	73	69	95	93	110	*
XIX. Transport	45	45	41	41	38	*
XX. Local Authorities	32	32	37	37	33	*
XXI. Government Departments	20	20	19	19	22	*
Total	1,632	1,549	1,505	1,504	1,576	1,599†
XXII. Dyeing, cleaning, etc.	16					
Duties included in 1924 total	95	*	*	*	*	*
	1,743					

* Not available. † Total, using Column C where necessary.

at a sum calculated to cover the cost of labour and materials, with such a proportion of the general establishment charges as was attributable to the services concerned; the element of profit is, therefore, absent from the value both of the gross and of the net output. This method of calculating net output applies to Transport and Communication, Trade Group XIX, to the

Local Authorities, Group XX, and to the Government Departments, Trade Group XXI. As regards Gas, Electricity and Water, Trade Group XVIII, the position was as follows: the net output value was obtained for the most part on the basis of the selling value of the gas and electricity supplied and included the profits derived from their sale; as regards water undertakings, the revenues of which are frequently obtained by the levy of a rate on the annual value of the premises served, the receipts may not bear any necessarily fixed relation to working costs.

Certain classes of *maintenance* belonging to the Local Authorities Trade Group, such as street cleaning and watering; house refuse, sewage, etc., are not considered as production and are excluded.

APPENDIX II

EXCISE, CUSTOMS AND SUBSIDIES

The problem of including in or excluding from the net output figures such items as subsidies, excise duties and customs duties is not a clear-cut one, and it depends to a large extent on the problem in hand. The accompanying table summarizes the situation in respect of these items. It presents them in a form which is handy and which can easily be fitted into the main totals or trade-group totals obtained from the Censuses of Production.

The arrangement of the table is such as to bring it in as close correspondence as possible with the table on pp. 124–5. The trade groups in which subsidies, excise or customs duties occur bear the same numbers as in that table.

The information is drawn from two sources, viz. from the Censuses of Production and from the Finance Accounts of the United Kingdom. On the whole there is here a close agreement between the same facts as recorded in the different Censuses of Production. Where such divergences exist, they are shown.

The entries in the table refer to the three Census years, 1924, 1930 and 1935, and are derived from the Censuses of Production estimates. The data from the Finance Accounts cover the two financial years ended on 31 March of the year of each Census and a similar period ended on the same day the year immediately following.

All entries in the table can be classed under one of three distinct headings: subsidies, excise duties and customs duties.

Excise and Customs Duties, Subsidies, etc. in 1924, 1930, 1935

CP, From Censuses of Production.
FA, From Finance Accounts of the United Kingdom for financial years ended 31 March.
(G) Gross duty. (Dr) Drawbacks, Rebates, etc. (N) Net duty.

Trade group	Name of trade	1924			1930			1935		
		CP	FA 1923–4	FA 1924–5	CP	FA 1929–30	FA 1930–1	CP	FA 1934–5	FA 1935–6
		(In £000,000's)								
I	Coal mining									
	Subsidy	ns	1·3	(c)	(c)	(c)	(c)	(c)	(c)	(c)
IV	Chemical and allied trades									
	Excise	3·2	3·2	3·2	3·2	3·3	3·2	2·9	2·9	2·9
	Customs (Petroleum)	(a)	(a)	(a)	2·1	15·1	16·0	ns	42·4	45·2
VIII	Silk and artificial silk									
	Excise (G)	(b)	(b)	(b)	—	2·7	2·4	—	3·1	2·9
	(Dr)	—	—	—	—	1·0	0·8	—	1·3	0·7
	(N)	—	—	—	1·6	1·7	1·6	2·1	1·8	2·2
	Customs (G)	(a)	(a)	(a)	ns	5·7	5·9	—	4·4	4·2
	(Dr)	—	—	—	—	1·1	0·8	ns	0·9	0·6
	(N)	—	—	—	—	4·6	5·1	ns	3·5	3·6
XI	Cocoa and sugar confectionery									
	Customs (G)	—	1·5	0·8	—	0·8	0·9	—	1·0	1·2
	(Dr)	ns	0·2	0·1	ns	0·1	0·1	ns	0·2	0·2
	(N)	—	1·3	0·7	—	0·7	0·8	—	0·8	1·0
	Sugar, glucose and molasses									
	Subsidy	(c)	(c)	(c)	6·0	6·0	6·0	2·2	2·2	2·2
	Excise	15·7	0·8	0·4	2·1	1·7	2·4	2·5	2·5	2·3
	Customs (G)	—	37·8	20·6	—	13·5	14·7	—	13·3	13·5
	(Dr)	ns	0·8	0·6	ns	2·6	3·3	ns	4·1	4·3
	(N)	—	37·1	20·0	—	10·9	11·4	—	9·2	9·2

XII	Brewing and malting									
	Excise (G)	ns	77·3	76·9	—	73·0	70·8	ns	54·7	56·6
	(Dr)	ns	1·2	1·1	ns	1·8	1·5	—	1·1	1·2
	(N)	75·8	76·1	75·8	70·0	71·2	69·3	55·3	53·6	55·4
	Spirits (distilling and rectifying and compounding)									
	Excise (G)	ns	53·1	51·5	ns	47·6	44·2	ns	35·8	38·9
	(Dr)	—	8·0	8·7	—	11·0	9·0	—	7·5	8·5
	(N)	—	45·2	42·8	—	36·6	35·2	—	28·3	30·4
	Aerated waters, British wines, cider, etc.									
	Excise	0·4	0·7	0·5	0·4	0·6	0·5	0·7	0·6	0·7
XIII	Tobacco									
	Customs (G)	ns	59·5	59·6	ns	88·1	88·1	ns	96·8	102·2
	(Dr)	—	7·5	7·6	—	25·2	23·9	—	26·0	27·1
	(N)	—	52·0	52·0	—	62·9	64·2	—	70·8	75·1
XV	Printing, binding, etc.									
	Excise	0·1	0·0	0·1	0·1	0·1	0·1	0·1	0·1	0·1
XX	Road fund									
	Subsidy	ns	14·1	14·5	ns	21·9	22·8	ns	26·4	25·8
	Totals									
	Subsidies	0·0	15·4	16·7	6·0	27·9	28·8	2·2	28·6	28·0
	Excise duties (G)	—	135·3	132·7	—	129·0	123·7	—	99·8	104·5
	(Dr)	—	9·3	9·9	—	13·7	11·4	—	10·0	10·4
	(N)	95·2	126·0	122·8	77·4	115·3	112·3	63·6	89·8	94·1
	Customs duties (G)	ns	98·8	81·0	ns	123·1	125·7	ns	158·1	166·7
	(Dr)	—	8·4	8·3	ns	29·0	28·2	ns	31·6	32·6
	(N)	—	90·4	72·7	ns	94·1	97·5	ns	126·5	134·1

ns, Not stated. sc, Subject to correction. (a) No customs duties in force.
(b) No excise duties in force. (c) No subsidy in force.

The *subsidies* which occur in the table are in respect of the Coal Mining Industry, the Sugar, Glucose and Molasses Trade, and payments to the Road Fund (under 10 and 11 Geo. V, c. 72, sec. 2; 16 and 17 Geo. V, c. 22, sec. 42; 19 Geo. V, c. 17, sec. 87; 19 and 20 Geo. V, c. 25, sec. 54; and 24 and 25 Geo. V, c. 52), on account of the net proceeds of Motor Vehicle Duties, etc.

The subsidies to the Coal Mining Industry and the payments to the Road Fund do not appear in the Censuses of Production, while the subsidies on home-grown beet sugar do not appear in the Finance Accounts of the United Kingdom.

We present the Road Fund payment together with Trade Group XX (Local Authorities). This is the sum of payments to the Road Fund on account of the net proceeds of Motor Vehicle Duties. The reason for doing this is that, though a large part of the road and highway construction is carried out by private contractors, the subsidy as such was not available to the Building and Contracting Trades for distribution in the form of wages, rents, rates, interest, salaries, etc. It did not add any additional funds to the industry beyond their gross receipts expressed in the contracted competitive prices. The issue is different in the case of Local Authorities, which from this point of view act in the double capacity of agencies ordering the construction and repairing of roads and highways as well as of contractors building them in their own administration. In this latter capacity they act as their own contractors. It is clear that this method of classifying the Road Fund grants is not a watertight one, if only for the reason that a considerable proportion of constructional work, repairs and renewals of highways, bridges, etc. is carried out by private contractors. Allocating, however, a part of the Road subsidy to private Building and Contracting, or leaving it completely out of account, would probably be open to even graver objections. A similar problem arises with the subsidy on building.

In 1924 there was no subsidy paid to beet-sugar manufacturers. The subsidy was instituted in 1925 under the British Sugar (Subsidy) Act. Both in 1930 and in 1935 the subsidy exceeded the net output of firms to which it was paid and which were mainly engaged in beet-sugar production.

In the Finance Act 1924–5 and in 1930 and 1935 there was no subsidy in force in the Coal Mining Industry. In the Finance Accounts 1923–4 the 'total issue in the year' under the heading Coal Mines Deficiency was £1,309,603 and no issues were made for the Coal Mining Industry Subvention. In the Finance Accounts 1924–5 no issues were made under either of the two headings.

Negligible amounts of subsidies under the Trade Facilities Act 1921 (11 and 12 Geo. V, c. 63) have been left out of account. Other very small subsidy items have been omitted, e.g. Export Credit Guarantees, where the effective amount of the subsidy is probably equal only to the difference between the insurance premiums which the firms in question would have to pay to the insurance companies and the effective insurance premiums paid under the official scheme.

Only the Sugar Subsidy has been included in our net output figures presented in the table on pp. 124–5. In doing this we follow the practice of the Censuses of Production. The Coal subsidy and Road Fund payments have not been added as neither of them seems to appear in the Censuses of Production.

Excise

We have tabulated all the excise duties paid on the products of the Trade Groups recorded by the Censuses of Production. The latter show in one way or another all the excise duties, with the exception of duties on spirits. Those in the table (pp. 166–7) cover the bulk of the excise duties returned in the Finance Accounts of the United Kingdom, the most important exceptions being the Entertainment Duty and the Licence Duties. E.g. out of a total of £166·7 mn. of net excise duties returned in the Finance Accounts 1935–6, the table on pp. 166–7 covers £94·1 mn. Motor Vehicle Duties are not included.

The excise duties in the table are returned only at their *net* receipt value except in those cases in which there is a large item of Drawbacks, Rebates, Repayments and Allowances repayable to the industries mostly on articles exported. In the latter cases also the excise duties are returned at their gross recepit value, and the Drawbacks, etc. are given separately.

In the Chemical and Allied Trade Group (IV) the duties affected Saccharine, Patent Medicines (Labels), Petroleum and Matches. In the table they are all lumped together. In the Censuses of Production these duties were returned under the headings of two sub-groups: No. 1, 'Chemicals and Dyestuffs', and No. 8, 'The Match Trade'. The petroleum excise duty, which was very small, is left out of account.

The excise on Artificial Silk has been charged since July 1925.

In the case of excise on Sugar in 1924, owing to the practice of refining foreign raw sugar imported in bond, it is difficult to state which part of the total excise duty returned by the Census authorities belongs to import duties. In 1930 the estimated excise on sugar was paid from the following sources: £1·3 mn. was paid on the product of firms primarily engaged on beet-sugar production and £0·8 mn. on the products of other firms entering into the Sugar, Glucose and Molasses Trade Sub-Group. In 1935 the former contributed £1 mn. and the latter £1·5 mn.

The excise on beer, falling on the Brewing and Malting Sub-Group, is the largest of all such duties. In the 1924 Census it was estimated net at £75·8 mn. and it was included in the net output of the Sub-Group, thus swelling it compared with all other items of Trade Group XII (Drink).

In the case of both the Sub-Groups Spirit Distilling and Spirit Rectifying, Compounding, etc. the Censuses of Production did not state the amount of excise. In neither of the Censuses of Production was the duty included in the net output. In the case of Spirit Distilling the value of spirits was returned exclusive of duty. In the case of Spirit Rectifying, Compounding, etc. the amount of duty was included both in gross output and in the cost of materials, and consequently automatically excluded from the net output values. The gross value of dutiable spirits rectified, compounded, etc. for home consumption was returned inclusive of duty, whilst the value of spirits exported was recorded less drawbacks.

A small duty was collected on Aerated Waters, British Wines, Cider, etc., the amount of which was not stated in the 1924 Census, though it was included in the net output figure.

A very small amount of excise was collected on Home-grown Tobacco. The amount is not stated in the table.

A small amount of duty was collected in the Trade Sub-Group (XV), Printing, Binding, etc., on Playing Cards. Though its amount was not stated in the 1924 Census, the duty was included in net output.

On the whole the excise duties returned for the same years by the Censuses of Production agree very closely. The largest difference occurs in 1924 in the case of excise on Beer, which in the 1924 Census is returned at £75·8 mn., while in the 1930 Census and in the final report of the 1935 it is returned at £74·1 mn.

In 1935 the Preliminary Report of the 1935 Census returned £56·1 mn. of excise on Beer; the Final Report reported £55·3 mn.

Minor differences occur in 1924 in the case of sugar duty, which in the 1924 Census was returned at £15·8 mn. and at £15·7 mn. in the other two Censuses. In 1930, the 1930 Census reported £2·1 mn. of duty on sugar while the Preliminary Report and the Final Report of the 1935 Census returned £2·3 mn. A similar minor disparity was observed in 1935 between the Preliminary Report of the 1935 Census, which recorded £2·4 mn. of excise duty on sugar, and the Final Report (of the 1935 Census), in which the duty was £2·5 mn.

The returns of excise in the Censuses of Production and in the Finance Accounts agree fairly closely. The widest disagreement was observed in the Sugar, Glucose and Molasses Group in 1924, where the excise duty in the Census of Production was returned at £15·7 mn. and at £0·8 mn. in the Finance Accounts 1924–5. The chief reason for this discrepancy is that the excise in the Finance Accounts covered only duties on glucose. In the case of the Aerated Waters, etc. Trade Sub-Group, in 1924 the value of excise was reported in the Census as £0·4 mn., while it was higher in both the Finance Accounts for 1923–4 and 1924–5. In 1930 the Census returned £0·4 mn. and in the two Finance Accounts 1929–30 and 1930–31 the duty was returned at a higher value.

Customs

Sources. All the data referring to Customs are derived from the Finance Accounts of the United Kingdom; none seem to be available in the Censuses of Production except in the case of petroleum.

Gross and Net Values. With the exception of Petroleum, where the Drawbacks are relatively very small and which are returned net, the table (pp. 166–7) presents the customs duties at their gross value and states separately the amounts of Drawbacks, Rebates, Repayments and Allowances as reported in the respective Finance Accounts.

Trades Covered. The table covers the customs duties in the following trades: Trade Group IV (Chemicals, etc.), Petroleum; Trade Group VIII (Textiles), Silk and Artificial Silk; Trade Group XI (Food), Cocoa and Sugar Confectionery; and Sugar; Trade Group XIII, Tobacco. Those duties cover a large part of all customs receipts; thus e.g. in the financial year 1935–6 the table covers £134·1 mn. of net customs receipt out of a total of £196·6 mn. returned in the Finance Accounts 1935–6. The duty on sugar includes customs on refined and unrefined sugar, molasses and glucose, saccharine and articles containing sugar. The duty on cocoa includes cocoa preparations, cocoa butter, and husks. The duty on tobacco includes snuff. The duty on petroleum returned in the 1930 Census of Production referred to duty paid by firms on oil purchased and refined by them.

In selecting the customs duties included in the table we have had in mind only those articles which mainly constitute the materials entering into further stages of production in this country. It would seem that the duties paid on imported goods ready for consumption should not be added under any conceivable definition into the net output of the factory and non-factory trades.[1]

The distinction which has been drawn between goods entering into further stages of production in the United Kingdom and goods entirely ready for use is not clear cut. Only a part of the total petroleum imported is subjected to further treatment in this country; similarly with silk and artificial silk, cocoa, tobacco and sugar. Sugar refining since April 1928 received a special encouragement in the form of reduction of the duty on raw sugar with the maintenance of full protection on refined sugar. This increased immensely the amount of foreign raw sugar refined in Great Britain.

After 1931 the classification into the two groups becomes gradually more difficult, owing to the impossibility of splitting up such items as 'Abnormal Importations', Customs Duties, 'General Ad Valorem Duties Goods' appearing in the Finance Accounts 1931–2. These items, however, are not very large and they have been excluded from the table. In the 1932–3 Finance Accounts the goods liable under the Import Duties Act 1932 make their appearance for the first time; and in 1934–5 we find a new item, 'Duties on certain imports from the Irish Free State'. All these duties, which amount to some £35 mn., have been excluded from the table for reasons stated above.

Subject to the corrections just mentioned, the customs duties in the table represent the duties on the bulk of materials and semi-manufactured goods used in the United Kingdom.

All the entries of the net output in the table in Chapter III (p. 164) are net of excise duties. In the 1924 Census of

1 In estimates of Real Income, however, they have their place. See Chapter IV, pp. 187–8.

Production a number of excise duties were included in the net output figures, viz. £1·4 mn. in the Chemicals, Dyestuffs and Drugs Sub-group; £1·8 mn. in the Match Trade; £15·7 mn. in the Sugar, Glucose and Molasses Group; £75·8 mn. in Brewing and Malting; £0·4 mn. in Aerated Waters, etc.; £0·1 mn. in the Playing Cards, Printing, Binding Group, etc. Their total value was £95·3 mn. Excise duties on spirits formed a prominent exception.

The data derived from the Censuses of Production and from the Finance Accounts do not cover precisely the same period. The excise derived from the Censuses are estimates of the duties collected in the Census year. The information from the Finance Accounts corresponding to each datum from the Census covers the financial year ended 31 March of the Census year and an analogous period of the year following the Census. On the whole the figures of excise given in the Censuses lie within each pair of figures from the corresponding Finance Accounts, as one would expect prima facie. The only exception was the excise on Aerated Waters, etc. in 1924 and in 1930, when the Census figures were lower than either of the figures in the corresponding pairs of figures in the Finance Accounts. The differences, however, are small.

Subsidies on dwelling-houses raise so many problems both of a statistical and of an economic character that it has not been possible to treat them on the same lines as those followed in this Appendix. In the table, pp. 126, the value is that of the finished product, less materials, etc., and therefore includes any subsidies on building in the same way that the value of the net output of sugar includes the sugar subsidy.

The totals represent the *aggregates* of the returns from each source for any particular year. In some cases these totals are incomplete in so far as e.g. the Censuses of Production provide no information as to some subsidies, while the Finance Accounts leave out others. In other cases, such as sugar, the 1924 Census of Production returned some of the customs duties under the heading of excise duties, as has been already mentioned.

The large *fluctuations* in the totals are due partly to cyclical fluctuations and partly to changes in the rates of duties charged, e.g. there was a heavy increase in the customs duty on hydrocarbon oil between 1930 and 1935. In the case of beer the quantity on which duty was paid (home made) fell from 21 mn. standard barrels in 1924 to 18½ mn. in 1930 and 16 mn. in 1935. The excise duty per barrel at 1055° amounted to 80*s*. in 1924–25, 83*s*. in 1930–31, and 80*s*. in 1935–36.

APPENDIX III

NUMBERS EMPLOYED AND NET OUTPUT OF SMALL FIRMS

The table on pp. 176–7 refers to the net output of and the numbers employed by firms employing on the average ten or less persons in Great Britain and five or less persons in Northern Ireland. It covers the three Censal years 1924, 1930 and 1935.

The main trades in which small firms are important are: Building and Contracting; Building materials; Chains, nails and screws; Motor and Cycle; Carriage, cart and wagon; Plate and Jewellery; Tailoring; Boots and Shoes; Bread and Cakes; Timber saw-milling; Furniture and Upholstery; Printing and Binding; Blacksmithing (in 1924).

Repair work. In some trades a considerable proportion of the net output contributed by the small firms consisted of repair work. This applies to Building where a considerable proportion consisted of repair work and re-decorating. Some 43 per cent of small firms in 1924 in Tools and Implements were doing repair work, the corresponding percentage in 1930 was 45.

Of all small firms in Group VI (Engineering, etc.) in 1924 some 60 per cent of their total net output was contributed by repair and other work and 40 per cent by manufacturing output. In the same year the repair work constituted 16 per cent of the total repair work of *all* firms in the group, while the manufacturing output constituted only some 2 per cent of the whole group.

About 10 per cent of the net output of the small firms in 1924 in the Finished Brass Sub-group (Group VII) consisted of repair work, while in the Plate and Jewellery Trade the same constituted 32 per cent. In the Watch and Clock Trade some 75 per cent of all repair work done by *all* the firms went to the small firms. In addition to that some repair work was carried out by retail trade firms employing one or two assistants for fulfilling repair orders of customers.

In 1924 some 33 per cent of the net value of repair work of *all* firms in the Coopering Trade (Group XIV) was contributed by the small firms.

Apart from that many small firms are engaged in manufacturing goods which often differed considerably in type and quality from those manufactured by larger concerns.

Allowances and Omissions

In several cases small allowance was made for Northern Ireland, e.g. in Trade Group VIII, Linen and cotton, and Group X (especially in the case of Tailoring); Trade Group XI, Food, Butter; Fish-curing; and Trade Group XII (Beer); Saw-milling, Furniture and Upholstery (Group XIV). In most cases when allowances were made they varied between 1 and 3 per cent.

A small allowance has also been made where there was some industrial activity which was not recorded by the Census, such as the output of the inmates of philanthropic institutions. This refers in the first line to Coir Fibre, Horse-hair and Leather in Group VIII, and to Timber, Group XIV, Cane and Wicker Furniture, Upholstery and Basketware. A number of firms engaged in repair work in the Building Trade in 1930 were classed in 1924 together with Electrical Engineering.

The net output of collieries excluded collieries in the process of development.

In none of the cases was the net output of outworkers added to the net output of the small firms, as it was impossible to find out what proportion of the outworkers were employed in the various sub-groups. In some of the industries, e.g. Tailoring, the number of outworkers was a considerable proportion of the total number of workers.

Method of Computation

The data referring to the net output of the small firms employing less than ten persons are scanty and scattered over various parts of the Censuses of Production. Whenever the net output was not available directly from the Census, it was estimated as follows:

In some cases the gross output of the small firms *not making* returns in 1924 was estimated by the Census authorities. From those gross output figures the net output figures were computed by assuming that in the case of small firms the net output bears the same relation as that of the larger firms.

For the other years the net output of the small firms not furnishing returns has been arrived at on the assumption that the net output per person employed in the small firms employing less than ten persons was equal to that in the nearest size-class of firms available in the Census (in most cases 11–24 workers). In those cases, however, in which the latter was larger than the

Numbers Employed and Net Output of Small Firms in the Main Industrial Groups

Inset: numbers, etc. of smaller groups in which 5,000 or more were employed

Industrial group or sub-group	Numbers employed* (000's)					
	1924		1930		1935	
I, II. Mines	10		10		9	
Non-metalliferous		5		8		8
III. Building, etc.	151		183		275	
Materials		6		10		11
Building and contracting		140		167		257
IV. Chemicals	11		12		12	
V. Iron and steel	39		38		32	
Hardware		9		11		11
Chains, nails, screws		20		18		14
VI. Engineering	87		110		106	
Mechanical		33		26		[illegible]
Electrical		6		7		[illegible]
Motors, etc.		30		63		[illegible]
Carriages, etc.		15		12		[illegible]
VII. Non-ferrous metals	14		16		12	
Plate, jewellery		6		8		[illegible]
VIII. Textiles	15		19		15	
IX. Leather	8		8		7	
Leather goods		6		5		[illegible]
X. Clothing	161		141		109	
Tailoring		123		107		[illegible]
Boots and shoes		30		25		[illegible]
XI. Food	91		99		101	
Bread		72		75		[illegible]
XII. Drink	11		13		12	
Aerated waters		5		6		[illegible]
XIII. Tobacco	0		0		0	
XIV. Timber	49		72		69	
Saw-mills		23		36		[illegible]
Furniture		21		32		[illegible]
XV. Paper	29		33		33	
Printing		26		28		[illegible]
XVI, XVII. Rubber, miscellaneous	12		15		14	
XVIII–XXI. Gas, transport, Government	11		12		11	
Total: All	696		780		816	
Firms making returns	474		716		791	
Firms not making returns	222		64		25	

* Administrative and operative.

Numbers Employed and Net Output of Small Firms in the Main Industrial Groups

Inset: numbers, etc. of smaller groups in which 5,000 or more were employed

Industrial group or sub-group	Net output (£ mn.)					
	1924		1930		1935	
I, II. Mines	2		2		2	
Non-metalliferous		1		1		2
III. Building, etc.	25		32		50	
Materials		1		2		3
Building and contracting		23		30		46
IV. Chemicals	3		4		5	
V. Iron and steel	5		7		6	
Hardware		1		2		2
Chains, nails, screws		2		3		3
VI. Engineering	14		15		18	
Mechanical		5		5		5
Electrical		1		1		1
Motors, etc.		6		7		10
Carriages, etc.		2		2		2
VII. Non-ferrous metals	2		3		3	
Plate, jewellery		1		1		1
VIII. Textiles	4		3		2	
IX. Leather	1		1		1	
Leather goods		1		1		1
X. Clothing	24		22		17	
Tailoring		18		16		12
Boots and shoes		5		4		4
XI. Food	19		19		23	
Bread		15		14		18
XII. Drink	3		4		4	
Aerated waters		1		1		2
XIII. Tobacco	0		0		0	
XIV. Timber	8		11		14	
Saw-mills		3		5		7
Furniture		4		5		5
XV. Paper	5		5		7	
Printing		—		—		—
XVI, XVII. Rubber, miscellaneous	2		3		2	
XVIII–XXI. Gas, transport, Government	4		4		4	
Total: All	120		135		159	
Firms making returns	87		124		155	
Firms not making returns	33		11		4	

average for the whole Industrial Group, e.g. in the case of woollen and worsted in 1935, linen and hemp in 1930, tailoring, etc., the more conservative estimate was used by taking, instead, the average net output for the industry as a whole. By multiplying such average net output by the number of workers in the small firms under ten in each trade, the net output was estimated for the whole industry. For the reason above and owing to the exclusion of outworkers the net output of the small firms is probably somewhat under-estimated by some 7 to 10 per cent.

In the case of small firms *making returns* the net output in 1930 and 1935 for each trade group, for which data concerning the size distribution are available in the Final Reports of the Censuses of Production, has been arrived at in the same way as in the case of firms not furnishing returns. In the case of those industries for which the Final Report of the 1935 Census is not yet available, it was necessary to use the Preliminary Reports and assume that the net output per person was equal to the average net output per person for the trade as a whole.

In the case of Building and Contracting, since it is a very important group, a greater degree of accuracy was attempted as follows:

We have the number of persons employed in firms making and not making returns. That figure was multiplied by the net output per man. The latter is not available in the Preliminary Report for 1935 and had to be assumed. We assumed a similar distribution of net output per man in 1935 in the groups of firms of various sizes as in 1930 and we took the output per man in 1930 in the smallest size group, which we deflated in the same ratio as that in which the average net output per man in 1935 has fallen compared with 1930, viz. (199/207). By multiplying the result by the total employment we obtained the net output of the small firms for the industry.

At the foot of the table are shown the numbers employed and the net output of firms from which returns were obtained separately from others. It is seen that the returns were more complete in successive Censuses.

Employment. Inclusions and Omissions

The employment figures in the small firms include the owners of the establishments when themselves engaged in productive processes. They include all persons whether belonging to the operative or administrative staff, but exclude persons engaged in retail and selling operations. In 1930 the employment figure in the small firms in the Bread and Cakes Group excludes some 11,400 employees estimated to be engaged on retail functions in bakeries. We excluded likewise all outworkers employed by the various trades on the ground that it was impossible to assess how many of them were connected with the small firms. This is unfortunate, since a large proportion of the outworkers recorded were not improbably engaged by small firms.

Where no direct information was available from the Census of Production as to the number of persons engaged in the firms not furnishing returns, it was assumed as in the Census Reports that on the average those firms employed the same number as the small firms furnishing returns in their respective trades.

The average number employed per firm in all industries together appears not to exceed four in either year.

Chapter IV

PRICE MOVEMENTS: INDEX OF REAL INCOME

It is the usual practice, after estimates of money income (on any definition) have been made for two or more years, to adjust them by index-numbers of prices, so as to obtain some measurement of the change of 'real income'. The price index-numbers are generally weighted by reference to the relative importance of different categories of expenditure at the first year under consideration. The result is often expressed in some such phrase as 'income in year *B* in dollars of year *A*'.

Though there is no more appropriate method possible than this or some development of it, it should be acknowledged that the result has only a numerical or formal meaning, and is not an exact measure of increased well-being, which is a hedonistic or psychological concept, and not measurable by statistics. If in a period every price increased 20 per cent, and every income 50 per cent, this method would show an increase of 'real income' of 25 per cent,[1] and it would be possible (if supplies were available) for each individual to increase his purchase of each article by 25 per cent. But he would not in fact do this and his re-arrangement of his purchases would depend on his relative preferences for the particular goods. His aggregate satisfaction would be greater, but not by 25 per cent or any other numerical measure. We could say that he could purchase his former budget of commodities and have one-fifth of his money left; or we might reach such a conclusion as 'the partly skilled workman to-day with 55*s*. could make the same purchases as the artisan some decades ago with 40*s*.'

Formally at least we get closer to the problem by averaging two price index-numbers, one based on purchases at the first date, the other on purchases at the second date, thus getting over some numerical difficulties caused by abnormal changes in prices of particular goods.

The usual procedure is best expressed in notation. Write K for expenditure at the first date on Q_1, Q_2, ... units of various goods whose prices per unit are P_1, P_2, ...

1 $1{\cdot}50 \div 1{\cdot}20 = 1{\cdot}25$.

Write k, $q_1, q_2, \ldots, p_1, p_2, \ldots$ for the corresponding quantities at the second date. Then $K = \Sigma QP$, $k = \Sigma qp$.

The price index-numbers are

$$I_1 = \frac{\Sigma Qp}{\Sigma qP}, \text{ based on the earlier budget,}$$

and $$I_2 = \frac{\Sigma qp}{\Sigma qP}, \text{ based on the later budget.}$$

k is then reduced to its presumed value at the earlier prices by dividing by I_1 or I_2, or by $I = \sqrt{(I_1 I_2)}$ (Irving Fisher's 'ideal index-number') or some other average, e.g.

$$\tfrac{1}{2}(I_1 + I_2) \quad \text{or} \quad \frac{\Sigma(Q+q)\,p}{\Sigma(Q+q)\,P}.$$

The ratio of 'real' incomes is then taken as

$$\frac{\text{Real income second year}}{\text{Real income first year}} = \frac{k \div I_1}{K} = \frac{\Sigma qp}{\Sigma QP} \div \frac{\Sigma Qp}{\Sigma QP} = \frac{\Sigma qp}{\Sigma Qp} = J_2 \text{ (say)}$$

or $$\frac{k \div I_2}{K} = \frac{\Sigma qP}{\Sigma QP} = J_1 \text{ (say)},$$

or generally $k/K \div I$.

It is clear that J_1 and J_2 are weighted index-numbers of change of quantities purchased, and that they may be calculable without the intermediate step of forming price index-numbers.

Write $r_1 = q_1/Q_1$, $r_2 = q_2/Q_2, \ldots$, so that $r_1, r_2, \ldots$ are ratios of quantities. Write $L_1 = Q_1 P_1$, $L_2 = Q_2 P_2, \ldots$, $l_1 = q_1 p_1$, $l_2 = q_2 p_2, \ldots$, so that L, l are the sums expended and $K = \Sigma L$, $k = \Sigma l$. Then

$$J_1 = \frac{\Sigma rQP}{\Sigma QP} = \frac{\Sigma rL}{\Sigma L} = \frac{\Sigma Lr}{K} \quad \text{and} \quad J_2 = \frac{\Sigma qp}{\Sigma qp/r} = \frac{\Sigma l}{\Sigma l/r} = \frac{k}{\Sigma l/r}.$$

All we need to know for this procedure is the expenditure at each date on each kind of goods, and the ratio for each kind of the quantity purchased in the second to that purchased in the first year.

The method is applicable to an individual or to a group of individuals or to a nation considered as a unit; but in the latter case it takes no account of the variation caused by the changed prices and incomes as between persons, families or classes.

Before the method is used we must, of course, have a clear definition of national income, in respect both to the separate or corporate incomes included in the nation, and to the items that are counted as income for this purpose. Such questions were considered in Chapter 1.

Particular difficulties are found in connection with goods subject to customs, excise or purchasing tax, goods the production of which is subsidized, goods produced or services rendered freely by Government (Central or Local), direct taxation, indirect taxation, and by transfer of money by tax from one group of persons to another. Agreement has not been reached as to the appropriate treatment of these problems, and the method described below is the subject of some controversy.[1]

We need further notation:

Take three classes of goods:

	Quantity	Cost	Cost price	Selling price
Produced privately; no excise	Q_1	L_1	$\Pi_1 = L_1/Q_1$	P_1
Produced privately; tax on sale	Q_2	L_2	$\Pi_2 = L_2/Q_2$	P_2
Public production, not charged to users	Q_3	L_3	$\Pi_3 = L_3/Q_3$	P_3

Write $P_2 = \Pi_2(1+T)$, so that $\Pi_2 T$ is a tax per unit sold. Write $E = Q_2\Pi_2 T = L_2 T$ for the yield of this indirect taxation. We have

$$P_1 = \Pi_1, \quad P_3 = 0, \quad K = L_1 + L_2 + L_3.$$

Write D for the amount of direct taxation.

For the second year use small letters, k, p, q, π, t, d, e. In general

$$J_1 = \frac{\Sigma qP}{\Sigma QP}, \quad J_2 = \frac{\Sigma qp}{\Sigma Qp}.$$

Case I. Direct taxation only, applied wholly to the production of Q_3 and q_3.

$$E = e = 0, \quad P_2 = \Pi_2, \quad D = \Pi_3 . Q_3 = L_3.$$

$$J_1 = \frac{q_1 P_1 + q_2 P_2 + q_3 P_3}{Q_1 P_1 + Q_2 P_2 + Q_3 P_3} = \frac{r_1 L_1 + r_2 L_2 + 0}{L_1 + L_2 + 0} = \frac{r_1 L_1 + r_2 L_2}{K - D},$$

when $r_1 = q_1/Q_1, \ldots$.

Here and throughout it is assumed that in every case the cost of production equals the income of the producers (profits, rents, salaries and wages), and that there are no imports or exports[2], and that all income is spent (in any proportion) on the goods

1 This is re-worked, with some change of notation, from a paper read to the Manchester Statistical Society, November 1939.

2 The effect of external trade is considered below.

produced in the first two classes. The treatment of depreciation is left open for the present.

$$J_2 = \frac{q_1 p_1 + q_2 p_2 + q_3 p_3}{Q_1 p_1 + Q_2 p_2 + Q_3 p_3} = \frac{l_1 + l_2 + 0}{l_1/r_1 + l_2/r_2} = \frac{k - d}{l_1/r_1 + l_2/r_2}.$$

This method in this case, however, leads to an absurdity. For if direct taxation is increased so as to absorb a great part of income, the denominator of J_1 becomes small, J_1 is great, and J_2 is small. In a communistic state naturally the method would not apply.

An alternative method is to regard D as transferred from private to communal expenditure, so that the goods are furnished to the community without further payment. We impute a price equal to the cost price, and write $P_3 = \Pi_3$, $p_3 = \pi_3$. Then

$$J_1 = \frac{r_1 L_1 + r_2 L_2 + r_3 L_3}{K} \quad \text{and} \quad J_2 = k \Big/ \left(\frac{l_1}{r_1} + \frac{l_2}{r_2} + \frac{l_3}{r_3}\right).$$

This method does not lead to inconsistent or ambiguous results, and comes directly from the assumption that a community decides freely to employ jointly a group of people (say for road-making, police protection, etc.) instead of hiring watchmen and men for making up their own roads, etc. In such cases evidently real income is not affected except by changes in efficiency. The same argument applies in a democratic community to all public services. Transfers of income (not in return for services) are considered later.

Case II. Indirect taxation only.

Here the sum $Q_2 P_2$ is spent on goods of class 2, of which $Q_2 \Pi_2 = L_2$ is kept by the producers and $L_2 T = Q_2 \Pi_2 T = E$ handed to the Government. E is then spent on the production of Q_3, so that also $E = L_3$.

As in Case I it is assumed that the community decides to provide goods or services (such as teaching or street-lighting) acting as a single employer. But the individuals actually spend all their money on goods, and decide how much to buy at the price P_2 by the same considerations as in buying the untaxed goods (Q_1 at price P_1). If all goods were taxed at a uniform rate, it would be completely indifferent whether the sum was raised by direct or indirect taxation, unless the incidence of taxation on different classes was changed, except in so far as the change in quantities bought or produced varied from one commodity to another, and this result should appear in our formula.

In this case

$$J_1 = \frac{\Sigma qP}{\Sigma QP} = \frac{q_1\Pi_1 + q_2\Pi_2(1+T) + q_3 \times 0}{Q_1\Pi_1 + Q_2\Pi_2(1+T) + Q_3 \times 0} = \frac{r_1 L_1 + r_2 L_2 + r_2 L_2 T}{L_1 + L_2 + L_2 T}$$

$$= \frac{r_1 L_1 + r_2 L_2 + r_2 L_3}{K},$$

and $$J_2 = \frac{q_1\pi_1 + q_2\pi_2(1+t) + q_3 \times 0}{Q_1\pi_1 + Q_2\pi_2(1+t) + Q_3 \times 0} = \frac{k}{l_1/r_1 + l_2/r_2 + l_3/r_2}.$$

If T and t were also imposed on class 1, and $r_1 = r_2 = r_3$, then

$$(r_1 L_1 + r_2 L_2)T = r_1(L_1 + L_2)T = r_1 E = r_1 L_3;$$

$J_1 = r_1 = J_2$ both in direct and indirect taxation.

The difference between the effects of direct and indirect taxation is therefore to be found in the difference between the relative amounts bought when the price of one or more, but not every, commodity is raised by excise.

To simplify the problem assume that there is no change in the total number of occupied persons or of number of incomes or of average income. These assumptions detract little from the generality of the argument.

Take the case where $T = 0$, but taxation (t) is imposed in the second year. Write $q_1 = Q_1(1+u)$, $q_2 = Q_2(1-v)$, $q_3 = Q_3$. Here u and v are positive if (as is normally the case) there is a transfer of production from the taxed to the untaxed article. It is assumed that the quantity of Government products is the same as under private enterprise and that the pre-tax price equals cost price. Then

$$J_1 = \frac{q_1\Pi_1 + q_2\Pi_2 + q_3\Pi_3}{Q_1\Pi_1 + Q_2\Pi_2 + Q_3\Pi_3} = 1 + \frac{L_1 u - L_2 v}{K},$$

$$\frac{1}{J_2} = \frac{Q_1\pi_1 + Q_2\pi_2(1+t) + Q_3 \times 0}{q_1\pi_1 + q_2\pi_2(1+t) + q_3 \times 0}$$

$$= \frac{\dfrac{l_1}{1+u} + \dfrac{l_2}{1-v}(1+t)}{l_1 + l_2(1+t)} = \frac{\dfrac{l_1}{1+u} + \dfrac{l_2 + l_3}{1-v}}{k},$$

since $l_2 t = l_3$,

$$= 1 + \frac{1}{k}\left(-\frac{l_1 u}{1+u} + \frac{(l_2 + l_3)v}{1-v}\right).$$

The simplest case is when there is no change in the cost of unit production owing to the change in output in either class 1 or class 2. Then

$$\frac{L_1}{Q_1}=\frac{l_1}{q_1}, \quad \frac{L_2}{Q_2}=\frac{l_2}{q_2}, \quad \frac{L_3}{Q_3}=\frac{l_3}{q_3}.$$

$$\therefore\ l_1=L_1(1+u), \quad l_2=L_2(1-v), \quad l_3=L_3.$$

Since it is assumed that there is no change in total income,

$$L_1+L_2+L_3=l_1+l_2+l_3,$$

$$L_1u=L_2v.$$

The income (or wages, profits, etc.), L_2v, is transferred from producers in class 2 to producers in class 1, L_1u. Then

$$J_1=1 \quad \text{and} \quad \frac{1}{J_2}=1+\frac{1}{k}\left(-L_1u+L_2v+\frac{L_3v}{1-v}\right)=1+\frac{L_3}{k}\cdot\frac{v}{1-v}.$$

Thus, since v is to be taken as positive, J_2 is less than unity and there is a loss of real income owing to the transfer.

But if the untaxed article is produced under conditions of diminishing or constant return while the taxed is under increasing return, then l_2/q_2 is greater than L_2/Q_2, while l_1/q_1 is equal to or greater than L_1/Q_1. Write

$$l_2/q_2=(1+x)\ L_2/Q_2 \quad \text{and} \quad l_1/q_1=(1+y)\ L_1/Q_1.$$

Then, neglecting products uy and vx, the equation of incomes gives

$$L_1(u+y)-L_2(v-x)=0$$

and

$$J_1=1-\frac{L_2x+L_1y}{K},$$

$$\frac{1}{J_2}=1+\frac{1}{k}\left\{L_1y+L_2x+L_3\frac{v}{1-v}\right\}.$$

Then both J_1 and J_2 are less than unity, that is, real income decreases.

But if L_1 is produced under conditions of increasing return (y negative) and L_2 under constant or diminishing return (x zero or negative), real income decreases.

These results are believed to be consistent with those first stated by Marshall (*Principles of Economics*, 1936, Book v, Chap. xiii, especially pp. 468 seq.).

Case III. There is no additional assumption needed for the general case where there are both direct and indirect taxation.

The imputed price per unit in class 3 is now D/Q_3.

$$D+E=\text{whole cost of } Q_3=L_3, \text{ and } E=L_2T \text{ as before.}$$

The formula is simplified by writing $D=RL_3$ and $E=(1-R)L_3$. Then

$$J_1=\frac{r_1L_1+r_2\{L_2+L_3(1-R)\}+r_3L_3R}{K}$$

and

$$J_2=\frac{k}{\frac{1}{r_1}l_1+\frac{1}{r_2}\{l_2+l_3(1-r)\}+\frac{1}{r_3}l_3r}.$$

When $R=1=r$ we have Case I; when $R=0=r$ we have Case II.

The conclusions about the effect of transfer from class 2 to class 1 apply in a modified form, which it is not necessary to elaborate here.

There is no need to restrict the analysis to three commodities, one in each group. Each class may be regarded as containing any variety of goods and prices, and in class 2 the rates of customs or excise may vary. The complete formulae may then be written:

$$KJ_1=\Sigma\{r_{1.s}.L_{1.s}\}+\Sigma\{r_{2.s}.L_{2.s}.(1+T_s)\}+R.\Sigma\{r_{3.s}.L_{3.s}\},$$

$$\frac{k}{J_2}=\Sigma\left\{\frac{l_{1.s}}{r_{1.s}}\right\}+\Sigma\left\{\frac{l_{2.s}(1+t_s)}{r_{2.s}}\right\}+r.\Sigma\left\{\frac{l_{3.s}}{r_{3.s}}\right\}.$$

Each summation is extended over $s=1, 2, \ldots n$, where n is the number of separate goods in a class, and $R=D/(D+E)$, $r=d/(d+e)$, as before.

If one or more of the goods is subject to subsidy, we can relegate it to class 2 with a negative value for a T_s or t_s.

It is interesting to show how Government goods in class 3 form the limiting case when $t=-1$. Thus if there are only three commodities and no direct taxation:

$$KJ_1=r_1L_1+r_2L_2(1+T)+r_3L_3(1-S),$$

$$\frac{k}{J_2}=\frac{l_1}{r_1}+\frac{l_2}{r_2}(1+t)+\frac{l_3}{r_3}(1-s),$$

where S, s are the rates of subsidy per unit value cost.

Here the tax is used to subsidize other goods and $L_2T=L_3S$, $l_2t=l_3s$. When $S=1=s$, we come to Case II above, with $L_2T=L_3$.

We can treat depreciation either as subtractive from income throughout, or include its amount in income and goods allotted to replacement under expenditure, thus merging them with savings, taken as devoted to purchase of capital goods.

In the formula in Case II there is no term r_3, the ratio of Government products at the two dates, and it might have been expected that the result would be affected by any change in efficiency in passing from private enterprise to public production. Take the case where $T=0$, but t is not zero, so that

$$KJ_1 = r_1 L_1 + r_2 L_2 + r_3 L_3.$$

Write $$r_3 = \frac{q_3}{Q_3} = \frac{fq_2}{Q_2} = fr_2.$$

Then $$\frac{k}{J_2} = \frac{l_1}{r_1} + \frac{l_2}{r_2} + \frac{l_3}{fr_3},$$

in which equivalent form any change in efficiency appears explicitly.

The restriction of the formulae to a closed economy where there are no exports or imports may now be removed. If at the two dates we have (assuming value of $E=1$)

	Exports		Imports	
Price	P	p	P'	p'
Quantity	Q	q	Q'	q'
Value	L	l	L'	l'

where $PQ = L = L' = P'Q'$, $pq = l = l' = p'q'$.

Write $q = r_e Q$ and $q' = r_i Q'$. Then in the numerator of J_1, when we consider consumption rather than production, we must substitute $\Sigma_e qP$ for $\Sigma q'P'$, where this expression stands for the part of the product that is exported, that is, $\Sigma r_i L' = \Sigma r_i L$ for $\Sigma r_e L$. Now, as we cannot allocate particular imports to particular exports, this must be generalized by writing $r_i \Sigma L'$, $r_e \Sigma L$ for $\Sigma r_i L'$ and $\Sigma r_e L$, where

$$r_i = \frac{\Sigma q'P'}{\Sigma Q'P'} = \frac{l'}{L'} \times \frac{\Sigma q'P'}{\Sigma q'p'} = \frac{l'}{L'} \div I_i = \frac{l}{L} \div I_i,$$

$$r_e = \frac{\Sigma qP}{\Sigma QP} = \frac{l}{L} \div I_e,$$

and I_i and I_e are import and export price indices.

Hence $r_e = r_i \times F$, where $F = I_e \div I_i$ and measures the 'terms of trade'.

Thus, finally, we write $F.\Sigma r_e L$ instead of $\Sigma r_e L$ for exports, as perhaps might have been seen without the analysis.

Similarly, in the denominator of J_2 write $\frac{1}{F}.\Sigma\frac{l}{r_e}$ for $\Sigma\frac{l}{r_e}$, where

$$F' = \frac{\Sigma Q'p'}{\Sigma Q'P'} \div \frac{\Sigma Qp}{\Sigma QP}.$$

F and F' are weighted respectively with q, q' and Q, Q'.

There remains the question of transfers of income by taxation, where the proceeds are devoted to payment for past services (interest on the national debt) or for no services (old-age pensions).

Where, as in this country, the proceeds of direct and indirect taxation are pooled, and there is seldom any allocation of a particular tax to a particular object, the only unambiguous treatment seems to be to suppose that these expenses are met from direct and indirect taxation in the same proportion, $R:1-R$, as are those for Government production.[1] If L_4, l_4 are the sums transferred in the two years, we have to subtract RL_4, rl_4 (the contributions of direct taxation) from total income (including pensions) and insert terms $L_4(1-R)$, $l_4(1-r)$ in the terms depending on indirect taxation. The results are

$$J_1 = \frac{r_1 L_1 + r_2\{L_2 + (L_3 + L_4)(1-R)\} + r_3 L_3 R}{L_1 + L_2 + L_3 + L_4(1-R)},$$

$$J_2 = \frac{l_1 + l_2 + l_3 + l_4(1-r)}{l_1/r_1 + 1/r_2\{l_2 + (l_3 + l_4)(1-r)\} + 1/r_3\, l_3 r}.$$

To recapitulate the principal assumptions that are novel in the foregoing analysis:

Direct taxation is the transfer of income from personal to communal expenditure, and the effective or imputed price of communal production is determined by the relation of the quantities communally produced to the amount of direct taxation. If there is no indirect taxation, this price is the cost price.

1 Other hypotheses are worked out in the paper at Manchester referred to above (p. 182). Admittedly there is an unresolved difficulty in this treatment. But a compromise method by which specific taxes for a specific object are credited to D or to E as the case may be, and the rest are pooled, is not unreasonable.

Indirect taxation is included in the selling price of taxed goods; its proceeds are directed to cheapening Government-produced goods, so that their imputed price is determined by direct taxation only. If there is no direct taxation, then the cost of Government goods has been included in the prices of the taxed articles and their effective price is zero.

Mr Colin Clark and others include in the numerator and denominator of J_1 not only the price in class 2 after taxation, but also Government goods at cost price. In our notation this gives

$$K_1 = L_1 + L_2 + E + L_3, \quad k_1 = l_1 + l_2 + e + l_3,$$

$$J_1 = \frac{r_1 L_1 + r_2 (L_2 + E) + r_3 L_3}{L_1 + L_2 + E + L_3},$$

where

$$I_2 = \frac{l_1 + l_2 (1 + t) + l_3}{r_1 L_1 + r_2 L_2 (1 + T) + r_3 L_3} = \frac{k_1}{r_1 L_1 + r_2 (L_2 + E) + r_3 L_3}.$$

In order to make this harmonize with the usual method of deflating the second year's income by an index-number of prices so that

$$\frac{\text{Real income in 2nd year}}{\text{Real income in 1st year}} = \frac{\text{Money income in 2nd year}}{\text{Money income in 1st year}} \div I_1,$$

an entity is created called 'gross income', to obtain which the yield of indirect taxation is added to personal incomes. By some writers it is then assumed that this gross income is spendable on commodities with the apparent conclusion that a government can increase income by indirect taxation on any commodities. This seems to the writer to arise from confusion of thought or of definition. For simplicity take the case where there is no direct taxation. Then the whole of the income of the nation, including that of those engaged in Government production, is spent on goods of classes 1 and 2:

$$K = L_1 + L_2 + L_3 = Q_1 P_1 + Q_2 P_2 = L_1 + L_2 + E.*$$

E, the amount of taxation, is the source of the income L_3, and $E = L_3$. There seems to be no justification for the creation of a fictitious income to harmonize with a particular price index-number. The objective is not money income, but a weighted index of production or consumption. Some of the writers who use this method do not appear to have offered any reasons for taking Government goods at cost price, while taxed goods are

* Since P_1 = cost price, and P_2 = cost price $(1 + T)$.

taken at their selling price. But Professor J. R. Hicks (*Economica*, May 1940, pp. 116–18) goes further into the question. He arrives at the definition 'Social Income including public services = all private incomes + indirect taxes − subsidies − pensions', including public services at their cost price.

He argues that a commodity should not be valued at zero unless it is provided in unlimited quantities. 'Now hardly any of the Public Services are such that no additional satisfaction would result from extra expenditure upon them—which is the condition for it to be appropriate to value them at zero.' But in the treatment developed above, it is the *selling price* that (in the absence of direct taxation) is placed at zero, while their *value* is taken at the amount of indirect taxation which equals cost price. It is *not* assumed that no further satisfaction would be obtained by increasing these services. The position is that the community is (for example) willing to pay more for its tobacco in order to provide more teaching. Equilibrium is at the point where additional teaching is balanced against less tobacco, and this is on all fours with the balance between the prices and consumption of other commodities. Professor Hicks's and Mr Colin Clark's methods result in the paradox that social income can be increased indefinitely by increasing direct taxation. In the method adopted above indirect taxes are part of private incomes, namely the incomes of persons rendering public services. Fortunately it is not necessary here to decide on the merits of the rival formulae, since in the period 1924–38 the results of the two methods differ very slightly[1] (resulting in any case only from differences in weighting the quantity

1 Write ${}_0J_1$ for J_1 in Case I (p. 182).

Let $E = \lambda . K$, i.e. λ is the ratio of indirect taxation to the total of incomes. Then the measurement in the text, p. 184, is

$$ {}_1J_1 = {}_0J_1 \left\{ 1 + \lambda \frac{r_2 - r_3}{{}_0J_1} \right\}. $$

If $r_2 < r_3$, that is, if production of the taxed commodity diminishes relatively to that on the group transferred to Government,

$$ {}_1J_1 < {}_0J_1, $$

but the relative difference depends on the product of two fractions each of which is usually small.

Mr Clark's measurement reduces to

$$ {}_2J_1 = {}_0J_1 \left\{ 1 + \lambda \frac{r_2 - {}_0J_1}{{}_0J_1} \right\}, $$

when λ^2 is neglected. This differs from ${}_1J_1$ by a quantity which is very small, unless ${}_0J_1 - r_3$ is abnormally great.

relatives), while the margin of uncertainty in other factors, especially those relating to services as contrasted with goods, is quite considerable. When, as in 1941, indirect and direct taxation form large proportions of total income, it may be that the differences would be significant.

It is clear that the formulae for the ratio of real incomes depend on weighting quantity changes and that price movements do not enter explicitly. Prices only enter in the choice of weights applied to quantity movements. But if the change in the value of £1, though its measurement depends on arbitrary definitions, is regarded as being of interest and importance, it can be deduced from relating the measurement of changes of real income to that of the changes of money income.

APPLICATION OF THE FORMULAE TO THE NATIONAL INCOME OF THE UNITED KINGDOM, 1924 TO 1938

In the accompanying tables index-numbers of quantity are given with (A) 1924 as base and (B) 1935 as base. These index-numbers are weighted with the estimated income in each class, in (A) that of 1924 (L), in (B) that of 1935 (l).

The results[1] are given on the basis of Cost price (line 9) and on the basis of the formula developed above (line 12).

It will be seen that the two different formulae give results varying by less than 1 per cent from each other in most cases. For the period 1924 to 1935 we have:[2]

	Cost price	Formula	Mr Clark's method
(A) Forward working J_1	100 : 123·1	100 : 121·7	100 : 121·4
(B) Backward working J_2	100 : 118·7	100 : 119·0	100 : 118·3

But the backward working (1935 base) gives a perceptibly smaller increase than does the forward working.

1 The formulae are:

(A) line 9, $100\,\Sigma L \frac{m}{M} \div \Sigma L$,

line 12, $100\left(\Sigma L_1 \frac{m_1}{M_1} + \Sigma \frac{m_2}{M_2}(L_2+E) + \Sigma \frac{m_3}{M_3} L_3 R\right) \div \Sigma L$,

where E is the amount of indirect taxation, R the ratio of direct to total taxation. ΣL_1 includes lines 4, 7, 8; ΣL_2 lines 10, 11; ΣL_3 lines 5, 6.

(B) The formulae are as in (A) with small and capital letters interchanged.

2 In the calculations the first decimal place was used. In the table the nearest units are given.

Mr Clark, if I understand him rightly, includes indirect taxation *and* Government goods at cost price. The difference made is quite small.

The averages of J_1 and J_2 are 120·9, 120·3 and 119·9, differences which are quite insignificant.

Thus, as was to be expected, the differences that arise from different systems of weighting at one date are quite small, but those from variation of the base year are significant, though within the kind of margin of error that must attach to this kind of estimate.

On the other hand considerable importance attaches to the measurement of the changes of quantity. Physical production (lines 4 and 6) accounts for 43 per cent of the value in 1924 and is credited with an increase of 35 per cent in 1935, while Services (lines 6 and 8) account for 50 per cent of the value and are credited with a rise of only 10 per cent. Below it is shown how difficult and doubtful is the change to be attributed to Services; and the effect of different hypotheses on the final index-numbers is discussed.

After the table there are given explanations and details of all the estimates, so that it is possible for a student to compute the results on various formulae or after different judgment of treatment of the basic series.

PRICES

We can deduce an index-number of prices in general by dividing the index of money income by that of quantity.

Index-numbers

Years	Total quantity	Total income	Quotient or price	Prices Board of Trade	Cost of living	Wage rates
1924	100	100	100	100	100	100
1925	102	98	96	96	100	101
1926	99	96½	98	89	98	101½
1927	107	100	93	85	95	101½
1928	107	101	94	84	94	101
1929	111	101	91	82	94	100
1930	107½	98	91	72	94	99
1931	105	88½	84	62½	90	98
1932	105	85½	81	61	84	96
1933	109½	91	82	62	79½	95
1934	115	95½	83	63	80½	95
1935	120½	101	84	64	81½	96
1936	125	107	85	68	84	98½
1937	127	112	88	78	88½	102
1938	124	112	90	73	89	105½

The Quantity index used is the average of (A) line 12 and (B) line 13, viz. $\frac{1}{2}(J_1+J_2)$.

The money income series is computed from Total B, Table IX (p. 81 above).

For comparison the Board of Trade index of Wholesale Prices is given and the Cost of Living index. Except in 1931–33 the new index lies very close to the Cost of Living.

Also the Wage-Rate index of the London and Cambridge Economic Service is entered. The Cost of Living index is approximately half-way between Wholesale Prices and Wage Rates, except in 1929–32, when it is nearer the Wage Rate index.

A rough comparison is possible between the increase in the Quantity index discounted for the growth of population, and the increase of real wages as estimated from the quotient of the Wage index by the Cost of Living index. But we should use, instead of the Wage index in the table above, one modified to allow for increased earnings, as discussed on pp. 64, 65 above. This revised index of earnings is:

1933	1934	1935	1936	1937	1938
95	95½	99	100½	103	106

We then have:

Year	Quantity index adjusted to population	Quotient of earnings per head by Cost of Living index
1924	100	100
1925	101	101
1926	98	103
1927	106	107
1928	106	107
1929	109	106
1930	105	105
1931	102	109
1932	102	114
1933	106	119
1934	111	119
1935	115	121
1936	120	120
1937	121	116
1938	117	119

Over the whole period the increase is nearly the same on both sides. But between 1927 and 1932 the Cost of Living index-number falls rapidly and causes an increase which is not confirmed by the index of Quantity. The fall of prices in this period was in primary foods and materials, not in services or cost of manufacture.

Table A

National Income. Index-numbers of Quantity: 1924 base

	1924 Value *L* (£ mn.)	1924	1925	1926	1927	1928	1929	1930	1931	1932	1933	1934	1935	1936	1937	1938
1. Industry	1,455	100	100	88	112	108	117	107	97	97	107	121	130	141	149	134
2. Agriculture	170	100	101	101	106	107	105	103	106	115	120	123	123	122	120	122
3. Together	—	100	100½	89	111	108	115½	107	98	99	108	121	129	139	145½	133
4. *Together	1,625	100	99	90	111½	108	115	111	107½	108	120½	134	141	150	152	146
Government:																
5. Products	50	100	101	92	118	117	128	120	111	112	122	137	146	158	166	153
6. Services	500	100	102	104	104	106	104	104	102	104	104	104	110	108	107	107
7. Houses	220	100	101	102	104	107	110	112	114	116	119	121	124	128	132	136
8. Services	1,495	100	102	104	104	106	104	104	102	104	104	104	110	108	107	107
Total	3,890															
9. Index-number Cost price	—	100	100	98	107	107	110	108	105	107	112	118	123	128	128	126
10. Customs	100	100	104	103	103	106	110	110	110	109	106	110	114	120	124	127
11. Excise	135	100	100	94	91	86	91	87	77	67	69	72	77	78	81	82
12. Index-number by formula	—	100	101	97	107	106	109	107	104	105	111	117	122	127	127	125

* Allowing for effect of changing 'terms of trade'.

Table B

National Income. Index-numbers of Quantity: 1935 *base*

	1935 Value *l* (£ mn.)	1924	1925	1926	1927	1928	1929	1930	1931	1932	1933	1934	1935	1936	1937	1938
1. Industry	1,535	80	80	71	90	87	94	86	80	80	86	94	100	108	115	102
2. Agriculture	165	81	82	82	86	87	85	84	86	93	97	101	100	100	98	100
3. Together	—	80	80	72	90	87	93	86	81	81	87	95	100	107	113½	102
4. *Together	1,700	77	78	70	86	84	92	86	81	81	86	95	100	106	112	102
Government:																
5. Products	55	68	70	63	81	80	88	82	75	76	84	95	100	108	114	105
6. Services	665	92	94	96	96	98	97	95	94	96	96	96	100	102	99	101
7. Houses	330	80	81	82	83	86	88	90	92	94	96	98	100	103	106	110
8. Services	1,170	92	94	96	96	98	97	95	94	96	96	96	100	102	99	101
Total	3,920															
9. Index-number Cost price	—	84	86	83	90	91	94	90	88	89	91	95	100	104	106	102
10. Customs	200	79	83	89	92	91	96	90	98	89	90	98	100	108	121	116
11. Excise	105	132	132	123	119	113	120	114	100	89	90	94	100	102	106	106
12. Index-number by formula	—	84	85	82	90	90	94	90	87	89	91	97	100	104	107	107
13. Re-written with 1924=100	—	100	103	100	108	108	113	108	103	105	108	113	119	124	127	123

* Allowing for effect of changing 'terms of trade'.

Explanation of the Table

Weights (*L and l*). For Industry the net output (including small firms and excluding Government Products) has been taken in 1930 and 1935 after deducting 10 per cent as an allowance for depreciation and any rates that enter into cost.

For Agriculture (which has little weight in the total so that exact computation is not necessary) one of the estimates for net output, as discussed on pp. 95–101 above, is adopted for 1924, and after consideration of Schedules A and B of the income tax and the numbers and wages of agricultural labourers a slightly lower figure has been taken for 1935.

For Government Products the net output of physical production by the Central and Local Authorities has been written in for 1924 and 1935. For Government Services in 1924 and 1935, Total Expenditure chargeable against Revenue has been added to estimated total local rates, and then the interest (and other service) of the National Debt and the value of Post Office services has been deducted. From this remainder the amount already included as Products has been subtracted.

For Houses it has been arbitrarily assumed that the annual value of houses, as distinct from business premises, already taken into account in line 4, is 71 per cent of the assessed value of buildings in Schedule A. This estimate has no authority, except that Mr Flux appears to have used it in his work on the 1907 Census of Production. The weight is so small a proportion of the total, and the Quantity index moves so closely with the general index-number, that an exact valuation is of little importance.

The totals of *L* and *l* are the estimates of National Income in the table on p. 81 above, obtained by subtracting Pensions, National Debt interest and Income due to Foreigners from the total of personal and corporate incomes. The difference between this total and lines 4, 5, 6, 7 is entered in line 8, and is attributable to activities outside the Census of Production and Government Production. It includes transport, distribution, wholesale and retail, other commerce and banking, professions, domestic and restaurant service.

In considering these estimates, it is to be remembered that they are only necessary as weights for the Quantity index-numbers, and precision is only of importance in the larger categories.

Index-numbers of Quantity. In (A) line 1 is the annual index of the London and Cambridge Economic Service after Agriculture is detached. In (B) the change shown by Dr Rhodes (see pp. 141, 142 above) between 1930 and 1935, on the basis of 1935, gives 86 in 1930. For the years between 1930 and 1935 the changes shown in (A) are damped down proportionately to yield the smaller increase over the five years. Before 1930 and after 1935 the changes in (B) are proportional to those in (A).

Line 2. For Agriculture series are formed of the annual production of wheat, barley, potatoes, sugar, cattle (dairy and other), sheep, pigs and fowls, each equated to 100 in 1924, and an index-number is formed by using as weights the estimated value of their products in 1924.

Line 3 is a weighted average of lines 1 and 2.

In lines 2, 5, 6, 7 and 8 the index-numbers in (B) are the same as in (A), reduced proportionally to give 100 in 1935.

Since the results to the home consumer of production for export are found in quantities imported in exchange for them, it is proper to include in the index-numbers of quantities consumed (which are those with which we are concerned when considering income) a quantitative measure of imports. Line 4 shows the result, and since the adjustment from line 3 is small a rough method is sufficient.

Average price index-numbers of imports and exports are available in the statistical abstract. The ratios of the export to the import price index are approximately

Year	Ratio	Year	Ratio	Year	Ratio
1924	100	1929	100	1934	121
1925	99	1930	108	1935	119
1926	102	1931	120	1936	116
1927	101	1932	120	1937	110
1928	100	1933	124	1938	118

That is, the 'terms of trade' improved considerably from 1929 to 1931 and deteriorated from 1934 to 1938.

In 1924 exports of British Produce were valued at £800 mn., that is, 48 per cent of the Net Output of Industry and Agriculture.

The revised Quantity index for 1935 (e.g.) is thus computed from line 3:

$$129(1+0{\cdot}48 \text{ of } 0{\cdot}19)=141.$$

In (B) the difference between lines 3 and 4 is smaller since Exports were only 23 per cent of the Net Output.

For line 5 in (A) we have the numbers for 1924, 1930, 1935 from the Tables pp. 148, 150 above. For the years 1925–29 it has been assumed that the greater increase in Government Products than for others from 1924 to 1930 was evenly distributed through the five years. After 1935 the rate of increase is taken as the same as in line 1. Since the weight attributed in line 5 is so small, it is not important to aim at exact interpolation.

Lines 6 and 8 may be taken together, for we cannot separate clearly the numbers of persons paid by the Government from all others rendering services. There is no quantitative measurement of the change in the amount of service rendered by an individual, and the only available method seems to be to estimate the number of persons and, assuming that the quantity of service per head is unchanged, to take the total amount of service as proportional to the numbers.

The numbers employed in this group cannot be estimated from the Unemployment or Health Insurance Statistics, since the former exclude domestic service and most railway employees, in the latter there is no division by occupation, and both exclude persons with incomes over £250. In default of a better method the numbers presumed to have an occupation are taken from the table on p. 56 and discounted for unemployment, arbitrarily at half[1] the percentage applicable to wage-earners. From these are subtracted the estimated numbers employed in the Census of Production industries and Agriculture. Thus:

000's omitted

	1924	1935
Numbers 'occupied'	2,040	2,208
Less unemployed	180	292
Less Production and Agriculture	938	916
Services	922	1,000
Index-number	100	108

There is little doubt that the whole occupied and employed population increased more rapidly than those engaged in production, so that the table which gives an increase from 1924 to 1935 of 3 per cent for all employed, a decrease of 2 per cent for production, and an increase of 8 per cent for services, is a priori reasonable. But these results are hardly consistent with the amounts of income credited to the persons in lines 6 and 8, viz.

1 If the same proportion were subtracted for both classes, the index-numbers for Services in 1935 would be 110 instead of 108.

£1950 mn. in 1924 and £1835 mn. in 1935, a decrease of 6 per cent; for this could mean that salaries or earnings per head had fallen 14 per cent in the period. On p. 92 above it is estimated that salaries had fallen about 3 per cent, including the wages of shop-assistants. In the same period railwaymen's earnings had fallen 3 per cent.

There are many elements of approximation both in taking the residual income as applying to services and in using the occupation figures. But the discrepancy between the fall in income and the increase in numbers is too large to explain away.

If we took 100 instead of 108 in 1935 in lines 6 and 8, the index in line 9 would become 118 instead of 123, and there would be a corresponding change of about the same amount in other index-numbers summarized on pp. 192–3.

The basis of calculation for Housing (line 7) is the number of dwelling-houses in Great Britain in 1931, adjusted to other years by the number of houses built in each year. This makes no allowance for demolitions, but on the other hand does not include any estimate for the increase in hotels and other buildings, which are not private dwelling-houses nor factories, etc. accounted for in the Census of Production. From 1924 to 1937 it is thus estimated that the quantity of houses increased 32 per cent, while the assessed value increased 64 per cent; on this basis rent increased 24 per cent, while the rents (including rates) used in the Cost-of-Living index increased 8 per cent, dominated by controlled rents.

For Customs (A) (line 10) the receipts in 1924 are used as weights for series of quantities taxed (1924 to 1938) for beer, wine, spirits, tea, cocoa, sugar, currants, tobacco and matches separately. Sugar and tobacco dominate the reckoning. For (B) it was necessary to take account also of the duties on oil and the various new general import taxes. For oil a rough estimate is possible of the quantities imported. For the change in quantity of other goods newly taxed there is no obvious method. It is assumed that the change in the values liable to tax is proportional to the value of all imported manufactured goods, and that the corresponding quantities are measurable by deflating or inflating the values by the import price index based on all imports. No doubt this method could be improved on by more detailed work, but no reasonable revision could affect the general index-number of quantity (line 12) significantly.

For Excise (line 11) only spirits and beer have been taken into account. Index-numbers of the quantities taxed weighted in (A) and (B) respectively by the excise receipts in 1924 and 1935. The numbers so obtained are applied to total excise receipts, for (together with liquor licences) they account for the great part of excise, other than the entertainments tax, which does not lend itself to any easy quantitative treatment.

When the whole calculation is reviewed and the margins of error attachable to the items that enter into it are considered, we can express some opinion about the precision of the main result, that is, the progress of real income. Naturally it applies only to income as defined for in Chapter II (Table IX, Total B), and it is subject to the vagueness that is intrinsic when an objective measurement is applied to a subjective entity. The margins that are of importance to the result are those attaching to the Index of Production in line 4 and that of Services in lines 6 and 8, and to a much smaller extent to the weights given to these lines. From 1924 to 1938 we may write the increase in line 4 at 38 ± 6 per cent, so including the estimates in (A) and (B). For Services the assumption was unchanged efficiency and there is perhaps a margin of 5 per cent to be applied to the numbers; if the increase is stated at 10 ± 8 per cent we allow for both uncertainties. Then for the whole (line 12) the increase may be estimated as between 18 and 30 per cent in the fifteen years, and the index-numbers as 124 ± 6. The extreme limits are improbable and the central figure 124 may be used as a reasonable approximation.

The margin given for 1938 may be regarded as cumulative during the 15 years, so that the earlier entries have the greater accuracy. The dates and relative amounts of variation from period to period, for example the rapid rise after 1932, are more reliable than the numerical measurements of the changes.

BIBLIOGRAPHY OF BOOKS, JOURNALS AND OTHER PUBLICATIONS RELATING TO NATIONAL INCOME

The sections of the bibliography are arranged alphabetically, but the countries are separated. All sections start with United Kingdom.

CLASSIFICATION

A card index of the Bibliography is preserved by the National Institute of Economic and Social Research. The cards show in most cases in what Library the books can be found, and some of them indicate what topics are discussed.

A. THEORY AND/OR SYSTEM

A I. *NATIONAL INCOME*

United Kingdom

A. L. Bowley. *National Progress in Wealth and Trade.* 1904.

—— The definition of national income. *Econ. Journ.* March 1922.

—— Evidence before the Select Committee on Income Tax, 1905–6. (U.K. Sel. Com. on Inc. Tax.)

—— *Three studies on the National Income*: being 'The Division of the product of Industry'; 'The Change in the Distribution of the National Income, 1880–1913'; 'The National Income, 1924' (with Lord Stamp). London, 1938.

—— *Wages and Income in the United Kingdom since* 1860. Cambridge, 1937.

—— The measurement of Real Income. Manchester. *Stat. Soc.* 1939.

—— Some constituents of the National Income (Valedictory address). *Journ. of R. Stat. Soc.* 1940, Pt iv.

Morgan Browne. Sir R. Giffen's indiscretion. *New Liberal Review*, April 1902.

Edwin Cannan. *Wealth.* 1914.

A. M. Carr-Saunders and D. Caradog Jones. *A Survey of the Social Structure of Income of England and Wales.* 1937.

Colin Clark. Income and the theory of production. *Econ. Journ.* June 1933.

—— Internationaler Vergleich der Volkseinkommen. *Weltwirtschaftliches Archiv*, 1938.

—— *The Conditions of Economic Progress*, 1940.

H. Clay. *Property and Inheritance* (post 1933).

F. Y. Edgeworth. Income. Palgrave's *Dictionary of Political Economy.*

A. W. Flux. Industrial productivity in Great Britain and the United States. *Quart. Journ. of Econ.* Nov. 1933.

—— Irving Fisher on capital and interest. *Quart. Journ. of Econ.* Feb. 1909.

Sir Robert Giffen. *Economic Enquiries and Studies.* 1904.

W. J. Harris. A comparison of the growth of wealth in France and England. *Stat. Journ.* 1894.

J. R. Hicks. *Value and Capital.* London, 1939.

C. K. Hobson. *Work and Wealth, a human valuation.* 1914; rev. ed. 1933.

George Howell. *The Conflict of Capital and Labour.* 1878.

E. Huncke. Die Entwicklung von Einkommensteuer und Einkommensverteilung in England. *Finanz-Archiv*, 1905.

F. Ireson. *The People's Progress.* 1910.

R. F. Kahn. The relation of home investment to unemployment. *Econ. Journ.* June 1931.

M. A. Kalecki. A theory of commodity, income and capital taxation. *Econ. Journ.* 1937.

J. M. Keynes. *The General Theory of Employment, Interest and Money.* Cambridge, 1936.

A. Marshall. *Principles of Economics.* 1907.

—— *Economics of Industry.* 1907.

J. S. Nicholson. Capital and labour, their relative strength. *Econ. Journ.* 1892.

R. Inglis Palgrave. An enquiry into the economic condition of the country. *Inst. of Bankers' Journ.* 1904.

A. C. PIGOU. *The Economics of Welfare.* 1929.
—— *Wealth and Welfare.* 1929.
—— Net income and capital depletion. *Econ. Journ.* June 1935.
—— Measurement of real income. *Econ. Journ.* 1940.
G. R. PORTER. *The Progress of the Nation.* 1847.
G. L. S. SHACKLE. *Expectation, Investments and Income.* 1938.
G. FINDLAY SHIRRAS. *Volkseinkommen und Besteuerung.* Ed. by M. J. Bonn. Jena, 1926.
A. SOETBEER. *Zur Einkommensstatistik Preussens, Sachsens und Grossbritanniens.*
U.K. Select Committee on the Depression of Trade and Industry. Report and Evidences of Sir Robert Giffen and Mr Algernon West. B.P.P. 1886.

AUSTRIA

H. MAYER (Editor). *Die Wirtschaftstheorie der Gegenwart.* Wien, 1928.

BELGIUM

FERNAND BAUDHUIN. Le revenu national en 1930. *Bulletin d'Information et de documentation, Banque Nationale de Belgique,* Vol. v, No. 10.
—— Les finances belges en 1937. *Bulletin de l'institut de recherches économiques,* 1937–8.
—— Les finances belges en 1938. *Bulletin de l'institut de recherches économiques,* 1938–9.

CANADA

Canada Year Book. National Wealth and Income. Ottawa (annual).

FRANCE

M. HUBER. *La Population de la France pendant la Guerre, avec un appendice sur le revenu avant et après la guerre.* Paris, 1932.
J. C. L. SIMONDE DE SISMONDI. *Du Revenu Social. Études sur l'Économie politique.* 1837–8.
A. R. J. TURGOT. *Réflections sur la Formation et la Distribution des Richesses.* 1788.

GERMANY

BIEDERMANN. Einkommens- und Vermögensverhältnisse in Preussen. *Zeitschrift des Preuss. Stat. Landesamts,* 1918.
L. v. BORTKIEWICZ. Die Grenznutzenlehre als Grundlage einer ultraliberalen Wirtschaftspolitik. *Jahrbuch f. Gesetzgebung, Verwaltung und Volkswirtschaft* (Schmoller), 1898.
K. DIEHL. Volkseinkommen und Volksvermögen. Beiträge zur Wirtschaftstheorie. *Schriften des Vereins für Sozialpolitik,* 1926.
A. EMMINGHAUS. Einkommen. Renzsch's *Handwörterbuch.* Leipzig, 1870.
R. FRICKE. *Konjunktur und Einkommen, eine Grundlegung zur dynamischen Konjunkturtheorie.* Halberstadt, 1927.
E. v. GOTTL-OTTILIENFELD. Volkseinkommen und Volksvermögen. *Weltwirtschaftliches Archiv,* 1927.
B. HARMS. *Kapital und Kapitalismus,* Bd. 1, Heft II. Berlin, 1931. (Vorlesungen gehalten in der Deutschen Vereinigung für Staatswissenschaftliche Fortbildung.)
F. B. W. HERMANN. *Staatswirtschaftliche Untersuchungen.* Leipzig, 1924.
E. KLEINSCHMITT. Articles on 'Volkseinkommen' in *Germania,* 25 Nov. 1924; *Hamburgischer Correspondent,* 24 May 1925.
A. LANSBURGH. Volkseinkommen und Sozialprodukt. *Die Bank,* 1926.

H. Losch. *Volksvermögen, Volkseinkommen und ihre Verteilung*. Leipzig, 1887.

Walter Lotz. Kapitalbildung und Besteuerung. *Schriften des Vereins für Sozialpolitik*, Bd. 174, Heft 4. München, 1929.

F. Lutz. *Der Begriff Volksreichtum in der volkswirtschaftlichen Literatur, vornehmlich Deutschlands*. Erlangen, 1922.

H. C. Mangoldt. Einkommen. Article in *Deutsches Staatswörterbuch* (Bluntschli und Brater), Bd. iii. Stuttgart, 1857–70.

R. Meyer. Einkommen. *Handwörterbuch der Staatswissenschaften*, 1. Aufl. 1892–3. Aufl. 1909.

H. Nies. *Achille Lorias wesentliches wirtschaftliches Gesetz*. Vohwinkel, 1926.

R. Nitschke. *Einkommen und Vermögen in Preussen und ihre Entwicklung seit Einführung der neuen Steuer mit Nutzanwendung auf die Theorie der Einkommensentwicklung*. Jena, 1902.

O. Pfleiderer. *Die Staatswirtschaft und das Sozialprodukt*. Jena, 1930.

I. Pierstorff. *Die Lehre vom Unternehmergewinn*. Berlin, 1875.

—— Unternehmer und Unternehmergewinn. Article in *Handwörterbuch der Staatswissenschaften*, 3. Aufl., Bd. viii.

H. Roesler. Zur Lehre vom Einkommen. *Jahrbüch für Nationalökonomie und Statistik* (Conrad).

W. Röpke. Sozialökonomische Betrachtungen über den abnehmenden Bevölkerungszuwachs. *Der Economist*, 1930.

G. Rümelin. *Beiträge zur Vermittlung des Volksvermögens und Volkseinkommens. Das Königreich Württemberg*. Stuttgart, 1863.

Samter. Das Einkommen der Bevölkerung in Preussen. *Kgl. Phys. Oek. Gesellschaft*, Königsberg, 1873.

G. Schmoller. On National Income. *Evangelisch-sozialer Kongress*. Leipzig, 1897.

G. Schnapper-Arndt. *Sozialstatistik*. Leipzig, 1908.

E. Schuster. *Die Einkommen: eine kritische Untersuchung*. Tübingen, 1926.

—— *Einkommen und Volkseinkommen*. v. Diehl, above.

K. Singer. Kapitalbedarf und Kapitalbildung in Deutschland. Ein statistischer Versuch. *Schriften des Vereins für Sozialpolitik*, Bd. 174. München, 1929.

A. Soetbeer. *Zur Einkommensstatistik Preussens, Sachsens und Grossbritanniens. Vierteljahrsschrift für Volkswirtschaft, Politik und Kulturgeschichte*, 1887–88.

H. Storch. *Betrachtungen über die Natur des Nationaleinkommens*. Halle, 1825.

W. Winkler. Einkommen. Article in *Handwörterbuch der Staatswissenschaften*, 4. Aufl., Bd. iii.

Württembergisches Statistisches Landesamt. *Volksvermögen, Volkseinkommen und Steuerbelastung in Deutschland vor und nach dem Krieg*. Mitteilungen Nr. 6.

E. Würzburger. Die Sächsische Einkommensstatistik als Masstab für die Beurteilung der Einkommensverhältnisse. *Zeitschrift d. kgl. Sächs. Stat. Büros*, 1904.

Holland

De Bruyn-Kops. Report on the 'revenu annuel de la nation'. *Int. Stat. Congress*, Pt I, The Hague, 1869.

J. Ort. *Het Inkomensbegrip*. Amsterdam, 1911.

India

V. K. R. V. Rao. *The National Income of British India*. 1940.

IRELAND

ERSKINE CHILDERS. *Irish Fiscal Authority*. In 'The Fiscal Relations of Great Britain and Ireland'. Conference of the Royal Economic Society, Jan. 1912.

ITALY

DETTORI. *Lezioni de Statistica economica*. 1918.

L. EINAUDI (Spectator). Gli indici della vita italiana in cinquantennio (1861–1911). Articles on Italy's National Income in *Corriere della Sera*, April 1911, Feb. 1916.

—— Rivista economico-finanziaria dell' Italia nel periodo 1885–1901. *Riforma soziale*, 1902.

A. GARELLI. *Il concetto di reddito nella scienza financiaria*. Milano, 1917.

C. GINI. *A Comparison of the Wealth and National Income of Several Important Nations before and after the War*. 1925.

—— Quelque chiffres sur la richesse et les revenus nationaux de quinze états. *Metron*, Vol. III, 1923.

—— Untersuchungen über den Einfluss des Krieges auf das Volksvermögen. Basel, 1924. Reprint from *Zeitschrift für Schweiz. Stat. und Volkswirtschaft*.

A. LORIA. *The Economic Synthesis*. 1913.

V. PARETO. *Manuel d'Économie politique*. Paris, 1909.

G. E. PRATO. *Di alcuni recenti Teorie sul Capitale e sul Reddito e delle loro consequenzi tributarie*. Turin, 1912.

POLAND

Birmingham Information Service on Slavonic Countries. *The National Income of Poland*. Birmingham, 1937.

RUSSIA

Birmingham University. Bureau of Research on Russian Economic Conditions, Memoranda No. 3: *National Income of the U.S.S.R.* Birmingham, 1931.

S. FALKNER. Ponyate narodnogo dokhada i ego elementi. The Concept of National Income and its elements. *Sotsialisti cheskve Khozyastro*, Vol. II, Pt IV, 1929.

V. KATS. *Narodny dokhod U.S.S.R. i ego raspredeleine*. (National Income of the U.S.S.R. and its distribution.) Moskow, 1932.

SPAIN

Banco de Espana. Servicio de Estudios. *La determinacion de la renta nacional*. 1937.

J. VANDELLOS. La richesse et le revenu de la Péninsule ibérique. *Metron*, Vol. V, No. 4, 1925.

SWITZERLAND

W. EGGENSCHWYLER. Die Bestimmung des Einkommens und die Finanzierung des Krieges. *Jahrbücher für Nationalökonomie und Statistik*, 1915.

E. LAUR. Wechselbeziehung zwischen privatwirtschaftlichen und volkswirtschaftlichen Einkommen unter Berücksichtigung der Landwirtschaft. *Zeitschrift für Schweiz. Stat. und Volkswirtschaft*. 1924.

P. MORI (Bern). Das Schweizer. Volkseinkommen. *Bulletin de L'institut international de Statistique*, Vol. XXV, 1931.

A. Reichlin. Das schweizerische Volkseinkommen, seine Quellen und ihre Bedeutung. *Journ. de Statistique Suisse*, 1927.

J. Wyler. Das schweizerische Volkseinkommen im Jahre 1924. *Zeitschrift für Schweiz. Statistik und Volkswirtschaft*, 1927.

Union of S. Africa

S. H. Frankel and S. D. Neumark. Note on the National Income of the Union of South Africa. *South African Journ. of Econ.* 1940.

U.S.A.

B. M. A. Anderson. *The Income of the American people and the ratio of foreign to domestic trade*, 1890–1924. Chase National Bank, Economic Bulletin, 1925.

M. R. Benedict. *Studies in Income and Wealth.* Vol. I, Part 8. New York, 1937.

J. D. Black. *Ibid.* Vol. I, Part 8. New York, 1937.

R. Blough. *Ibid.* Vol. I, Part 4. New York, 1937.

Brookings Institution. Institute of Economics, Publ. No. 56:

M. Leven and others. *America's Capacity to Consume.* Washington, 1934. (Pt II of the 'Distribution of Wealth and Income'.)

Brookings Institution. Institute of Economics, Publ. No. 68:

H. G. Moulton. *Income and Economic Progress.* Washington, 1935. (Pt IV of the 'Distribution of Wealth and Income'.)

Brookings Institution. Institute of Economics, Publ. No. 74:

M. Leven and C. Wright. *The Income Structure of the United States.* Washington, 1938.

A. F. Burns. *Quarterly Journal of Economics*, May 1936. Review of the Brookings 'Inquiry into the Distribution of Wealth and Income'.

—— *Journal of Political Economy*, October 1935. Review of the Brookings 'Inquiry into the Distribution of Wealth and Income'.

T. N. Carver. *The Distribution of Wealth.* New York, 1925.

J. M. Clark. *Studies in Income and Wealth.*

G. Colm. Review of C. H. Simms, *Personal Income Taxation*; *The Definition of Income as a problem of fiscal policy*, Chicago, 1938. *Social Research*, 1938.

—— *Studies in Income and Wealth.*

J. R. Commons. *The Distribution of Wealth.* New York, 1893.

M. A. Copeland. National wealth and income; an interpretation. *Journal of the American Statistical Association*, June 1935.

—— Some problems in the theory of national income. *Journ. of Polit. Econ.* 1932.

W. L. Crum. The national income and its distribution. *Journ. Amer. Stat. Assoc.* March 1935.

R. R. Doane. *The Measurement of American Wealth.* New York, 1933.

Irving Fisher. Der Einkommensbegriff im Lichte der Erfahrung (The income concept in the light of experience). See H. Meyer, *Die Wirtschaftstheorie der Gegenwart.* 1928.

—— *The Nature of Capital and Income.* New York, 1912.

—— The role of capital in economic theory. *Econ. Journ.* 1897.

—— What is Capital? *Econ. Journ.* Vol. VI, 1896.

D. Friday. Taxable income of the United States. *Journ. of Polit. Econ.* 1918.

G. Harrison and F. C. Mitchell. *The Home Market; a Handbook of Statistics.* 1936.

The Index New York Trust Co. *The National Income. Recent Changes in its Distribution.* Feb. 1937.

A. C. MILLER. War finance and inflation. *Annals of the American Academy of Political and Social Science*, Jan. 1918: 'Financing the War'.

National Bureau of Economics. Research No. 3:

O. W. KNAUTH. *Distribution of Income by States in* 1919.

C. C. PLEHN. Income as recurrent consumable receipts. *American Econ. Review*, 1924.

H. STAEHLE. Review of Federal Trade Commission on Wealth and Income; Senate Document No. 126, 69th Congress, 1st Session. *Jahrbücher für Gesetzgebung und Verwaltung* (Schmoller), 1926.

A I *a*. *Total representations or estimates only*

UNITED KINGDOM

R. D. BAXTER. *Direct Taxation of Property and Income*. 1871 (?).

—— *National Income: the United Kingdom*. London, 1868.

H. BEEKE. *Observations on the produce of the Income Tax and on its proportion to the whole Income of Great Britain, including important facts respecting the extent, wealth and population of this Kingdom*. London, 1799.

G. H. BLUNDEN. A new property tax. *Econ. Journ.* Dec. 1897.

A. L. BOWLEY. The census of production and the national dividend. *Econ. Journ.* March 1913.

—— *A Short Account of English Foreign Trade in the Nineteenth Century*. 1922.

—— *Some Economic Consequences of the Great War*. 1930.

—— The national income of the United Kingdom in 1924. *Economica*, May 1933.

—— Some constituents of the national income. *Statistical Journ.* 1940.

—— The measurement of real income. *The Manchester School*, April 1940.

—— The measurement of real income. *Econ. Journ.* June-Sept. 1940.

A. L. BOWLEY and Sir JOSIAH STAMP. *The National Income*, 1924. A Comparative Study of the Income of the United Kingdom in 1911 and 1924. Oxford, 1927.

A. J. BROWN. *Resources available for war: A Comparison*. Oxford Economic Papers, no. 3, 1940.

Sir GEORGE CHALMERS. *An Estimate of the Comparative Strength of Great Britain*. 1802.

COLIN CLARK. *The National Income*, 1924–1931. Cambridge, 1932.

—— The national income and the net product of industry. *Stat. Journ.* 1933, Pt 4.

—— The national income, 1932. *Econ. Journ.* June 1933.

—— Further data on the national income. *Econ. Journ.* Sept. 1934.

—— *National Income and Outlay*. London, 1937.

—— National income at its climax. *Econ. Journ.* 1937.

W. COATES. *The Citizen's Purse*. Manchester Statistical Society, 1931.

T. A. COGHLAN. See United Kingdom Select Committee on Income Tax, 1906.

PATRICK COLQUHOUN. *Treatise on the Wealth, Power and Resources of the British Empire in every quarter of the world, including the East Indies, etc*. London, 1815.

L. R. CONNOR. On certain aspects of the distribution of income in the United Kingdom in 1913 and 1924. *Journ. Stat. Soc.* 1928.

E. CRAMMOND. The economic position of Scotland and her financial relation with England and Ireland. *Stat. Journ.* 1912.

E. Crammond. The economic relations of the British and German Empires. *Stat. Journ.* 1914.

C. Crowther. *Ways and Means.* Twelve Broadcast Talks. A study of the economic structure of Great Britain of to-day. 1936.

Myra Curtis. National income and expenditure and the measurement of savings. *Econ. Journ.* Sept. 1935.

Chas. Davenant. *The Discourses of the Public Revenue and on the Trade of England.* 1698.

—— *An Essay on Ways and Means of Supplying the War.* Reprinted in the *Political and Commercial works of the Celebrated writer Ch. Davenant.* London, 1771.

W. Farr. *Vital Statistics.* 1885.

Sir Alfred Flux. The national income. *Stat. Journ.* 1929.

—— Review of Colin Clark, *The National Income,* 1924–1931. *Econ. Journ.* June 1933.

—— See United Kingdom Report on Census of Production, 1907, Cd. 6320.

F. A. Hayek. Review on *How to pay for the War,* by J. M. Keynes. *Econ. Journ.* June to Sept. 1940.

J. M. Keynes. Income and fiscal potential of Great Britain. *Econ. Journ.* Dec. 1939.

—— *The Revision of the Treaty.* London, 1922, pp. 81, 82. (M. J. Elsas' *Estimate of Germany's National Income.*)

—— *How to pay for the War.* London, 1940.

—— The Concept of national income (Supplementary Note). *Econ. Journ.* March 1940.

Gregory King. *Two Tracks. National and Political Observations and Conclusions upon the State and Condition of England.* 1696. Reprint, 1936.

G. F. Kolb. *The Condition of Nations.* London, 1880.

P. D. Leake. Evidence before the Treasury Committee on National Debt and Taxation, 1927.

Leone Levi. Statistics of the revenue of the United Kingdom, 1859 to 1882. *Stat. Journ.* 1884.

Liberal Industrial Enquiry. *Britain's Industrial Future.*

Lord Liverpool. Debate on Agricultural Distress in the House of Lords. *Hansard,* 1822.

A. Loria. *The Economic Synthesis.* A study of the law of income. 1914.

J. Lowe. *The Present State of England in regard to Agriculture, Trade and Finance.* 2nd ed. 1823.

T. P. McQueen. Estimate for England, 1828, in Tait's *Edinburgh Magazine,* July 1839.

B. Mallet and H. C. Strutt. The multiplier and capital wealth. *Stat. Journ.* 1915.

M. G. Mulhall. *Balance Sheet of the World for Ten Years,* 1870–1880. Printed 1881.

—— *Progress of the World.* 1880.

Rich. Paget. See U.K., B.P.P. 1884/5, XLV, Session 345. Re Paget's Return.

P. de Pebrer. *Histoire Financière générale et Statistique de l'Empire Britannique.* Paris, 1839.

Sir William Petty. *Political Arithmetic.* 1690.

E. H. Phelps-Brown and G. L. S. Shackle. *Statistics of Monetary Circulation in England and Wales* 1919 *to* 1937. London and Cambridge Economic Service, Special Memoranda 46.

E. C. SNOW. Reviews of Colin Clark's *The National Income*, 1924–1931. *Stat. Journ.* 1933.

Sir EDGAR SPEYER. Some aspects of national income. *Inst. of Bankers' Journ.* 1905.

J. C. STAMP. *British Incomes and Property*. London, 1916. 2nd ed. 1920.

—— Review of Maurice Leven, *Income in the Various States—its Sources and Distribution*, National Bureau of Economic Research, 1925. *Stat. Journ.* 1927.

RICHARD STONE. Review of *Studies in Income and Wealth* (see Bowley and Stamp). *Econ. Journ.* 1938.

U.K. Report on Financial Relations between Great Britain and Ireland. B.P.P. 1895, XXXVI, C. 7720–21 and 8008; B.P.P. 1896, C. 8262, XXXIII, Final Report. Evidences: Sir Alfred Milner, Sir Robert Giffen, Thos. Lough and Sir Edw. W. Hamilton; Memoranda: Prof. Henry Sidgwick and Prof. C. F. Bastable.

—— Report of the Royal Commission on the Income Tax (Colwyn Committee). B.P.P. 1920, XVIII, Cmd. 615. Evidences: Prof. Bowley, J. C. Stamp, Sir L. G. Chiozza Money and Prof. Edgworth.

—— Report from the Select Committee on Income Tax together with the Proceedings of the Committee. Minutes of Evidence and an appendix, 1906. Evidences: Sir Henry Primrose, Sir Bernard Mallet, Sir L. G. Chiozza Money, Prof. Bowley and T. A. Coghlan.

—— Royal Commission on Local Taxation, 1899. B.P.P. 1899, XXXV, C. 9141; B.P.P. 1899, XXXVI, C. 9150, 9319, 9528. Answers to questions by Sir Robert Giffen, Prof. Sidgwick, Prof. Marshall, Prof. Bastable and Prof. Cannan. Memoranda by Sir Edw. W. Hamilton. Reprint of an Article on 'A new property tax' by G. H. Blunden in the *Econ. Journ.*

—— An Analysis of the Sources of War Finance and an Estimate of National Income and Expenditure in 1938 and 1940 (Cmd. 6261).

Sir FREDERIC WISE. Evidence before the Treasury Committee on National Debt and Taxation, 1927.

PRITCHARD-WOOD and partners. *A Commercial Barometer*. 1930 to date, quarterly.

ARTHUR YOUNG. *The question of Scarcity plainly stated*. 1800.

AUSTRALIA

COLIN CLARK and J. G. CRAWFORD. *National Income of Australia*. Sydney, 1938.

T. A. COGHLAN. *A Statistical Account of Australia and New Zealand*, 1902–3. Printed 1903.

—— *A Statistical Account of the Seven Colonies of Australasia*, 1861–1896. Sydney, 1897.

D. B. COPLAND. National income and economic prosperity. *American Acad. of Political and Soc. Science Annals*, Vol. CLVIII, 1931.

J. T. SUTCLIFFE. *The National Dividend*. Melbourne, 1926.

G. L. WOOD. Survey of production and the national income. *American Acad. of Political and Soc. Science Annals*, Vol. CLVIII, 1931.

AUSTRIA

K. v. BALES. *Theorie der Einkommens- und Zahlungsmachtverteilung*. Wien, 1927.

A. BEER. Given in de Foville, The Wealth of France and other Countries. *Stat. Journ.* 1893.

F. v. Fellner. *Die Schätzung des Volkseinkommens.* 1903.

—— Die Schätzung des Volkseinkommens. *Bull. de l'Inst. Int. de Stat.* Vol. xiv, 1905.

—— Das Volkseinkommen Oesterreichs und Ungarns. *Stat. Monatsschrift.* 1916.

—— *Das Volkseinkommen Oesterreichs und Ungarns.* Mainz, 1917.

A. Gürtler. Das Volkseinkommen Oesterreichs und Ungarns. Kritische Ergänzungen zu dem gleichnamigen Buch von F. v. Fellner. *Weltwirtschaftliches Archiv,* ii. Bd. 1918.

F. O. Hertz. *Kapitalbedarf, Kapitalbildung und Volkseinkommen in Oesterreich.* Wien, 1928.

—— Zahlungsbilanz und Lebensfähigkeit Oesterreichs. *Schriften des Vereins fur Sozialpolitik.* Vol. clxvii. München, 1925.

R. Meyer. *Das Wesen des Einkommen.* 1887.

Monatschrift Oesterr. Institut f. Konjunkturforschung (26 April 1937). *Die Entwicklung d. Einkommens in Oesterreich,* since 1929.

E. Waiszner. Das Volkseinkommen Altösterreichs und seine Verteilung auf die Nachfolgerstaaten. *Metron,* Vol. vii, 1928.

Belgium

F. Baudhuin. La fortune, le revenu et l'épargne de la Belgique en 1924. *Revue cath., soc. et jur. Brussels,* Dec. 1924 and Jan. 1925.

Belgia. Proceedings of the Chamber of Representatives. 8 March 1892.

Armand Julin. The economic progress of Belgium, 1880–1908. *Stat. Journ.* Feb. 1911.

E. Maham (Editor). *La Belgique restaurée. Études Sociologiques.* Institut Solvay, Brussels, 1926.

Ministry of Finance:

Lord Stamp, *Wealth and Income of the Chief Powers.*

Bulgaria

P. Kiranoff. *National Income of Bulgaria.* 1929 and 1932.

Kiril G. Popoff. *La Bulgarie Économique,* 1879–1911. Sofia, 1920.

A. Tchakanoff. *National Income of Bulgaria,* 1924–1935. Stat. Inst. for Economic Research. Sofia, 1937.

Canada

Dominion Bureau of Statistics. General Statistical Branch. *The National Income of Canada.* Ottawa, 1934.

Czecho-Slovakia

S. Prokopovic. Répartition du revenu national en Bohème, Moravie et Silésie au cours de 1913 à 1917. *Revue Stat. Tchéchoslovaque,* 1926.

P. Smutny. Revenu National. *Revue Stat. Tchéchoslovaque,* 1930.

Denmark

A. Liegaard. La fortune nationale du Danemark. *Journ. de la Société de Stat. de Paris,* 1876.

Egypt

J. Baxter. Notes on the estimate of the national income of Egypt. *Égypte Contemporaine,* 1923.

J. Craig. National income of Egypt. *Égypte Contemporaine,* 1924.

I. G. Levi. Évaluation du revenu national de l'Égypt. *Égypte Contemporaine,* 1923.

FINLAND

W. LINDBERG. Incomes in Finland. *Bank of Finland Monthly Bulletin*, Nov. 1926.

FRANCE

DELAI D'AGIER. *French Income of Personal Property*. 1791.

A. AMELIN. *L'Écho Agricole*. Aug.-Sept. 1878.

VICOMTE d'AVENEL. *Decouvertes d'histoire sociale, etc.* 1200–1910. Paris, 1910.

—— *Histoire Économique de la Propriété, des Salaires et des Denrées*. 1909.

BALLUE. Est. in National Assembly Chambre des Députés, No. 1314. *Journal Officiel*, 1886.

COCHUT. Enchérissement des marchandises et des services. *Revue des Deux Mondes*, 1883.

—— The wealth of France and other countries. *Revue des Deux Mondes*, 1849.

DUGÉ DE BERNONVILLE. Les revenus privés. *Revue d'Économie Politique*, 1933.

E. DE EICHTHAL. Revenus privés et revenu national. *Journ. de la Société de Stat. de Paris*, 1917.

A. DE FOVILLE. L'évaluation de la richesse nationale. *La France Économique*, 1899.

F. LEROY-BEAULIEU. La lenteur de l'accroisement de la fortune des classes aisées et opulentes en France. *Économiste français*, 23 Jan. 1892.

E. LEVASSEUR. *La Population française*. Paris, 1884.

A. NEYMARCK. The distribution of personal property in France. *Stat. Journ.* 1896.

H. PASSY. *On large and small farms and their influence on the social economy including a view of the progress of the division of the soil in France since* 1915. London, 1848.

C. PELLETAN. *Report on the Financial Situation of France*.

POUSSIELGUE. *French National Income*. 1817.

CH. RIST. Article in *Revue de Paris*, Dec. 1915.

L. WELEWSKI. Est. in National Assembly Chambre des Députés. *Journal Officiel*, 22 Dec. 1871.

GERMANY

TH. BALOGH. The national economy of Germany. *Econ. Journ.* 1938.

V. BÖHMISCH. Die Ergebnisse des sächsischen Einkommens-Abschätzungen in den Jahren 1875–77. *Zeitschrift d. kgl. Sächs. Stat. Büros*, 1878.

COLIN CLARK. Internationaler Vergleich der Volkseinkommen. *Weltw. Arch.* 1938.

Dresdner Bank. *The Economic Forces of the World*. Berlin, 1930.

M. J. ELSAS. *Germany's National Income*. (J. M. Keynes, *The Revision of the Treaty*. London, 1922, pp. 81, 82.)

—— Volkseinkommen. *Magazin der Wirtschaft*, Jahrg. 1.

E. ENGEL. Die Klassensteuer und die klassifizierte Einkommensteuer und die Einnahmenverteilung im preussischen Staat in den Jahren 1852–1875. *Zeitschrift d. kgl. Preuss. Stat. Büros*, 1875.

E. FUHRMANN. *Das Volksvermögen und Volkseinkommen im Königreich Sachsen*. Leipzig, 1914.

B. GLEITZE. Der Streit um die Höhe des deutschen Volkseinkommens. *Die Arbeit*, 1930.

Gothaer Almanach. Average income per head in different European States. 1928 edition.

F. Guth. *Die Lehre vom Einkommen in dessen Gesamtzweigen.* Prag, 1869.

K. Helfferich. *Das deutsche Volkseinkommen vor und nach dem Krieg.* Berlin, 1932.

—— Volksvermögen; Volkseinkommen und Steuerlast einst und jetzt. *Weltpolitik und Weltwirtschaft*, Bd. I, 1926. (Since 1926 *Zeitschrift für Geopolitik.*)

Institut für Konjunkturforschung. *Konjunkturstatistisches Jahrbuch.* Berlin.

Journal of the Royal Statistical Society (Editorial). Distribution of incomes in Germany. Account of Engel's Address in the 'Volkswirtschaftliche Gesellschaft', Berlin; probably reprinted in *Volkswirtschaftliche Zeitfragen. Stat. Journ.* 1888.

A. Kühner. Deutschlands Volksvermögen und Volkseinkommen vor dem Krieg und heute. *Wirtschaftswissenschaftliche Vierteljahrshefte.* I. *Zeitschrift des Verbandes katholischer kaufmännischer Vereinigungen Deutschlands.*

A. Lansburgh. Die finanzielle Tragfähigkeit Deutschlands. *Die Bank*, 1919.

F. List. *Das nationale System der politischen Oekonomie.* Stuttgart, 1841.

Magazin der Wirtschaft (Editorial). Das Volkseinkommen nach der Steuerstatistik. *Magazin der Wirtschaft*, 5. Jahrg., Nr. 23, 1929.

R. E. May. Das deutsche Volkseinkommen im Jahre 1900. *Jahrbuch f. Gesetzgebung, Verwaltung und Volkswirtschaft* (Schmoller), 1909.

—— Das deutsche Volkseinkommen und der Zuwachs des deutschen Volksvermögens im Jahre 1907. *Jahrbuch f. Gesetzgebung, Verwaltung und Volkswirtschaft* (Schmoller), 1909.

R. Meerwarth. *Nationalökonomie und Statistik.* 1925.

J. v. Miquel. *Mitteilungen des kgl. Preussischen Finanzministeriums.* Nov.-Dec. 1892.

National Industrial Conference Board. Studies No. 236:

V. Trivanovitch. *Economic Development of Germany under National Socialism.* New York, 1937.

Klara Perls. *Die Einkommensentwicklung in Preussen seit* 1896. Berlin, 1911.

Reichsverband der deutschen Industrie. *Deutsche Wirtschafts- und Finanzpolitik*, Heft 29, 1925.

E. Rogowski. *Das deutsche Volkseinkommen.* Berlin, 1926.

A. Soetbeer. Das gesamte Einkommen und dessen Verteilung im preussischen Staat. *Arbeiterfreund*, 1875.

—— *Umfang und Verteilung des Volkseinkommens im preussischen Staate*, 1872–1878. Leipzig, 1879.

—— Veränderungen in der Zusammensetzung des Volkseinkommens in Grossbritannien. *Vierteljahrsschrift für Volkswirtschaft, Politik und Kulturgeschichte*, 1884.

—— Volkseinkommen im preussischen Staate 1876 und 1888. *Jahrbücher für Nationalökonomie und Statistik* (Conrad), 1889.

Statistisches Reichsamt. *Das deutsche Volkseinkommen vor und nach dem Kriege. Einzelschriften zur Statistik des deutschen Reichs.* Berlin, 1932.

—— *Das Volkseinkommen in den Ländern und preussischen Provinzen.* (Annual since 1932 for 1931.)

A. Wagner. Statistik des Volks- oder Nationaleinkommens. *Bull. de l'Inst. Int. de Stat.* 1905.

W. Winkler. *Statistisches Handbuch für das gesamte Deutschtum.* Berlin, 1927.

—— Statistik des Volkseinkommens. *Handwörterbuch der Staatswissenschaften*, Bd. VIII.

H. Wolff. *Wirtschafts-Statistik. Grundriss zum Studium der Nationalökonomie.* Herausg. v. K. Diehl und P. Mombert. Jena, 1927.

Greece

G. Kafandaris. Minister of Finance Budget, 1927/28. (See Rediadis.)

P. D. Rediadis. The Greek national income and wealth in 1929. *Metron*, June 1930.

G. Sacalis. Private estimate. (See Rediadis.)

S. Skiadas. Estimate, 1890. (See Rediadis.)

X. Zolotas. *National Income of Greece*, 1929. (See Rediadis.)

Hungary

F. v. Fellner. Le revenu national de la Hongrie actuelle. *Bull. de l'Inst. Int. de Stat.* Vol. xxv, Part III, 1931.

D. de Laky. *The National Income of Hungary*, 1924/25–1936/37. London, 1938.

M. Matolcsy and St Varga. *The National Income of Hungary*, 1924/5–1936/7. London, 1938.

India

Fred. J. Atkinson. A statistical review of the income and wealth of British India. *Stat. Journ.* 1902.

G. Findlay Shirras. India's national income. *Revue de l'Inst. Int. de Stat.* Vol. 1936, Jan. 1937.

Ireland

T. J. Kiernan. The national income of the Irish Free State in 1926. *Econ. Journ.* March 1933.

C. H. Oldham. Public finances of Ireland. In 'The Fiscal Relations of Britain and Ireland'. Conference of the Royal Economic Society, Jan. 1912.

Italy

A. Balbi. *Bilancia politica del Globo.* Padua, 1837.

C. Gini. L'évaluation de la richesse et du revenu de l'Italie avant et après la guerre. *Int. Inst. of Statistics*, xix Sess. 1930.

L. Meliadò. Il reddito privato degli Italiani nel 1928. *Metron*, 1932.

J. Tivaroni. *Patrimonio e Reddito di alcune Nazione Civili.* Turin-Rome, 1901.

Wiseman. Article in *Nuova Antologia de Scienze, Lettere ed Arti.* Florence, 1915.

Japan

Bureau of Statistics of the Cabinet. *The estimated National Income of Japan in* 1925.

K. Mori. Estimate of the national wealth and income of Japan proper. *Bull. de l'Inst. Int. de Stat.* Vol. xxv, Pt II, 1931.

Charles V. Sale. Some statistics of Japan. *Stat. Journ.* 1911.

S. Shiomi. Japan's national income. *Kyoto University Economic Review*, 1930.

—— Japan's wealth and income. *Kyoto University Economic Review*, 1930.

—— Survey of the distribution of the peoples' income in the light of the household rate. *Kyoto University Economic Review*, 1934.

Netherlands

C. A. Verijn-Stuart. Volksvermögen und Volkseinkommen in den Niederlanden. *Bull. de l'Inst. Int. de Stat.* 1931.

Russia

Amtorg Trading Corporation. *Economic Statistics of the Soviet Union.* New York, 1928.

S. Prokopovitch. *The World War and National Economy.* Moskow, 1917.

Spain

Corriani. *Economista,* Aug. 1918.

Sweden

E. Lindahl and others. *National Income of Sweden.* London, 1937.

Sweden. *Officiella statistik Folkräkningen,* 1911–1920. Stockholm, 1929.

Switzerland

P. Mori. Das Schweizerische Volkseinkommen. *Zeitschrift für Schweizerische Statistik und Volkswirtschaft,* 1926.

Union of S. Africa

R. A. Lehfeldt. *The National Revenue of South Africa.* 1922.

United States

Bankers' Trust Company of New York City. *What is my share?*

H. E. Fisk. Some new estimates of national income. *American Econ. Review,* March 1930.

W. I. King. Das Einkommen der Vereinigten Staaten. See H. Meyer, *Die Wirtschaftstheorie der Gegenwart.*

—— *The Wealth and Income of the People of the U.S.A.* 1915.

S. Kuznets. National income. *Encycl. of the Social Sciences.*

—— *National Income in the United States* 1929–1935. U.S.A. Department of Commerce.

A. R. March. Taxable income in the United States in 1923. *Economic World,* 1929.

R. F. Martin. National Industrial Conference Board. No. 227. *National Income and its Elements.* New York, 1936.

—— National Industrial Conference Board. No. 241. *National Income in the United States,* 1799–1938. New York, 1939.

National Bureau of Economic Research, New York.

National Income Totals. Bulletin 35.

W. I. King. *The National Income and its Purchasing Power.* Publication No. 15. 1930.

S. Kuznets. *National Income,* 1929–1932. Bulletin 49. 1934.

National Income, 1919–1935. Bulletin 66. 1937.

National Income and Capital Formation. Publication No. 32. 1937.

National Income and its Composition. Publication No. 40. 1941.

Maurice Leven and W. I. King. *Income in the Various States: its Sources and Distribution,* 1919, 1920 and 1921. Publication No. 7. 1925.

W. C. Mitchell. *Business Cycles: the Problem and its Setting.* Publication No. 10. 1927.

W. C. Mitchell, W. I. King, F. R. Macaulay and O. W. Knauth. *Income in the United States, its Amount and Distribution.* Vol. 1, 1921, Vols. 2 and 3, 1922.

S. NEARING. *Income: An examination of the returns for services rendered and from property owned in the U.S.* New York, 1915.

R. STONE. Review of S. Kuznets' *National Income and Capital Formation.* (See National Bureau.) *Econ. Journ.* 1938.

U.S.A. Department of Commerce. The national income, 1929–1932. *Survey of Current Business,* Feb. 1934.

—— ROBERT F. MARTIN. The national income, 1933. *Survey of Current Business.* 1935.

—— Bureau of Foreign and Domestic Commerce. *National Income in the United States,* 1929–1935. Washington, 1936.

—— ROBERT R. NATHAN. Expansion in the national income (continued in 1935). *Survey of Current Business,* July 1936.

—— —— National income increases five billion dollars in 1934. *Survey of Current Business,* Aug. 1935.

—— —— National income in 1936 largest of recovery period. *Survey of Current Business,* June 1937.

—— —— National income 1937 largest since 1929. *Survey of Current Business,* June 1938.

—— —— The national income produced, 1929–1934. *Survey of Current Business,* Nov. 1935.

U.S.A. Treasury Department. Bureau of Internal Revenue. *Statistics of Income.* Reports of Individual and Corporation tax returns. *Annually.*

See also A I. H. MAYER. *Die Wirtschaftstheorie der Gegenwart.*

A I *b*. *Higher Incomes*

ANONYMOUS. The super-tax and some other branches of inland revenue. *Economist,* Oct. 1913.

C. HEISS. Die grossen Einkommen in Deutschland und ihre Zunahme in den letzten Jahrzehnten. *Hirth's Annalen,* 1893.

LORD STAMP. The influence of the price level on the higher incomes. *Stat. Journ.* 1936.

A I *c*. *Incomes below Tax Limit.*

A. L. BOWLEY. Report of a Committee of the British Association. The amount and distribution of income (other than wages) below the income-tax exemption limit in the U.K. *Journ. of the Stat. Soc.* 1910–11.

VISCOUNT GOSCHEN. The increase of moderate incomes. *Stat. Journ.* 1887.

P. I. STRAYER. *The Taxation of Small Incomes.* New York, 1939.

A II. *DIVISION OF INCOME. THEORY*

UNITED KINGDOM

A. L. BOWLEY. *The Change in the Distribution of the National Income,* 1880–1913. Oxford, 1920.

—— *The Division of the Product of Industry.* An Analysis of National Capital before the War. Oxford, 1919.

EDWIN CANNAN. The division of incomes. *Quart. Journ. of Econ.* 1905.

—— Review of A. L. Bowley, *The Division of the Product. Econ. Journ.* 1919.

R. McG. CARSLAW and P. E. GRAVES. The Labour Bill and output on arable farms. *Stat. Journ.* 1935.

COLIN CLARK. How the consumer used his £5,000,000,000 this year. *Marketing Survey of the United Kingdom*, 1936.

H. CLAY. Distribution of capital in England and Wales. *Trans. of the Manchester Stats. Soc.* 1924–25.

MYRA CURTIS. National income and expenditure and the measurement of savings. *Econ. Journ.* 1935.

HUGH DALTON. *Some Aspects of the Inequality of Incomes in Modern Communities.* L.S.E. Studies in Econ. and Pol. Sci. No. 59, 1925.

CHARLES DAVENANT. *An Essay upon the probable methods of making people gainers in the balance of trade.* 1699.

Fabian Tracts: revised by MAX BROWN. *Facts for Socialists showing the distribution of the National Income and its results.* No. 5, 14th ed. 1937.

A. E. FEAVEARYEAR. Spending the national income. *Econ. Journ.* March 1931.

—— Spending the national income. *Econ. Journ.* 1931.

Sir ROBERT GIFFEN. The expenditure of national capital. *Inst. of Bankers' Journ.* 1901.

R. JONES. *An Essay on the Distribution of Wealth and on the Sources of Taxation.* 1831.

WALTER LAYTON. Some statistical aspects of the labout unrest. *Economist*, Aug. 1911.

W. H. MALLOCK. *The Landlords and the National Income*, a chart showing the proportion borne by the rent of the landlords to the gross income of the people. 1884.

MERCATANTE. Profits, Wages and Taxes. Answer to Layton's 'Some statistical aspects of the labour unrest'. *Economist*, Sept. 1911.

Sir L. G. CHIOZZA MONEY. La distribution de la richesse en Angleterre. *Revue Econ. Intern.* Oct. 1908.

A. C. PIGOU and COLIN CLARK. *The Economic Position of Great Britain.* L. and C.E.S. Special Memoranda No. 43, April 1936.

NASSAU SENIOR. *Political Economy.* 3rd ed. 1845.

W. SMART. *The Distribution of Income.* 3rd ed. 1923.

CHARLES B. SPAHR. *An Essay on the Present Distribution of Wealth in the United Kingdom.* New York, 1896.

AUSTRIA

F. LEITER. *Die Verteilung des Einkommens in Oesterreich.* Wien, 1907.

E. v. PHILIPPOVICH. Die Regelung der Einkommensverteilung durch die Wirtschaftspolitik. *Zeitschrift für Volkswirtschaft, Sozialpolitik und Verwaltung*, XVL, 2, 1907.

FRANCE

J. BERTILLON. Répartition de la richesse en France selon l'âge des habitants. *Journ. de la Société de Stat. de Paris*, 1909.

E. CHATELAIN. La répartition de la richesse en France. *Revue Sociale*, Oct. 1909.

J. DITENS. *Essai comparatif sur la formation et la distribution du revenu de la France en* 1815 *et* 1835. Printed 1843.

A. DE FOVILLE. *Le Morcellement.* Paris, 1885.

—— La statistique de la division de la propriété en France et dans la Grande Bretagne. *Bull. de l'Inst. Int. de Stat.* I, 1886.

A. LEROI-BEAULIEU. *Essai sur la Répartition des Richesses.* Paris, 1883.

P. LEROY-BEAULIEU. Les successions et la répartition de la richesse en France. *Économiste français*, 5 and 12 Dec. 1908.

Germany

Alfred Amonn. *Grundzüge der Volkswohlstandslehre.* I. Teil. Der Prozess der Wohlstandsbildung. Jena, 1916.

E. Angelopoulos. *Die Einkommensverteilung im Lichte der Einkommenssteuerstatistik.* Leipzig, 1931.

Fr. Kleinwachter. *Das Einkommen und seine Verteilung.* Leipzig, 1896.

C. Landauer. Theorie der Verteilung. See H. Mayer, *Die Wirtschaftstheorie der Gegenwart.*

W. Lexis. Verteilung. *Handwörterbuch der Staatswissenschaften,* 3. Aufl. Bd. viii, Jena, 1911.

R. Michaelis. *Die Gliederung der Gesellschaft nach dem Wohlstand auf Grund der neueren deutschen Einkommens- und Wohnungsstatistik.* Leipzig, 1878.

Th. Mithoff. Das Einkommen und seine Verteilung. In *Schönberg's Handbuch der polit. Oekonomie,* Volkswirtschaftslehre i. Tübingen, 1896.

C. Rodbertus-Jagetzow. *Zur Beleuchtung der sozialen Frage.* Berlin, 1890.

G. Schmoller. Die Einkommensverteilung in alter und neuer Zeit. *Jahrbücher für Gesetzgebung, Verwaltung und Volkswirtschaft* (Schmoller), 1895.

A. Soetbeer. Die Klassen- und Einkommenssteuer und die Einkommensverteilung im preussischen Staate. *Concordia,* 1875.

—— Das souveräne Gesetz der Preisbildung. Ein Beitrag zur Kritik der Einkommensverteilung und zur Lehre von der Steuerprogression. *Hirth's Annalen,* 1875.

A. Wagner. Weitere statistische Untersuchungen über die Verteilung des Volkseinkommens in Preussen. *Zeitschrift des Preuss. Stat. Landesamts,* 1904.

Hungary

F. v. Fellner. *Die Verteilung des Volksvermögens und Volkseinkommens der Länder der ungarischen heiligen Krone zwischen dem heutigen Ungarn und den Sukzessionsstaaten.* Ferrara (no date).

Italy

C. Bresciani-Turoni. *Influenze dell' inflazione cartacea sulla distribuzione della richezza in Germania.* Triest, 1925.

V. Furlan. Neue Literature zur Einkommensverteilung in Italien. *Jahrbuch für Nationalökonomie und Statistik,* 3. Folge, Bd. xlii (Conrad).

C. Gini. Il diverso accrescimento delle classi sociali e la concentrazione della richezza. *Giornale degli Economisti,* 1900.

F. Vinci. Nuovi contributi allo studi della distribuzione dei redditi. *Giornale degli Economisti,* 1921.

—— Recenti redute sulle legge di distribuzione dei redditi. In R. Bacchi, *Problemi di finanza fascista.* 1937.

Japan

S. Shiomi. Form of the distribution of our national income. *Kyoto University Economic Review,* 1932.

Norway

A. N. Kiaer. Indtaegs- og Formnesforbold i Norge. *Statsokonomsk Tideskrif,* 1892–93. Distribution of Property and Incomes in Norway. Review in *Stat. Journ.* 1895.

A. N. KIAER. La répartition des revenus et fortunes privée. *Bull de l'Inst. Int. de Stat.* Vols. XIX, XX.

—— Répartition sociale des revenus. *Bull. de l'Inst. Int. de Stat.* Vol. XVIII, Pt I, 1909.

UNITED STATES

E. R. BECKWITH. Inequalities in the Distribution of Income, their Meaning and Measurement. Typewritten Harvard thesis. 1924.

A. G. HART. *How the National Income is divided.* Chicago, 1937.

W. I. KING. *Wealth and Income of the People of the U.S.A.* New York, published 1915, reprint 1917.

H. G. MOULTON. *Income Distribution under Capitalism.* 1930.

National Bureau of Economic Research, Bulletin 59:

S. KUZNETS. *Income Originating in Nine Basic Industries,* 1919–1934. Printed 1936.

F. H. STREIGHTOFF. *The Distribution of Incomes in the United States.* Studies in History, Economics and Public Law. Columbia University, New York, 1912.

See also A I. L. v. BORTKIEWICZ. Die Grenznutzenlehre als Grundlage einer ultraliberalen Wirtschaftspolitik.

A I. J. M. KEYNES. *The General Theory of Employment, Interest and Money.*

A I. A. LORIA. *The Economic Synthesis.*

A I. H. MAYER. *Die Wirtschaftstheorie der Gegenwart.*

A I. A. R. J. TURGOT. *Réflections sur la Formation et la Distribution des Richesses.*

A III. *NATIONAL WEALTH*

UNITED KINGDOM

ANONYMOUS, probably NEWMARCH. The annual accumulation of capital in the United Kingdom. *Economist,* 12 and 19 Dec. 1863; *Stat. Journ.* 1864.

ANONYMOUS. Growth of wealth and capital. *Economist,* 1911.

M. S. BOOKER. Review of S. Kuznets, *Commodity Flow and Capital Formation,* New York, 1939. *Economica,* May 1939.

A. L. BOWLEY. *National Progress in Wealth and Trade since* 1882. 1904.

British Association. Report 1910 ré National Wealth. See A. L. Bowley's Report, *Stat. Journ.* 1910–11.

H. CAMPION. *Public and Private Property in Great Britain.* London, 1939.

G. W. DANIELS and H. CAMPION. *The Distribution of National Capital.* Manchester, 1936.

P. H. DOUGLAS. An estimate of the growth of capital in the United Kingdom, 1865–1909. *Journ. of Economics and Business History,* Vol. II, 1929–30.

M. J. ELSAS. An index of prosperity. *Statist,* 1934, 1936.

RICHARD T. ELY. *Property and Contract in their relation to the Distribution of Wealth.* 1914.

Fabian Tracts. *Capital and Land.* 1890 (?).

Sir ALFRED FLUX. Review of Pareto's *Cours d'Économie Politique,* Vol. II. *Econ. Journ.* March 1897.

Sir ROBERT GIFFEN. *The Growth of Capital.* 1889.

A. E. FEAVEARYEAR. Capital accumulation and unemployment. *Econ. Journ.* June 1936.

W. J. HARRIS and K. A. LAKE. Estimates of the realisable wealth of the United Kingdom based mostly on the estate duty returns. *Stat. Journ.* 1906.

A. Hooke. *An Essay on the National Debt and the National Capital.* 1750.

J. M. Keynes. Fluctuations in net investment in the United States. *Econ. Journ.* Sept. 1936.

J. Landerdale (Maitland). *An Inquiry into the Nature and Origin of Public Wealth.* Edinburgh, 1804.

Leone Levi. *History of British Commerce.* London, 1880.

J. R. MacCulloch. *A descriptive and statistical account of the British Empire, exhibiting its extent, physical capacities, population, industry and civil and religious institutions.* 3rd ed. London, 1847.

W. H. Mallock. *Classes and Masses of Wealth, Wages and Welfare in the United Kingdom.* 1896.

—— *The Nation as a Business Firm.* London, 1910.

Sir L. G. Chiozza Money. *The Nation's Wealth. Will it endure?* 1914.

—— *Riches and Poverty.* 1914.

M. G. Mulhall. *Dictionary of Statistics.* 1892.

—— *Industries and Wealth of Nations.* 1896.

J. S. Nicholson. The living capital of the United Kingdom. *Econ. Journ.* 1891.

Sir William Petty. A gross estimate of the wealth of England (endorsed 'a gross estimate of the value of the lands, goods and people of England', 1685). *The Petty Papers*, I, 1927.

—— *Verbum Sapenti and the Value of the People.* The Economic Writings of Sir William Petty. Cambridge, 1899.

—— *Britannia Languens or a disclosure of Trade.* 1680.

G. D. Rokeling. The measurement of national prosperity. *Economist*, 6 Oct. 1928.

Nassau Senior. *On the National Property and on the prospects of the present administration and of their successors.* 3rd ed. London, 1835.

Lord Stamp. The Economic Distribution of the National Capital. In L. D. Stamp and S. H. Beaver, *An Introduction to Stratigraphy: The British Isles*, 2nd ed. 1934.

—— An estimate of the capital wealth of the United Kingdom in private hands. *Econ. Journ.* 1918.

—— Inheritance as an economic factor. *Econ. Journ.* Sept. 1926.

—— The national capital. *Stat. Journ.* 1931.

—— *The National Capital.* 1937.

—— *Wealth and Taxable Capacity.* 1922.

—— The Wealth and Income of the Chief Powers, 1914. In *Current Problems in Finance and Government.* 1924.

U.K. Select Committee on Increase of Wealth (War) Report. Minutes of Evidence, Appendices, B.P.P. 1920, VII (102). Evidences: A. H. Kilner, A. J. Hobson, Lord Stamp and F. W. P. Lawrence.

—— *Increase of Wealth (War).* Memorandum of the Board of Inland Revenue on the Methods of Graduation, on the practicability of levying a duty on War-time Wealth, etc. (different Memorandums). B.P.P. 1920, XXVII (275).

—— *Suggested Taxation of War-time Increases of Wealth.* Memoranda submitted by the Board of Inland Revenue to the Select Committee of the House of Commons on Increase of Wealth (War). B.P.P. 1920, XXVII, Cmd. (594).

Ch. de Varigny. *Les grands Fortunes aux États-Unis et en Angleterre.* Paris, 1889.

J. C. Wedgwood. *The Economics of Inheritance.* L.S.E. Studies No. 98. 1929.

LORD WELBY. The progress of the United Kingdom from the War of the French Revolution to 1913. *Stat. Journ.* 1915.

M. R. WEYERMANN. National Wealth. *Encyclopedia of the Social Sciences*, 1933.

AUSTRIA

F. v. FELLNER. *Ein Beitrag zur Frage der Schätzung des Volksvermögens.* 1930.

—— L'évaluation de la richesse nationale. *Bull. de l'Inst. Int. de Stat.* Vol. XIII, Pt II, 1902.

—— Das Volksvermögen Oesterreich und Ungarns. *Bull. de l'Inst. Int. de Stat.* Vol. XX, Pt II, 1913.

J. GRUNTZEL. *Die Lehre vom Volksreichtum.* Wien, 1926.

K. TH. v. INAMA-STERNEGG. Die Ergebnisse der Erbschaftssteuer in Oesterreich in den Jahren 1889–91 und ihre Bedeutung für die Schätzung des Nationalvermögens. *Stat. Monatsschrift*, Wien, 1893.

F. NEUMANN-SPALLART. Mesure des variations de l'état économique et social des peuples. *Bull. de l'Inst. Int. de Stat.* 1887.

J. v. ROSCHMANN-HOERBURG. *Veröffentlichungen des Stat. Landesamts der Bukowina.* Heft 2–6.

J. v. SODEN. *Die Nationalökonomie. Ein philosophischer Versuch über die Quelle des Nationalreichtums und über die Mittel zu dessen Beförderung.* Wien, 1815.

BELGIUM

F. BAUDHUIN. *Le Capital de la Belgique et le rendement de son industrie avant la guerre.* Louvain, 1924.

V. FALLON. La richesse de la Belgique 10 ans après la déclaration de guerre. *Revue cath., soc. et jur. Brussels*, Dec. 1924, Jan. 1925.

CZECHO-SLOVAKIA

F. BIBL. Évaluation de la richesse nationale d'avant-guerre. *Revue Stat. Tchéchoslovaque*, 1927 and 1928.

FRANCE

VICOMTE G. D'AVENEL. *La fortune privée à travers sept siècles.* Paris, 1904.

DUC D'AYEN (Comte de Noailles). Estimates de la richesse en France et en Angleterre. *Journ. des Économistes*, May 1875.

—— *Revenu salaire et capital, leur solidarité.* 1872.

M. BLOCK. *Statistique de la France.* Paris, 1875.

C. COLSON. *Cours d'Économie Politique.* Paris, 1918.

AD. COSTE. Études statistiques sur la richesse comparative des départments de la France. *Journ. de la Société de Stat. de Paris.* Feb. 1891.

—— L'évaluation de la fortune privée en France. *Journ. de la Société de Stat. de Paris*, 1901.

—— L'évaluation de la richesse nationale. *Journ. de la Société de Stat. de Paris*, 1901.

A. A. COURNOT. *Principes de la Théorie des Richesses.* 2nd ed. 1863.

P. DOUMER. La fortune de la France. *Je Sais Tout*, 15 June 1909.

S. FAUCONNIER. Les éléments de la fortune publique. *Économiste français*, 1879.

E. FOURNIER DE FLAIX. L'accroisement de la richesse depuis 1789 en France, en Angleterre et dans d'autres états. *Journ. de la Société de Stat. de Paris*, 1885.

—— The national wealth of France compared with other countries. *Stat. Journ.* 1886.

A. de Foville. La fortune de la France. *Journ. de la Société de Stat. de Paris*, 1883.

—— De quelques dévaluations récentes du capital national. *Économiste français*, 7 and 14 Dec. 1878; 4 and 18 Jan., 15 Feb. 1879.

—— Richesse. A. B. Say, *Dictionnaire du Finance*. Paris, 1894.

—— La richesse en France. *L'Opinion*, 23 Jan. 1909.

—— La richesse en France. *Revue Économique Internationale*, Vol. III, Pt 2, 1906.

—— La richesse en France et à l'étranger. *Journ. de la Société de Stat. de Paris*, 1893.

—— La richesse publique à l'étranger et en France. *Économiste français*, 12 Aug., 23 Sept., 21 Oct. 1882.

—— The wealth of France and other countries. Translation from *Dictionnaire de Finance. Stat. Journ.* 1893.

C. Gide and W. Oualid. *Le bilan de la guerre pour la France*. Paris, 1931.

E. de Girardin. *L'impôt*. 1853. See A. de Foville, 'The wealth of France and other countries', 1893.

Goudchaux. 1848. See A. de Foville, 'The wealth of France and other countries', 1893.

Y. Guyot. Évaluation de la fortune privée en France d'après les éléments fiscaux. *Bull. de l'Inst. Int. de Stat.* Vol. XIV, Pt III. Berlin, 1905.

A. de Lavergne and L. P. Henry. *La Richesse de la France, Fortune et Revenus Privées*. Paris, 1918.

A. Leroy-Beaulieu. Les fortunes en France d'après les dèclarations successorales. *Économiste français*, 25 July 1903; 5 and 12 Dec. 1908.

J. Lescure. *L'Epargne en France*. Paris, 1914.

E. Michel. *La Propriété. Évaluation de la fortune privée. Enquête sur la propriété non bâtie et bâtie. Enquête agricole*. Paris-Nancy, 1908.

S. Mony. *Étude sur le Travail*. 2nd ed. 1881.

H. C. Moulton and C. Lewis. See Brookings Institution, *The French Debt Problem*.

C. P. L'augmentation de la fortune de la France depuis 1826. Correspondence in *Économiste français*, 7 April 1877.

Peytral. Projected Law of 30 Oct. 1888, Appendices. Chambre des Députés.

R. Pupin. *La Richesse de la France devant la guerre*. Paris, 1916.

—— *La Richesse privée et les finances françaises de l'avant-guerre et l'après-guerre*. Paris, 1919.

A. Raffalovich. Frankreichs Nationalvermögen. *Bankarchiv*, 1911.

E. Reclus. *Nouvelle Géographie universelle*, Vol. II: La France. Paris, 1877.

J. H. Schnitzler. *Création de la Richesse*. Paris, 1842.

Talandier. *Journal Officiel*, 29 Jan. 1878.

E. Théry. *La Fortune Publique de la France*. Paris, 1911.

—— *Les progrès économiques de la France; Bilan du régime douanier de* 1892. Paris, 1908.

—— La situation économique et financière de la France avant, pendant et après la guerre. *Économiste Européen*, 18 Jan.–22 Feb. 1918.

H. le Tresor de la Roque. *Les Finances de la Republique. Les Chambres Prodigues*. Paris, 1884.

V. Turquan. Évaluation de la fortune privée de la France. *Revue d'Économie politique*. 1900.

B. Vacher. La fortune nationale en France. *Journ. de la Société de Stat. de Paris*, 1878.

L. Vacher. La fortune publique de la France. *Économiste français*, Dec. 1878.

E. Vignes. Estimate of Personal Property. See A. de Foville, 'The wealth of France and other countries', 1893.

Germany

J. W. Angell. *The Recovery of Germany*. Publication of the Council of Foreign Relations. Yale Univ. New Haven, 1929.

H. Benson and W. Genzmer. *Die Folgen der Markentwertung für uns und die andern*. Leipzig, 1923.

G. Colm and H. Neisser. Kapitalbildung und Steuersystem. *Verhandlungen und Gutachten der Konferenz von Eilsen*. Berlin, 1930.

Dresdner Bank. *Die wirtschaftlichen Kräfte Deutschlands*, 2. Aufl. Berlin, 1914.

M. J. Elsas. An Index of Prosperity (*Wohlstandsindices*). Blazek and Bergmann, Frankfurt a.M., bimonthly.

—— Wohlstandsindex u. sozialer Wohlstand. *Archiv f. Soz. Wissenschaft u. Soz. Politik*, 1928.

K. Elster. *Vom 'Volksvermögen'. Eine erkenntnistheoretische Studie*. Moskau, 1934.

G. Evert. Das deutsche Volksvermögen und sein jährliches Wachstum. *Die Woche*, 1913.

A. Friedmann. Die Wohlstandsentwicklung in Preussen 1891–1911. *Jahrbücher für Nationalökonomie und Statistik* (Conrad), 1914.

Ph. Geyer. Untersuchungen über Quellen und Umfang des allgemeinen Wohlstands in Deutschland. *Jahrbuch für Gesetzgebung, Verwaltung und Volkswirtschaft* (Schmoller), 1880.

K. Helfferich. *Deutschlands Volkswohlstand*, 1888–1913. Berlin, 1917.

A. Hesse. Das deutsche Volksvermögen. *Jahrbücher für Nationalökonomie und Statistik*, Jena, 1915.

J. Jastrow. *Deutschlands Volksvermögen im Krieg*. Berlin, 1919.

G. Kreiser und B. Bening. Kapitalbildung und Investitionen in der deutschen Volkswirtschaft, 1924–28. *Vierteljahrshefte zur Konjunkturforschung*, Sonderheft 22, Berlin, 1931.

L. Krug. *Betrachtungen über den Nationalreichtum des preussischen Staates*. 1805.

R. Kuczynski. Review of Helfferich, *Deutschlands Volkswohlstand. Allg. Stat. Archiv*, 1914.

W. Lexis. Volksvermögen. *Handwörterbuch der Staatswissenschaften*. 3. Aufl., Bd. viii. Jena, 1911.

R. Liefmann. *Vom Reichtum der Nationen*. Karlsruhe, 1925.

G. Losch. Lebendes und totes Volksvermögen. *Allg. Stat. Archiv*, 1898.

Prinz Fr. zu Löwenstein. *Volksvermögen und Kriegsentschädigung*. Berlin, 1918.

G. v. Mayr. Volksvermögen, Staatsvermögen und Statistik. *Allg. Stat. Archiv*, Bd. x, 1916–17.

E. Philippi. Schwankungen des Volkswohlstands im deutschen Reich. *Preuss. Jahrbücher*, 1883–85.

F. Popp. *Die Bedeutung der Volksvermögensrechnungen, ihr Gegenstand, ihre Methoden*. Bayreuth, 1929.

Reichs-Kredit-Gesellschaft. Aktiengesellschaft. *Deutschlands wirtschaftliche Lage an der Jahreswende*, 1927/28.

H. Ricken. *Das Volksvermögen*. Heidelberg, 1923.

H. Ritschl. See Walter Lotz, 'Kapitalbildung und Besteuerung'.

W. Röpke. Die Theorie der Kapitalbildung. In *Recht und Staat in Geschichte und Gegenwart*. Tübingen, 1929.

R. Rouse. Une évaluation allemande de la richesse publique de l'Allemagne. *Journ. des Économistes*, 1917.

A. Salz. Kapital, Kapitalformen, Kapitalbildung, Kapitaldynamik. *Grundriss der Sozialökonomie*, iv. Tübingen, 1925.

R. Schall. *Volksvermögen und Volkseinkommen. Das Königreich Württemberg.* Stuttgart, 1884.

H. Schmidt. *Der Wohlstandsindex im Dawes-Gutachten.* Erlangen, 1926.

E. Schnapper-Arndt. *Die Wohlstandsentwicklung in Deutschland. Denkschriftenband zur Reichsfinanzreform zusammengestellt im Reichsschatzamt.* Berlin, 1908.

R. Schnaudt. *Zur Methodologie des internationalen Steuerbelastungs-Vergleichs.* Köln, 1928.

S. Schott. *Der Volkswohlstand im Königreich Sachsen.* Leipzig, 1890.

A. Steinmann-Bücher. *Deutschlands Volksvermögen im Krieg.* 1916.

—— 350 *Milliarden deutsches Volksvermögen.* Berlin, 1909.

—— *Das reiche Deutschland. Ein Wehrbeitrag.* Berlin, 1914.

A. Wagner. Denkschrift zur Begründung des Entwurfes eines Gesetzes betreffend Aenderungen im Finanzwesen. III. Teil. Materialen zur Beurteilung der Wohlstandsentwicklung Deutschlands im letzten Menschenalter. *Zeitschrift des preuss. Stat. Bureaus*, 1904.

E. Walter. Wandlungen der deutschen Kapitalbildung. *Deutsche Sparkassenzeitung*, Berlin, 20 Sept. 1928.

F. Weinschenck. Das Volksvermögen. *Sammlung nationalökon. und stat. Abhandlungen*, Bd. xiii, 1896.

M. R. Weyermann. Sozialökonomische Begriffsentwicklung des Vermögens und Volksvermögens. *Jahrbücher für Nationalökonomie und Statistik* (Conrad), 1916.

—— Volksvermögen und Staatskredit in Krieg und Frieden. *Finanz und volkswirtschaftliche Zeitfragen*, Nr. 47. 1918.

Greece

P. D. Rediadis. The Greek national income and wealth in 1929. *Metron*, 1930.

Hungary

F. v. Fellner. La fortune nationale de la Hongrie actuelle. *Bull. de l'Inst. Int. de Stat.* Vol. xxiv, Pt II, 1930.

India

J. M. Datta. A wealth survey for Bengal. *Mysore Econ. Journ.* April 1934.

K. T. Shah and K. J. Khambata. *The Wealth and Taxable Capacity of India.* London, 1924.

Italy

R. Benini. Quote successorie di alcune specie di ricchezza. *Rendiconti della R. Acc. dei Lincei*, Rome, Feb. 1909.

C. Bresciani-Turoni. *La Ricchezza della Città.* Università di Palermo, 1912.

M. N. Colajamni. L'évaluation de la fortune de l'Italie. *Nuova Antologia*, 16 April 1917.

G. Solinas Cossu. Valore dei beni transferiti per successione e donazione nel quindicennio 1885–1899/1900. (Contributo allo studio sulla probabile ricchezza privata d'Italie.) *Boll. di Statistica, e di Legislazione comparata*, 1900.

A. degli Espinosa. La ricchezza privata degli Italiani, 1928. *Metron*, June 1929.

A. Garelli. *La Proprietà sociale*. Milano, 1898.

C. Gini. *L'Ammontare e la Composizione della Ricchezza delle Nazioni*. Turin, 1914.

—— La determinazione della ricchezza e del reddito delle nazioni nel dopo guerra e il loro confronto col periodo prebellico. *Bull. de l'Inst. Int. de Stat.* I, 1931.

—— Ueber Wohlstandsverteilung. *Deutsches stat. Zentralblatt*, 1911.

—— *La Ricchezza comparata delle Nazioni*. Milan, 1926.

D. Maroi. *Come si calcola e a quanto ammonta la Ricchezza d'Italia e delle altre principali Nazioni*. Rome, 1919.

G. Mortara. Intorno al calcola della ricchezza privata dell' Italia. *Giornale degli Economisti*, 1909.

F. S. Nitti. *La Ricchezza dell' Italia*. Torino-Rome, 1905.

M. Pantaleoni. Dell' ammontare probabile della ricchezza privata in Italia, 1872–1889. *Giornale degli Economisti*, 1890.

—— Dell' ammontare probabile della ricchezza privata in Italia. *Rassegna Italiana*, Rome, 1884.

—— Nota sul calcolo della ricchezza privata fatto L. Princivalle. *Scritti varii de Economia*, Series III, Rome, 1910.

—— Delle regioni d' Italia in ordine allo loro ricchezza ed al loro carico tributario. *Giornale degli Economisti*, Jan. 1891.

E. Porru. La concentrazione della ricchezza nelle diverse regioni d' Italia. *Studi Econ. Giurid. R. Università di Cagliari*. 1912.

Luigi Princivalle. Il calcolo della ricchezza privata. *Riforma Sociale*, 1909.

—— *La Ricchezza Privata in Italia*. Naples, 1909.

—— Review of M. N. Colajamni, 'L'évaluation de la fortune de l'Italie.' *Journ. des Economistes*, Aug. 1917.

Relazione della Amministrazione del Demanio. *La Ricchezza in rapporto alle successioni e donazioni*. Rome, 1887.

C. Santoro. *L' Italia nei suoi Progressi Economici de* 1860 *al* 1910. Printed 1911.

F. Savorgnan. L' ammontare e la composizione della ricchezza in Italia e nelle sue regioni. *Rivista Italiana di Sociologia*, 1916.

E. Sella. *La Vita della Ricchezza*. Turin, 1910.

G. Sensini. *Le Variazioni dello Stato Economico d' Italia*. Rome, 1904.

Japan

Bureau of Statistics of the Cabinet. *The Estimated National Wealth of Japan in* 1924. (Mentioned by Mori, *Bull. de l'Inst. Int. de Stat.* Vol. xxv, Pt II, 1931.)

Bureau of Statistics of the Cabinet:

Kokuseiin. *The Statistics of National Wealth before and after the Great War*. (Mentioned by Mori, *Bull. de l'Inst. Int. de Stat.* Vol. xxv, Pt II, 1931.)

Jgaraschi and Takahashi. *National Wealth of Japan*. 1906.

S. Shiomi. Interrelation between the wealth and the density of population in Japan. *Kyoto University Economic Review*, 1931.

—— On the national wealth of Japan in the year 1930. *Kyoto University Economic Review*, 1934.

—— On Japan's national wealth and income. *Kyoto University Economic Review*, July 1933.

Mexico

Official statistics of national wealth.

Netherlands

Boissevain. *Netherlands Statistische Ufficiale*, or *Bulletin de Statistique du Ministère de Finance*, Oct. 1892. See A. de Foville, 'The wealth of France and other countries'.

Russia

Economic Survey. Ekonomichestve Obozreme. *National Wealth of the U.S.S.R.* Jan. 1937.

U.S.S.R. Handbook, London, 1936.

Spain

Banco Urquijo. *La riqueza y el progreso de Espana.*

A. Barthe. Essai d'évaluation de la richesse de l'Espagne. *Journ. de la Société de Stat. de Paris*, May 1917.

A. Borrego. *Der Nationalreichtum Spaniens.* 1834.

Sweden

P. J. Fahlbeck. L'évaluation de la richesse nationale de la Suède. *Bull. de l'Inst. Int. de Stat.* Vienne, 1913, Vol. xx, Pt II.

—— La richesse nationale de la Suède. *Bull. de l'Inst. Int. de Stat.* Vienne, 1892.

Switzerland

F. Buomberger. Vermögensverhältnisse in Stadt und Landschaft Freiburg im Jahre 1845. *Journal de Stat. Suisse. Zeitschrift für schweiz. Statistik*, 1896.

M. Fahrländer. *Das Volksvermögen der Schweiz.* Basel, 1919.

C. Sergeev. *Die Verteilung der Güter in einigen Kantonen der Schweiz.* Basel, 1889.

M. R. Weyermann–W. Eggenschwyler. Zum Begriff des Volksvermögens. Replik und Duplik. *Zeitschrift für schweiz. Statistik und Volkswirtschaft*, Heft 4, 1916.

M. R. Weyermann. Zum Begriff des Volksvermögens. Erkenntnistheoretischer Beitrag zur nationalökonomischen Begriffslehre. *Zeitschrift für schweiz. Statistik und Volkswirtschaft*, Bern, 1916.

United States

Brookings Institution. Institute of Economics, Publication No. 59:

H. G. Moulton. *The Formation of Capital.* Washington, 1935. (Pt III of the 'Distribution of Wealth and Income'.)

Brookings Institution. Institute of Economics:

H. G. Moulton. *The Formation of Capital.* Pittsburg, 1935.

T. N. Carver. How ought wealth to be distributed? *Atlantic*, Vol. xcvii, 1914 (?).

J. A. Collins. *Distribution of Wealth in the United States.* Sen. Doc. 75, 55th Congress, 2nd Session, 1898.

R. R. Doane. Summary of the evidence on the National Wealth (U.S.A.). *Annalist*, 26 July-16 Aug., 15 Nov., 20 Dec. 1935; 31 Jan., 27 March, 15 May 1936.

W. W. Hewett. See National Bureau of Economic Research, *Studies in Income and Wealth.*

W. R. Ingalls. *Wealth and Income of the American People.* 2nd ed. York, Pa. 1923.

A. R. March. The national wealth and annual income of the American people. *Econ. World*, 1929.

B. C. MATTHEWS. *Our Irrational Distribution of Wealth.* New York, 1908.

R. MAYO-SMITH. *Statistics and Economics.* New York, 1899.

National Bureau of Economic Research:

S. KUZNETS. *Commodity Flow and Capital Formation,* Publication 34. 1938.

—— *Gross Capital Formation,* 1929–1933. Bulletin No. 52. 1934.

CHARLES B. SPAHR. *An Essay on the Present Distribution of Wealth in the United States.* New York, 1896.

G. TUCKER. *Progress of the United States in Population and Wealth in 50 Years.* New York, 1843.

C. A. TUTTLE. The real capital concept. *Quart. Journ. of Econ.* Boston, 1903.

Bureau of Statistics of Labour. *Distribution of Wealth.* 25th Annual Report, March, 1895.

Department of Commerce; Bureau of the Census. *Estimated Valuation of National Wealth,* 1850–1912. Washington, 1915.

Department of Commerce; Bureau of the Census. *Wealth, Public Debt and Taxation.* 1913 ed. 1915; 1922 ed. 1924. (Ten-yearly since 1850.)

Department of Commerce:

A. D. MOREHOUSE. The real property inventory of 1934. *Survey of Current Business,* Nov. 1934.

AUSTRALIA

C. H. KNIBBS. *The Private Wealth of Australia and its Growth.* 1918.

See also A I. EDWIN CANNAN. *Wealth.*

A I. A. M. CARR-SAUNDERS and D. CARADOG JONES. *A Survey of the Social Structure of Income of England and Wales.*

A I. G. R. PORTER. *The Progress of the Nation.*

A II. NASSAU SENIOR. *Political Economy.*

GERMANY

A I. K. DIEHL. Volkseinkommen und Volksvermögen.

A I*a*. E. FUHRMANN. Das Volksvermögen und Volkseinkommen im Königreich Sachsen.

A I. B. HARMS. *Kapital und Kapitalismus.*

A I*a*. K. HELFFERICH. Volksvermögen; Volkseinkommen und Steuerlast einst und jetzt.

A I*a*. A. KÜHNER. Deutschlands Volksvermögen und Volkseinkommen vor dem Krieg und heute.

A I. WALTER LOTZ. Kapitalbildung und Besteuerung.

A I. F. LUTZ. *Der Begriff Volksreichtum in der volkswirtschaftlichen Literatur.*

A I*a*. R. E. MAY. Das deutsche Volkseinkommen und der Zuwachs des deutschen Volksvermögens.

A I. R. NITSCHKE. *Einkommen und Vermögen in Preussen.*

GREECE

A I*a*. P. D. REDIADIS. The Greek national income and wealth in 1929.

ITALY

A I*a*. J. TIVARONI. *Patrimonio e Reddito di alcune Nazione Civili.*

JAPAN

A I*a*. K. MORI. Estimate of the national wealth and income of Japan proper.

A I*a*. S. SHIOMI. On Japan's wealth and income.

B. STATISTICAL METHOD

United Kingdom

R. G. D. Allen and A. L. Bowley. *Family Expenditure*, 1935. L.S.E. Studies in Statistics and Statistical Methods, No. 2, 1935.

A. L. Bowley. Criticism of official statistics. Address to the Economic Section of the British Association. Same reprinted as 'Improvement of official statistics', *Stat. Journ.* Sept. 1908.

—— The insufficiency of official statistics. Criticism of Mallock, 'The possibilities of an income tax according to the scheme of Pitt', *Nineteenth Century*, 1910.

—— *Nature and Purpose of the Measurement of Social Phenomena*. London, 1923.

—— *Official Statistics; what they contain and how to use them.* London, 1921.

—— Some tests of the trustworthiness of public statistics. *Economica*, Dec. 1928.

V. V. Branford. On the calculation of national resources. *Stat. Journ.* 1901.

Colin Clark. Determination of the multiplier from national income statistics. *Econ. Journ.* 1938.

W. L. Crum. Individual shares in the national income. *Review of Economic Statistics*, 1935.

F. Y. Edgeworth. Supplementary note on statistics. *Stat. Journ.* 1896.

C. Gini. Measurement of inequality of incomes. *Econ. Journ.* 1921.

—— See Italy: *Stat. Journ.* 1926.

International Labour Office:

Hans Staehle. *A Study of Certain Problems connected with the Making of Index Numbers, of Food Costs and of Rents.* 1934.

Harry Jerome. *Statistical Method.* New York and London, 1924.

J. C. Kapreyn. *Skew Frequency Curves in Biology and Statistics.*

Holt Mackenzie. Observations on the means of collecting information on various points of statistics. *Proceedings of the Stat. Soc. of London*, Vol. I, 1835–1836, No. 6.

Bernhard Mallet. A method of estimating capital wealth from the estate duty statistics. *Stat. Journ.* 1908.

W. H. Mallock. The possibilities of an income tax according to the scheme of Pitt. *Nineteenth Century*, March 1910.

H. Staehle. See International Labour Office.

Lord Stamp. Methods used in different countries for measuring national income. *Stat. Journ.* 1934.

—— A new illustration of Pareto's law. *Stat. Journ.* 1914.

Austria

E. Czuber. Beitrag zur Theorie der statistischen Reihen. *Versicherungswissenschaftliche Mitteilungen*, Neue Folge, Bd. IX. Wien, 1914.

Fr. v. Fellner. Das Volkseinkommen und dessen statistische Erfassung. Der internationale Kapitalismus und die Krise. *Festschrift für Julius Wolf*, hrsg. von S. v. Kardorff. Stuttgart, 1932.

F. Savorgnan. Di alcuni metodi per misurare la distribuzione dei redditi in Austria (1903–1910). *Bull. Inst. Int. de Stat.* 1931.

E. H. Vogel. Zur Methodologie der Einkommensstatistik. *Stat. Monatsschrift.* Wien, 1912.

France

J. Bertrand. See A. A. Cournot.

A. A. Cournot. *Recherches sur les Principes Mathématiques de la Théorie de la Richesse.* Nouvelle éd. avec les compliments de L. Walras, J. Bertrand et V. Pareto. Paris, 1938.

A. de Foville. Ce que c'est que la richesse d'un pays et comment on peut la mesurer. *Bull. de l'Inst. Int. de Stat.* Vol. xiv, Pt III. 1905.

M. G. François. La courbe de la répartition de la richesse. *Journ. des Économistes,* Sept. 1896.

R. Gibrat. *Les Inégalités Économiques.* Paris, 1931.

X. Heuschling. Mode d'évaluation du revenu national. *Journ. des Économistes,* 1871.

Germany

L. v. Bortkiewicz. Die Disparitätsmasse der Einkommensstatistik. *Bull. de l'Inst. Int. de Stat.* Vol. xxv, Pt III, 1931.

C. Brückner. Einkommensteuerstatistik und Wohlstandsverteilung. *Deutsches Statistisches Zentralblatt,* I, 1932.

M. J. Elsas. *Volkswohlstand und Volkseinkommen, Messung des Wohlstands und Dynamik des Lohns.* Leipzig, 1934.

H. Heckmann. Die Erfassung des Wohlstands einer Bevölkerung. *Heidelberger Studien,* II, 1932.

E. Huncke. Methodologisches zur Verwertung der Einkommensstatistik. *Allg. Stat. Archiv,* VII, 1907.

Paul Jostock. Wie weit sind Volkseinkommen international vergleichbar? *Weltwirtschaftliches Archiv,* 1939.

F. Kierdorf. *Volksreichtum und Berechnung des Volksvermögens.* Elberfeld, 1918.

R. Meyer. Ein Versuch auf dem Gebiet der Statistik der Einkommensteuer. *Allg. Stat. Archiv,* 1914.

Walter Schmidt. *Beiträge zur statistischen Erfassung des Volksvermögens.* Stralsund, 1914 (?).

K. Sorer. Ueber die Berechnung von Korrelationskoeffizienten zwischen den Symptomen der wirtschaftlichen Entwicklung in Oesterreich. *Allg. Stat. Archiv,* 1914.

Stat. Reichsamt. Ueber die Möglichkeiten einer kurzfristigen Einkommensbeobachtung. *Vierteljahrshefte zur Statistik des deutschen Reichs,* Heft 4, 1933.

C. A. Verijn-Stuart. Ueber die Methode der Berechnung des gesellschaftlichen Vermögens aus der Erbschaftsstatistik. *Allg. Stat. Archiv,* Tübingen, 1894.

E. Wagemann. Die statistische Erfassung der Kapitalbildung. See Colm and Neisser, 'Kapitalbildung und Steuersystem'.

A. Wagner. Zur Methodik der Statistik des Volkseinkommens und Volksvermögens. *Zeitschrift des Preuss. Stat. Landesamts,* Bd. XLIV, 1904.

—— Statistik des Volks- oder Nationaleinkommens. (Grösse, Arten, Verteilung, besonders mit Verwertung der Steuerstatistik.) *Bull. de l'Inst. Int. de Stat.* Berlin, XIV, 3, 4, 1905.

J. Wortmann. *Die Berechnung des Volkseinkommens: ein Beitrag zur Frage der statistisch-nationalökonomischen Begriffsbildung.* Emstetten, 1930.

E. Würzburger. Zur Frage der Einkommensstatistik. *Bull. de l'Inst. Int. de Stat.* XX, 1, 2, 1913.

N. Zabacovici. *Die Statistik der Einkommensverteilung mit besonderer Rücksicht auf das Königreich Sachsen.* Leipzig, 1913.

Italy

R. Benini. Ancora sul coefficiente pel calcolo della ricchezza privata. *Bolletino di Statistica e Legislazione comparata.* Rome, 1910.

—— Distribuzione probabile della ricchezza privata in Italia per classi di popolazione. *Riforma Sociale*, fasc. 9–10, anno 1, 1894.

—— *Quote successorie di alcune specie di ricchezza.* 1919.

—— Il totalizzatore applicato agli indici del movimento economico. *Giornale degli Economisti*, 1892.

L. Bodio. *Di alcuni indici misuratori del movimento economico in Italia.* Rome, 1891.

C. Bresciani-Turoni. La curva dei redditi. In R. Bachi, *Problema die Finanzy Fascista*, 1937.

—— Ueber einen quantitativen summarischen Ausdruck für die Ungleichmässigkeit der Einkommensverteilung. *Deutsches stat. Zentralblatt*, 1911.

—— *Di indice misuratore della disuguaglianza nella distribuzione della ricchezza.* Palermo, 1910.

—— Dell' influenze delle condizione economiche sulla forma della curva dei redditi. *Giornale degli Economisti*, Vol. xxxi, 1903.

—— Kritische Betrachtung über einige Methoden der Einkommensstatistik. *Stat. Monatsschrift*, 1915.

—— Ueber die Methode der Einkommensverteilungsstatistik. *Jahrbücher für Nationalökonomie und Statistik* (Conrad), 1907.

F. Coletti. La determinazione della durata della generazione e il calcolo della ricchezza privata di un paese. *Riforma Sociale*, xiv, Vol. xvii.

—— Nota sulla valutazione sintomatica del movimento economico e del benessere nazionale. *Rassegna di Scienze sociali e politiche*, 1892.

V. Furlan. Note sulla curva paretiana dei redditi. *Giornale degli Economisti*, 1909/II.

C. Gini. Il calcolo della ricchezza di un paese in base alle statistiche delle successioni e donazioni. *Atti dell' Ateneo di Treviso.* Treviso, 1908.

—— The contribution of Italy to modern statistical methods. *Stat. Journ.* 1926.

—— Methoden zur Erfassung und Verteilung der gegenseitigen Beziehungen statistischer Erscheinungen. *Deutsches stat. Zentralblatt*, 1911.

—— Sulla misura della concentrazione e della variabilità dei caratteri. *Rendiconti del Reale Istituto Veneto di Scienze, Lettere ed Arti*, Vol. liii, Pt II, Venice, 1914.

—— Variabilità e mutabilità, contributo allo studio delle distribuzioni e delle relazioni statistiche. *Studi economico-giuridici Università di Cagliari.* Bologna, 1912.

G. Mortara. Nozioni elementari intorno ad alcune categorie di rapporti statistici. *Giornale degli Economisti*, Serie III, Vol. xi, Feb. 1910.

V. Pareto. *La Courbe de la Répartition de la Richesse.* Lausanne, 1896.

—— La curva della entrate e le osservazioni del Prof. Edgeworth. *Giornale degli Economisti*, March 1896.

—— Il modo di figurare i fenomeni economici. *Giornale degli Economisti*, 1896.

G. Pietra. Delle relazioni tra gli indici di variabilità. *Rendiconti del Reale Istituto Veneto di Scienze, Lettere et Arti*, Vol. liv, Pt II. Venice, 1915.

L. P. (Luigi Princivalle). Alcune indagini sui passagi della proprietà fondiaria per causa di morte. *Bolletino di Statistica e Legislazione comparata*, 1908–9.

L. Princivalle. Il coefficiente per il calcolo della ricchezza privata. *Bolletino di Statistica e di Legislazione comparata*, 1909–10.

—— Intorno al coefficiente per il calcolo della ricchezza privata in base alle denuncie di successione. *Revista di Legislazione tributaria*, 1911.

U. Ricci. *L' Indice de Variabilità e la Curva dei Redditi*. Rome, 1916.

F. Savorgnan. Intorno all' approssimazione di alcuni indicti della distribuzione dei redditi. *Atti del Reale Istituto Veneto*, Vol. lxxiv, Pt II.

F. Vinci. Calcolo delle probabilità e distribuzione dei redditi nel pernsiero di Pareto. *Giornale degli Economisti*, 1924.

Netherlands

C. P. de Groot. *Methoden voor de berekening van het nat. inkomen, met een onderzoek naar de bruikbaarheid der Nederlandsche belastingsstatistieken*. Purmerend, 1936.

C. A. Verijn Stuart. See Germany.

I. van der Wijk. *Inkomens- en Vermogens-Verdeling*. Haarlem, 1939.

H. D. Dickinson. Review of Van der Wijk, *Inkomens- en Vermogens-Verdeling*, Haarlem, 1939. *Econ. Journ.* June-Sept. 1940.

Russia

A. N. Kiaer. *Mémoires...Essai sur la question d'une statistique du revenu national*. Petersburg, 1876.

Switzerland

W. Eggenschwyler. Sind Volksvermögen messbar? *Zeitschrift für schweizerische Statistik und Volkswirtschaft*, 1916.

L. Walras. *Théorie mathématique de la Richesse sociale*. Paris, 1883.

M. R. Weyermann. Die statistischen Versuche einer Erfassung des Volksvermögens. *Zeitschrift für schweizerische Statistik und Volkswirtschaft*, 1915.

—— Die statistischen Versuche einer Erfassung des Volksvermögens. *Zeitschrift für schweizerische Statistik und Volkswirtschaft*, Heft 3, 1916.

J. Wyler. Vom Tableau Economique zur volkswirtschaftlichen Einkommensbilanz. *Zeitschrift für schweizerische Statistik und Volkswirtschaft*, 1927.

United States

American Economic Association. *The Federal Census: Critical Essays*. New York, 1899.

Susan S. Burr. See J. Franklin Ebersole.

E. Day. The measurement of variations in the national real income. *Quarterly Publications of the American Statistical Association*, 1921.

J. Franklin Ebersole, S. S. Burr and George M. Petersen. Income forecasting by the use of statistics of income data. *Review of Economic Statistics*, 1929.

Irving Fisher. Income in theory and income taxation in practice. *Econometrica*, Jan. 1937.

G. H. Holmes. Computation of the value of the wealth in existence. *American Statistical Association Reports*, Dec. 1894.

G. K. V. Holmes. Review of Lorenz's method of measuring the inequality of income. *Quart. Publ. Amer. Stat. Assoc.* No. 71, 1905.

W. I. King. Desirable additions to statistical data on wealth and income. *American Statistical Association Publications*, 1916–17.

W. J. King. Income and wealth. How can they be measured? *American Econ. Review*, Sept. 1925.

M. O. LORENZ. Methods of measuring the concentration of wealth. *American Statistical Society*, No. 70, 1905.

W. C. MITCHELL. See National Bureau of Economic Research: R. C. Epstein, *Industrial Profits*.

W. C. MITCHELL and S. KUZNETS. Current problems in measurement of national income. *Bull. de l'Inst. Int. de Stat.* Vol. XXXVIII, 1935.

National Bureau of Economic Research. Conference on Research in National Income and Wealth. *Studies in Income and Wealth*, Vol. I, 1937.

National Bureau of Economic Research. Bulletin 60:

S. FABRICANT. *Measures of Capital Consumption*, 1919–1933. 1936.

W. M. PERSONS. The variability in the distribution of wealth and income. *Quart. Journ. of Econ.* 1909.

G. M. PETERSEN. See J. Franklin Ebersole.

E. SYDENSTRICKER and W. I. KING. Measurement of relative economic status of families. *Quart. Publ. Amer. Stat. Assoc.* Sept. 1921.

G. P. WATKINS. Comment on the method of measuring the concentration of wealth. *Quart. Publ. Amer. Stat. Assoc.* Bulletin 72, 1905.

—— An interpretation of certain statistical evidence of concentration of wealth. *Quart. Publ. Amer. Stat. Assoc.* March 1908.

—— The measurement of the concentration of wealth. *Quart. Journ. of Econ.* 1909.

D. B. YNTEMA. The Measurement of Inequality in the personal Distribution of Wealth and Income (typewritten). University of Michigan.

A. A. YOUNG. Do the statistics of the concentration of wealth in the United States mean what they are commonly assumed to mean? *American Statistical Association Publications*, Vol. XV, 1916–17.

See also A I. L. v. BORTKIEWICZ. Die Grenznutzenlehre auf Grundlage einer ultraliberalen Wirtschaftspolitik.

A I. A. EMMINGHAUS. Einkommen.

A I. V. PARETO. *Manuel d'Économie politique.*

C. PARTS OF NATIONAL INCOME

C I. *Agricultural Income*

UNITED KINGDOM

ANONYMOUS. Rent, wages and profits of British agriculture, 1913. *Economist*, 1913.

Sir JAMES CAIRD. General view of British agriculture. *Journ. of the Royal Agricultural Society*, Vol. XXXIX, 1878.

—— On the agricultural statistics of the U.K. *Stat. Journ.* 1868.

R. M. C. CARSLAW, A. W. MENZIES-KITCHIN and P. E. GRAVES. Cambridge University Department of Agriculture, Report No. 19. An Economic Survey of Agriculture in the Eastern Counties of England, 1931. Published 1932.

MAJOR CRAIGIE. Discussion of T. E. ELLIOTT's Paper. *Stat. Journ.* June 1887.

—— Taxation as affecting the agricultural interest. *Journ. of the Royal Agricultural Society*, 1878.

L. DRESCHER. Die Entwicklung der Agrarproduktion Grossbritanniens und Irlands seit Beginn des 19. Jahrhunderts. Bemerkungen zum Index der Agrarproduktion. *Weltwirtschaftliches Archiv*, March 1935.

R. H. Few. Farm revenue and capital. *Journ. of the Royal Agricultural Society*, 1895.

P. E. Graves and S. H. Carson. A cost index for miscellaneous farm expenses. *Journ. of the Ministry of Agriculture*, Nov. 1935.

Sir R. Griffith. *Thoughts and Facts relating to the Income of Agriculture, Manufacture, etc.* Dublin, 1895.

Journal of the Institute of Surveyors. 1884.

T. J. Kiernan. National income of the Irish Free State. *Econ. Journ.* March 1933.

J. R. MacCulloch. *Dictionary*, Appendix, Articles: Corn, Food, Animals. 1882.

J. S. Nicholson. *Rates and Taxes as affecting Agriculture*. 1905.

R. H. Inglis Palgrave. Estimates of agricultural lands in the United Kingdom in the last 30 years. *Stat. Journ.* 1905.

F. Purdy. On the earnings of agricultural labourers in England and Wales, 1860. *Stat. Journ.* 1861.

R. J. Thompson. An enquiry into the rent of agricultural land in England and Wales during the nineteenth century. *Stat. Journ.* 1907.

Ch. Turner. Income and Agricultural Owners. Letter to *The Times*, 24 Feb. 1914.

U.K. Royal Commission on Agricultural Depression, 1894–97. Reports of District Commissioners on different Counties; tables, mostly re gross and net output, rent, taxes, tithe, collected in B.P.P. 1894, xv, 1; 1895, xvi and xvii, together with 18 different C. numbers. Accounts summed up in Final Report, Appendix III, B.P.P. 1897, xv, C. 8541, by W. C. Little.

F. W. Wateridge. *Prosperous Agriculture*. 1911.

O. S. Wells. Thesis on Agricultural Production (unpublished). Cambridge, 1936.

L. W. Wilsden. The Census of Production and agriculture. *Econ. Review*, 1914.

Austria

F. v. Fellner. Der Wert des landwirtschaftlichen Grundbesitzes in Ungarn und Oesterreich. (Anmerkung zu Pribrams Artikel.) *Stat. Monatsschrift*, Neue Folge, Brünn, 1915.

K. Pribram. Der Wert des landwirtschaftlichen Grundbesitzes in Oesterreich. *Stat. Monatsschrift*, Neue Folge, Brünn, 1915, Nr. 7–8, 11–12.

Italy

S. Jacini. *La proprietà fondiaria e la popolazione agricola in Lombardia*. Milano, 1895.

S. Pugliese. *Due secoli de vita agricola. Produzione e valore dei terreni, contratti agrari, salari e prezzi nel Vercellese nei secoli XVIII e XIX*. Turin, 1908.

United States

A. B. Gennung. *Farm Management Demonstrator*, 1920.

E. A. Goldenweiser. The farmer's income. *American Econ. Review*, March 1916.

R. F. Martin. National Industrial Conference Board, 232. *Income in Agriculture*, 1929–1935. New York, 1936.

See also A I*a*. U.K. Royal Commission on Local Taxation. 1899.

C 2. *Income out of Real Property*

United Kingdom

E. Adam. *Land Values and Taxation.* London, 1907.

R. D. Baxter. *Local Government and Taxation and Mr Goshen's Report.* 1874.

A. L. Beck. Discussion of L. R. Connor's paper. *Stat. Journ.* 1928.

Ch. Bidwell. Changes in value of land since 1860. *Institute of Surveyors Transactions*, 1905.

John D. Black. The agricultural situation, March 1940. *Review of Econ. Stat.* May 1940.

G. H. Blunden. Some observations on the distribution and incidence of rates and taxes. *Stat. Journ.* 1896.

Sir James Caird. The British land question. *Stat. Journ.* 1881.

Chorlton. *Rating of Land Values.* Manchester University Publ. Econ. Series, No. 5. Manchester, 1907.

H. Cox. *Land Nationalisation.* London, 1892.

P. G. Craigie. Inaugural presidential address. *Stat. Journ.* 1902.

F. R. C. Douglas, A. R. McDougal and James Scott. *Agriculture and Land Value Taxation.* 1930.

F. Y. Edgeworth. The incidence of urban rates. *Econ. Journ.* 1900.

—— Recent schemes for rating urban land values. *Econ. Journ.* March 1906.

R. M. Garner. *History of English Landed Interest.* 1893.

Sir R. Giffen. Recent state finance and the budget. *Quarterly Review*, 1909.

Viscount Goshen. Report on Local Taxation.

Sir R. Griffith. Instructions to Valuers in Ireland. See R. B. O'Brien, *The Irish Land Question and English Public Opinion.*

—— *The Irish Land Question and English Public Opinion.* 1881.

G. Gunton. *Forum*, March 1887.

W. J. Harris. *Forum*, July 1887.

A. Hook. Rating and site valuation. *Econ. Review*, April 1906.

J. Hyder. *The Case of Land Nationalisation.* 1923.

London County. Assessment and Valuation Conference, 1893/4 to 1934.

Primrose McConnell. *Notebook of agricultural facts and figures for farmers and farm students.* 1883.

G. M'Crae. *Chambers' Journal*, Jan. 1901.

W. H. Mallock. Phantom millions. An inquiry into the actual amount of the annual increments of land values. *Nineteenth Century*, Nov. 1909.

Sir L. G. Chiozza Money. *Things that matter.* 1905.

Francis Newbury. *Observations on the Income Act, particularly as it relates to the Occupiers of Land.* 1801.

W. Newmarch. On the electoral statistics of the counties and boroughs in England and Wales, 1832–1853. *Stat. Journ.* 1857.

R. B. O'Brien. *The Irish Land Question and English Public Opinion.* 1881.

F. Purdy. Pressure of taxation on real property. *Stat. Journ.* 1869.

A. MacCallum Scott. *The International*, Feb. 1909.

H. W. Singer. Unpublished Cambridge Dissertation.

P. Snowden. *Social List Review*, 1909.

J. Calvert Spensley. The London valuation since 1871. *Stat. Journ.* 1903.

Lord Stamp. Land valuation and rating reform. *Econ. Journ.* March 1911.

N. J. Synnott. Revaluation of Ireland. *Journal of Statistical and Social Inquiry Society of Ireland*, August 1900.

Thomasson. Land nationalisation. *Westminster Review*, Aug. 1900.

U.K. Report from the Select Committee of the House of Lords on the Burdens Affecting Real Property, 1846. B.P.P. 1846, VI, Parts I and II.

—— Income Tax Commission. B.P.P. VII Session, 1861.

—— Select Committee on Income Tax. B.P.P. IX, 1852.

—— Copy of a letter dated 23rd Dec. 1850 addressed by the Commissioner for Valuation (Sir Richard Griffith) to the Lord Lieutenant of Ireland with reference to the present state and progress of the general valuation of Ireland. B.P.P. L Session, 1851.

Westminster Review. Thirty Years, 1902–3.

—— Whig and Tory. June 1899.

Sir THOMAS WHITTACKER. *Ownership, Tenure and Taxation of Land.* 1914.

AUSTRIA

W. SCHIFF. Les changes de la propriété foncière en Autriche. *Bull. de l'Inst. Int. de Stat.* 1893.

BELGIUM

J. MALOU. *Le Budget des Voies et Moyens de la Belgique de* 1831 *à* 1880. Brussels, 1881.

FRANCE

Y. GUYOT. L'évaluation des propriétés non baties. *Journ. de la Société de Stat. de Paris*, April 1914.

ITALY

L. SBROJAVACCA. Sul valore della proprietà fondiaria rustica e sulla gravezza delle imposteche la colposcono in alcuni stati. *Bull. de l'Inst. Int. de Stat.* I, 1886.

UNITED STATES

Harvard University. Business Research Studies, No. 13:

W. L. CRUM. *The Distribution of Wealth.* A factual survey based upon federal estate tax returns. Boston, 1935.

See also A I *a*. ARTHUR YOUNG. *The question of Scarcity plainly stated.*

A I *a*. H. PASSY. *On large and small farms.*

C 2. Sir THOMAS WHITTACKER. *Ownership, Tenure and Taxation of Land.*

C 1. U.K. Royal Commission on Agricultural Depression. 1894–97.

C 1. MAJOR CRAIGIE. Taxation as affecting the agricultural interest.

A II. Sir ROBERT GIFFEN. The expenditure of national capital.

A III. J. S. NICHOLSON. The living capital of the United Kingdom.

C 15. R. H. INGLIS PALGRAVE. Local Taxation.

C 3. *Wage Income*

A. L. BOWLEY. Changes in the average wages in the United Kingdom between 1880 and 1891. *Stat. Journ.* 1895.

—— Tests of national progress. *Econ. Journ.* 1904.

E. C. RAMSBOTTOM. Wage rates in the United Kingdom, 1921–1934. *Stat. Journ.* 1935.

See also C 1. ANONYMOUS. Rent, wages and profits of British agriculture.

A I. A. L. BOWLEY. *Wages and Income in the United Kingdom since* 1860.

C 1. F. PURDY. On the earnings of agricultural labourers in England and Wales.

C 4. *Professional Income*

U.S. Department of Commerce:
WALTER L. SLIFER. Income of independent professional practitioners. *Survey of Current Business*, April 1938.

C 5. *Industrial Income*

UNITED KINGDOM

A. L. BOWLEY. An Index of the Physical Volume of Production. *Econ. Journ.* 1921.

BOWLEY, SCHWARTZ and RHODES. *Output, Employment and Wages in the United Kingdom*, 1924, 1930, and 1935. L. and C.E.S. Spec. Mem.

G. W. DANIELS and H. CAMPION. *The Relative Importance of British Export Trade.* L. and C.E.S. Spec. Mem. No. 41, Aug. 1935.

WALTER HOFFMANN. Index of British industrial products. Annual 1780 onwards. *Weltwirtschaftliches Archiv*, Sept. 1934.

J. M. KEYNES. Efficiency in Industry. A Measure of Growth. *The Times*, 13 Sept. 1938.

J. W. F. ROWE. *The Physical Volume of Production.* L. and C.E.S. Spec. Mem. No. 8, 1924.

LORD STAMP. Index number of profits. *Stat. Journ.* 1932.

BELGIUM

See A III. F. BAUDHUIN. *Le Capital de la Belgique et le rendement de son industrie.*

UNITED STATES

National Bureau of Econ. Research, Bulletin No. 26:
R. C. EPSTEIN. *Industrial Profits in the United States.* 1934.

National Bureau of Econ. Research, Bulletin No. 45:
F. C. MILLS. *Changes in Physical Production.* 1933.

National Industrial Conference Board. Studies No. 213. *Costs and Profit in the Manufacturing Industry*, 1914–1933. New York, 1935.

See also C 1. Sir R. GRIFFITH. *Thoughts and Facts relating to the Income of Agriculture, Manufacture, etc.*
C 14. G. L. SCHWARTZ. Output, employment and wages, etc.

C 6. *Mining Income*

W. R. SORLEY. Mining royalties and their effects on the iron and coal trade. *Stat. Journ.* 1889.

C 7. *Trade Income*

IRIS DOUGLAS. Retail trade statistics in different countries. *Stat. Journ.* 1935.

H. J. H. PARKER. *Income of Small Shopkeepers and Independent Industrial Workers.* Dep. of Social Science, University of Liverpool.

LORD STAMP. The effects of trade fluctuations upon profits. *Stat. Journ.* 1918.

C 8. *Corporate Income*

UNITED KINGDOM

Economist. Regular analysis of companies' profits and losses.

UNITED STATES

Harvard University. Business Research Studies, No. 8:
W. L. CRUM. *The Effect of Size on Corporate Earnings and Conditions. An Analysis of* 1931 *Income-tax Statistics.* Boston, 1934.
National Bureau of Economic Research, Bulletin No. 50:
S. FABRICANT. *Recent Corporate Profits in the United States.* 1934.
National Bureau of Economic Research, Bulletin No. 55:
S. FABRICANT. *Profits, Losses and Business Assets,* 1929–1934. Published 1935.
National Bureau of Economic Research, Bulletin No. 26:
W. A. PATON. *Corporate Profits as shown by Audit Reports.* 1935.

See also A I. EDWIN CANNAN. *Wealth.*
A I*a*. COLIN CLARK. *National Income and Outlay.*
A I*a*. E. LINDAHL. *National Income of Sweden,* Pt I.
A I*a*. BOWLEY-STAMP. *The National Income,* 1924.
A I*a*. A. WAGNER. Statistik des Volks- oder Nationaleinkommens.

C 9. *Undivided Profits*

See C 2. A. L. BECK. Discussion of L. R. Connor's paper. *Stat. Journ.* 1928.

C 10. *Derivative Income*

E. BRESSON. Contribution à l'étude des doubles emplois dans l'évaluation des biens en France. *Journ. de la Société de Stat. de Paris,* 1901.
F. T. COLONJON. Des doubles emplois dans l'évaluation des biens en France. *Journ. de la Société de Stat. de Paris,* 1903.

See also A I. EDWIN CANNAN. *Wealth.*
A I*a*. COLIN CLARK. *National Income and Outlay.*
A I. M. A. COPELAND. *National Wealth and Income,* Pt I.
A I*a*. F. v. FELLNER. *Le Revenu National de la Hongrie actuelle.*
A I*a*. E. LINDAHL. *National Income of Sweden,* Pt II.
A I*a*. MATOLCSY and VARGA. *The National Income of Hungary.* 1938.
A I*a*. VERIJN-STUART. Discussion on Stamp's paper. *Stat. Journ.* 1934.

C 11. *Financial Income*

National Industrial Conference Board. Research Report No. 55. *Taxation and National Income.* New York, 1922.
C. H. SIMMS. *Personal Income Taxation. The Definition of Income as a problem of fiscal policy.* Chicago, 1938.
U.S.A. Department of Commerce. Revised estimate of monthly income payments in the United States, 1922–1938. *Survey of Current Business,* Oct. 1938.

C 12. *Income from Foreign Investments*

UNITED KINGDOM

HAROLD COX. The effect of the Corn Laws. *Nineteenth Century,* 1903. I.
FINANCIAL EXPERT. *Socialist Review,* March 1909.
C. K. HOBSON. *The Export of Capital.* 1914.
Sir ROBERT KINDERSLEY. British overseas investment. *Econ. Journ.* yearly 1928–34.
J. R. MACDONAL. *Financial Review of Reviews,* April 1909.

W. H. Mallock. The expatriation of capital. *Nineteenth Century*, March 1906.

Sir George Paish. Great Britain's capital investments in individual colonial and foreign countries. *Stat. Journ.* 1911.

Germany.

K. Helfferich. Auslandswerte. *Bankarchiv*, Vol. x, April 1911.

See also A I*a*. Bowley-Stamp. *The National Income*, 1924.
A I*a*. E. Lindahl. *National Income of Sweden*, Vol. iii, Pt II.
A I*a*. Matolcsy and Varga. *The National Income of Hungary.*

C 13. *Income in the Betting Industry*

Anonymous. Britain's betting industry. *Economist*, Feb. and March 1936.

C 14. *Public Income*

United Kingdom

Anonymous. British finance in the nineteenth century. *Edinburgh Review*, 1899.

Sir Gwilym Gibbon. The expenditure and revenue of local authorities. *Stat. Journ.* 1936.

W. R. Lawson. Two record budgets, 1860 and 1903. *Fortnightly Review*, May 1903.

Sir Bernard Mallet and George C. Oswald. *British Budgets*, Vol. i, 1888 (1887–1912/3); Vol. ii, 1929 (1913/14–1920/21); Vol. iii, 1933 (1921–22–1932/33).

Sir Herbert Samuel. The taxation of various classes of the people. *Stat. Journ.* 1919.

D. M. Sandral. The taxation of various classes of the people. *Stat. Journ.* 1931.

G. L. Schwartz. *Output, Employment and Wages in Industry in the United Kingdom.* L. and C.E.S. Spec. Mem. No. 26, 1924.

Charles Senior. *Handbook to Income Tax Law and Practice.* 1862.

G. Findlay Shirras. Taxable capacity and the burden of taxation and public debt. *Stat. Journ.* 1925.

Statistical Journal. Journal of the Royal Statistical Society. Miscellaneous. General results of the Census of 1861 of the United Kingdom, Progress of the Income Tax Assessments, 1853–1860. *Stat. Journ.* 1861.

W. M. J. Williams. Imperial Funds spent in Ireland. *Contemporary Review*, 1912.

Egypt

I. G. Levi. L'augmentation des revenus de l'état. *Égypte Contemporaine*, 1923.

France

F. de Colonjon. Composition et importance de la fortune de l'état en France. *Journ. de la Société de Stat. de Paris*, 1907.

Germany

F. Kühnert. Die Ergebnisse der staatlichen Einkommensbesteuerung der nichtphysischen Personen in Preussen im Zeitraum 1892–1905. *Zeitschrift d. kgl. Preuss. Stat. Büros*, 1906.

v. Mühlenfels. *Steuerkraft und Wohlstandsindex.* Leipzig, 1927.

W. Röpke. Deutschlands Leistungsfähigkeit. *Jahrbücher für Nationalökonomie und Statistik* (Conrad), iii. Folge, Bd. 66, 1923.

ITALY

F. S. NITTI. *Il Bilancio dello Stato dal 1862 al 1896–97. Primi linii de una inchiesta sulla ripartizione territoriale della entrate e della spese pubbliche in Italia.* Naples, 1900.

SWITZERLAND

C. BÜCHER. *Basel's Staatseinnahmen und Steuerverteilung*, 1878–1887. Basel, 1888.

See also C 2. Sir ROBERT GIFFEN. Recent state finance and the budget.

BELGIUM

C 2. J. MALOU. *Le Budget des Voies et Moyens de la Belgique de* 1831 *à* 1880.

GERMANY

A I*a*. TH. BALOGH. The national economy of Germany.

C 15. *Tax and Rate Questions*

UNITED KINGDOM

LORD ARNOLD. A capital levy. The problems of realisation. *Econ. Journ.* 1918.

J. ELLIS BARKER. British finances and the Budget. *Fortnightly Review*, May 1909.

C. F. BASTABLE. See U.K., Commission on Local Taxation, 1899.

—— See U.K., Report on Financial Relations between Great Britain and Ireland, 1895–96.

A. L. BOWLEY. The British super-tax and the distribution of income. *Quart. Journ. of Econ.* 1914.

—— Report of a Committee of the British Association. The amount and distribution of income (other than wages) below the income-tax exemption limit in the United Kingdom (1910–11). *Journ. of R. Stat. Soc.*

FREDERICK BROWN. Expenses of production in Great Britain. *Economica*, Dec. 1928.

EDWIN CANNAN. See Royal Commission on Local Taxation, 1899.

W. H. COATES. Evidence before the Treasury Committee on National Debt and Taxation, 1927.

S. DOWELL. *A History of Taxation and Taxes in England from the earliest times to the year* 1885. 2nd ed. London, 1888.

T. H. ELLIOTT. The annual taxes on property and income. *Stat. Journ.* 1887.

W. T. LAYTON. Evidence before the Treasury Committee on National Debt and Taxation, 1927.

League of Nations. International Financial Conference at Brussels. Report IV: Public Finance, 1920.

LEONE LEVI. On the reconstruction of the income and property tax. *Stat. Journ.* 1874.

Sir L. G. CHIOZZA MONEY. The possibilities of an income tax according to the scheme of Pitt. A reply to Mallock's article of the same title, same journal. *Nineteenth Century*, 1910.

R. H. INGLIS PALGRAVE. Local Taxation. *Dictionary of Political Economy.*

W. H. PRICE. The British income tax. *Quart. Journ. of Econ.* Feb. 1906.

D. H. ROBERTSON. The Colwyn Committee and the income tax and the price level. *Econ. Journ.* Dec. 1927.

Ed. R. A. SELIGMANN. *Essays in Income Taxation.* 1925.

—— *The Shifting and Incidence of Taxation.* 1899, 1921, 1932.

LORD STAMP. Economic aspects of income tax change. *Economic Review*, 1909.

—— The incidence of the taxation of leaseholds. *Economic Review*, July 1911.

—— *Fundamental Principles on Taxation.* 1921, 1936.

U.K. Select Committee on the Taxation of Ireland. Draft Report, B.P.P. xv, 1864.

—— Treasury. Committee on National Debt and Taxation, 1927. See W. H. Coates, W. T. Layton, P. D. Leake and Sir Frederic Wise.

—— Select Committee on the Taxation of Ireland. Report 1865, B.P.P. xii, 1865.

AUSTRIA

R. MEYER. Die ersten Ergebnisse der Personaleinkommensteuer in Oesterreich. *Zeitschrift für Volkswirtschaft, Sozialpolitik und Verwaltung*, VIII, 1899.

—— *Das Zeitverhältnis zwischen der Steuer und dem Einkommen.* Wien, 1901.

FRANCE

F. BAUDHUIN. *Finances belges: la stabilisation et ses conséquences.* 2nd ed. Paris, 1928.

P. LEROY-BEAULIEU. *Traité de la Science de Finance.* Paris, 1889.

GERMANY

G. COLM. *Volkswirtschaftliche Theorie der Staatsausgaben.* Tübingen, 1927.

EVERT. Sozialistische Streifzüge durch die Materialien der Veranlagung zur Staatseinkommensteuer. *Zeitschrift des Preuss. Stat. Büreaus*, 1902.

ADOLF HEIL. *Resultate der Einschätzung zur Einkommensteuer in Hessen, Sachsen und Hamburg.* Jena, 1887.

P. HERNBERG. *Volkswirtschaftliche Bilanzen, Probleme des Geld- und Finanzwesens.* Leipzig, 1927.

Internationaler Steuerbelastungsvergleich. *Einzelschrift z. Stat. d. Deutschen Reiches*, 1933.

B. KAUTSKY. Die Kapitalbildung der öffentlichen Hand seit dem Krieg in Deutschland und Deutschösterreich. *Schriften des Vereins für Sozialpolitik*, Bd. 174/IV. (See Walter Lotz, editor.)

R. E. MAY. Das Verhältnis zwischen Einkommen und Familienentfaltung. *Jahrbuch für Gesetzgebung, Verwaltung und Volkswirtschaft* (Schmoller). 1903.

G. SCHANZ. Der Einkommensbegriff und die Einkommensteuergesetze. *Finanz-Archiv*, 1896.

ITALY

C. GINI. Di alcuni circostanze che nei tempi moderni tendono a fare apparire l' incremento del reddito nazionale maggiore del vero. *Bull. de l'Inst. Int. de Stat.* II, 1935.

—— A quanto ammonta il reddito degli Italiani? *Tempo economico*, 1921.

B. GRIZOTTI. L' imposte sulla ricchezza dopo la guerra. *Giornale degli Economisti*, 1919.

C. JARACH. Come funziona la nostra imposta di ricchezza mobile. *Riforma soziale*, Vol. XVII.

R. MEYER. Direzione generale delle imposti dirette, Statistica del reddite accertato e tassato. *Bulletine ufficiale*, x, 1902; XIII, 1905.

Spain

F. Bernis. *La Hacienda Española. Los Impuestos.* Barcelona, 1918(?).

F. Y. Edgeworth. Review of F. Bernis, *La Hacienda Española. Econ. Journ.* 1919.

See also C 2. E. Adam. *Land Values and Taxation.*

C 2. G. H. Blunden. Some observations on the distribution and incidence of rates and taxes.

A I*a*. T. A. Coghlan. Evidence before the Select Committee on Income Tax.

C 2. Edgeworth. The incidence of urban rates.

C 2. Edgeworth. Recent schemes for rating urban land values.

A I. E. Huncke. Die Entwicklung von Einkommensteuer und Einkommensverteilung in England.

C 14. W. R. Lawson. Two record budgets.

C 1. J. S. Nicholson. Rates and Taxes as affecting Agriculture.

C 14. G. Findlay Shirras. Taxable capacity.

A I. G. Findlay Shirras. *Volkseinkommen und Besteuerung.*

C 2. Lord Stamp. Land valuation and rating reform.

C 2. U.K. Income Tax Commission.

C 1. U.K. Royal Commission on Agricultural Depression, 1894–97.

A I*a*. U.K. Royal Commission on Local Taxation, 1899.

A III. U.K. Suggested Taxation of War-time Increases of Wealth.

France

A III. E. Théry. *Les progrès économiques de la France.*

Germany

A II. A. Angelopoulos. *Die Einkommensverteilung im Lichte der Einkommensteuerstatistik.*

A I. Walter Lotz. Kapitalbildung und Besteuerung.

A II. A. Soetbeer. Das souveräne Gesetz der Preisbildung.

A I. Württembergisches Statistisches Landesamt. *Volksvermögen, Volkseinkommen und Steuerbelastung in Deutschland vor und nach dem Krieg.*

India

A III. K. T. Shah and K. J. Khambata. *The Wealth and Taxable Capacity of India.*

Italy

C 14. F. S. Nitti. *Il Bilancio dello Stato.*

Netherlands

A I. De Bruyn-Kops. Report on the 'revenu annuel de la nation'.

Switzerland

C 14. C. Bücher. *Basel's Staatseinnahmen und Steuerverteilung.*

C 16. *National Debt*

L. Einaudi. La inclusione del debito pubblico nelle valutazioni della ricchezza delle nazione. *Bull. de l'Inst. Int. de Stat.* II, 1935.

Brookings Institution. Institute of Economics, Publ. No. 8:

H. G. Moulton and C. Lewis. *The French Debt Problem.* New York, 1925.

See also A III. R. GIFFEN. *The Growth of Capital.*
A III. A. HOOKE. *An Essay on the National Debt and the National Capital.*
C 15. W. T. LAYTON. Evidence before the Treasury Committee on National Debt and Taxation.
A II. J. M. KEYNES. General Theory of Wages, Interest and Money.
C 2. Sir L. G. CHIOZZA MONEY. *Things that matter.*

C 17. *Depreciation and other questions of deductions, costs*

UNITED KINGDOM

G. T. JONES. *Increasing Returns.* 1932.

ITALY

A. CONIGLIANI. Sul preteso decremento del patrimonio nazionale italiano. *Giornale degli Economisti,* 1901.

UNITED STATES

National Bureau of Economic Research: Publication 35.
S. FABRICANT. *Capital Consumption and Adjustment.* New York, 1938.

See also C 15. FREDERICK BROWN. Expenses of production in Great Britain.
A I. A. C. PIGOU. Net income and capital depletion.

C 18. *Legal Questions*

UNITED KINGDOM

RAYMOND NEEDHAM. The distinction between capital and income. *Accountant,* 6 June 1925.

GERMANY

L. v. PETRAZYCKI. *Die Lehre vom Einkommen.* Berlin, 1893.

See also C 2. CHORLTON. *Rating of Land Values.*

C 19. *Population Questions*

UNITED KINGDOM

CHARLES BOOTH. Occupations of the people of the United Kingdom, 1801–1881. *Stat. Journ.* 1886.
A. L. BOWLEY. *Numbers occupied in the Industries of England and Wales,* 1911 *and* 1921. L. and C.E.S. Spec. Mem. No. 17*a.*

GERMANY

Einkommensteuergesetz vom 10. Aug. 1925. Reichsgesetzblatt v. 15. Aug. 1925, Nr. 39.
Körperschaftssteuergesetz vom 10. Aug. 1925. Reichsgesetzblatt, Nr. 39.
Reichsbewertungsgesetz vom 10. Aug. 1925. Reichsgesetzblatt, Nr. 39.

See also C 14. *Statistical Journal.* General results of the Census of 1861.

ITALY

C 1. S. JACINI. *La proprietà fondiaria e la popolazione agricola in Lombardia.*

JAPAN

A III. S. SHIOMI. Interrelation between the wealth and the density of population in Japan.

C 20. *Earned and Unearned Income*

R. Brunhuber. The taxation of the unearned increment in Germany. *Quart. Journ. of Econ.* 1907/8.

A. Hook. Earned and unearned income and income tax. *Westminster Review*, Feb. 1906.

C 21. *Income and Expenditure of Social Groups*

United Kingdom

A. L. Bowley. *Has poverty diminished?* L.S.E. Studies in Econ. and Pol. Sci. No. 82, 1925.

A. L. Bowley and A. R. Burnett-Hurst. *Livelihood and Poverty: a study in economic conditions of working-class households in Northampton, Warrington, Stanley and Reading.* 1915.

A. E. Feavearyear. The national expenditure 1932. *Econ. Journ.* 1934.

International Labour Office. *The Worker's Standard of Living.* Studies and Reports, Series B, No. 30, 1938.

Sir John Orr. *Food, Health and Income.* Report on a survey of adequacy of diet in relation to income. 1936.

S. U. Procopovitch. The distribution of the national income. *Econ. Journ.* March 1926.

G. D. Rokeling. A British index of national prosperity, 1920–1927. *Economist*, Suppl. 6 Oct. 1928.

Austria

E. v. Philippovich. Das Einkommen nach dem Berufe und nach der Stellung im Berufe in Oesterreich. *Zeitschrift für Volkswirtschaft, Sozialpolitik und Verwaltung*, xv.

F. Savorgnan. *La distribuzion dei redditi nelle provincie e nelle grandi città dell' Austria.* Triest, 1912 (?).

France

L. Dugé de Bernouille. Les revenus privés et les consommations. *Revue d'Économie politique*, 1935.

A. de Foville. Les valeurs successorales et la répartition territoriale de la richesse en France. *Économiste français*, 5 Nov. 1881.

M. A. Neymarck. La répartition et la diffusion de l'épargne françaises sur les valeurs mobilières françaises et étrangères. *Bull. de l'Inst. Int. d Stat.* 1892.

Germany

W. Böhmert. Die mittleren Klassen der Einkommensteuer in einigen deutschen Grossstädten in den Jahren 1880–1895. *Jahrbuch für Gesetzgebung, Verwaltung und Volkswirtschaft* (Schmoller), 1896.

—— *Die Verteilung des Einkommens in Preussen und Sachsen.* Dresden, 1898.

F. Freiherr v. Friedenfels. Die Höhe des Einkommens nach Geschlecht und Beruf der Zensiten des Personaleinkommens 1903. *Mitteilungen des Finanzministeriums*, 2, 1907.

—— Zur Statistik der Personaleinkommensteuer 1898; Höhe des Einkommens nach Geschlecht und Beruf des Zensiten. *Mitteilungen des Finanzministeriums*, xiii, 2, 1903.

W. Lederer. Was verbrauchen wir? *Die Arbeit*, 1931.

F. LEMMER. Die Grössenordnung des deutschen Arbeitseinkommens. *Arbeitgeber*, 1929.

E. WÜRZBURGER. *Das Einkommen der Haushaltungsvorstände*. 1906.

F. ZAHN. Die Probleme des Mittelstandindexes. Arztliche Mitteilungen. *Sozialwissenschaftliche Rundschau*, Nr. 40, 1928.

ITALY

C. GINI e R. D'ADDARIO. La distribuzione dei redditi mobiliari in Italia. *Bull. de l'Inst. Int. de Stat.* I, 1931.

JAPAN

S. SHIOMI. Survey of the distribution of the people's income in the light of the household rate. *Kyoto University Economic Review*, July 1933.

SWITZERLAND

C. MÜHLMANN. Untersuchungen über die Entwicklung der wirtschaftlichen Kultur und die Güterverteilung im Kanton Bern. *Mitteilungen des Bernischen statistischen Bureaus*, 1905.

UNITED STATES

U.S.A. Department of Commerce.

OSWALD NIELSEN. Survey of family income. *Survey of Current Business*, Dec. 1937.

ROBERT R. PETTENGILL. Division of the tax burden among income groups in the United States, 1936. *The American Econ. Review*, March 1940.

See also A II. WALTER LAYTON. Some statistical aspects of the labour unrest.

C 14. Sir HERBERT SAMUEL. The taxation of various classes of the people.

C 14. D. M. SANDRAL. The taxation of various classes of the people.

FRANCE

A III. C. COLSON. *Cours d'Économie Politique*.

GERMANY

A I*a*. TH. BALOGH. The national economy of Germany.

B. C. BRÜCKNER. Einkommensteuerstatistik und Wohlstandsverteilung.

A I*a*. E. ENGEL. Die Klassensteuer und die klassifizierte Einkommensteuer.

A I*a*. *Journal of the Royal Stat. Society*. Distribution of incomes in Germany.

ITALY

A III. E. PORRU. La concentrazione della ricchezza nelle diverse regioni d' Italia.

A III. F. SAVORGNAN. L' ammontare e la composizione della ricchezza in Italia e nelle sue regioni.

UNITED STATES

A I. Brookings Institution. LEVEN and WRIGHT. *The Income Structure of the United States*.

CZECHO-SLOVAKIA

A I*a*. S. PROKOPOVIC. Répartition du revenu national en Bohème.

C 22. *Valuation of Income, Money Value, Real Value*

UNITED KINGDOM

A. K. CAIRNCROSS. *Price Index for Iron and Steel Goods*. Glasgow University.

Sir ROBERT GIFFEN. Recent changes in prices and incomes compared. *Stat. Journ.* Dec. 1888.

International Labour Office. *A Contribution to the Study of International Comparisons of Costs of Living*, 1932.

U.K. Report from Select Committee on the General Valuation of Ireland. B.P.P. 1868–69, Session IX.

—— Select Committee on Irish Valuation. B.P.P. 1868–69, Session IX.

—— *Ministry of Labour Gazette*. The Cost of Living Index Number, Method of Compilation. B.P.P. 1931, Session O. 36–9999.

E. A. WINSLAW. *Budget Studies and the Measurement of Living Costs and Standards*, 1923.

FRANCE

A I*a*. A. NEYMARCK. The distribution of personal property in France.

GERMANY

F. SOLTAU. Wohlstandsindices. *Magazin der Wirtschaft*, 6. Jahrgang, Nr. 13, 1930.

—— Der Wohlstandsindex des Dawes Gutachtens und die Bedeutung seines Fortfalls im Young Plan. *Magazin der Wirtschaft*, 6. Jahrgang, 1930.

UNITED STATES

Bureau of Applied Economics, Inc. *Standards of Living. A compilation of Budgetary Studies*. (Revised Edition.) Bulletin No. 7, Washington, 1920.

U.S.A. Department of Commerce. Bureau of Foreign and Domestic Commerce. *Survey of Current Business*. Washington, Dec. 1936.

National Bureau of Econ. Research, Bulletin 62:

S. FABRICANT. *Revaluation of Fixed Assets*, 1925–1934. 1936.

See also C 21. International Labour Office. The worker's standard of living.

A I. J. M. KEYNES. *The General Theory of Employment, Interest and Money*.

A II. A. C. PIGOU and COLIN CLARK. *The Economic Position of Great Britain*.

C 23. *Inheritance and Death Duties*

UNITED KINGDOM

LORD STAMP. Inheritance—a sample inquiry. From the Report of the British Association, Sept. 1930. *Econ. Journ.* 1930.

H. C. STRUTT. Notes on the distribution of estates in France and the United Kingdom. *Stat. Journ.* 1910.

J. W. TYLER. Estate duty valuation and agricultural property. *Transactions of the Surveyors' Institute*, 1902–3.

J. C. L. ZORN. *The Incidence of the Income Tax*. London, 1909.

FRANCE

J. BERTILLON. Statistique des successions en France et à l'étranger. *Journ. de la Société de Stat. de Paris*, Sept. 1910.

M. J. SEAILLES. *La Répartition des Fortunes en France*.

ITALY

Bollettino di Statistica e Legislazione Comparata. Sciolgimento delle tasse di successione nel periodo 1877–1902. 1901–2.

Bollettino di Statistica e Legislazione Comparata. Le successioni e le donazioni nell' anno 1902–03. (Elementi per uno studio sulla natura e l' ammontare probabile della ricchezza privata nazionale e sulla sua ripartizione fra le diverse provincie e compartimenti.) 1903–4.

See also A II. H. CLAY. Distribution of capital in England and Wales.
A I*a*. T. A. COGHLAN. Evidence before the Select Committee on Income Tax.
A I*c*. VISCOUNT GOSCHEN. The increase of moderate incomes.
A III. W. J. HARRIS and K. A. LAKE. Estimates of the realisable wealth of the United Kingdom.
A I*a*. B. MALLET and H. C. STRUTT. The multiplier and capital wealth.

AUSTRIA

A III. K. TH. v. INAMA-STERNEGG. Die Ergebnisse der Erbschaftssteuer.

FRANCE

A III. C. COLSON. *Cours d'Économie Politique.*
C 21. A. DE FOVILLE. Les valeurs successorales et la répartition territoriale.
A I*a*. A. DE FOVILLE. L'évaluation de la richesse nationale.
A III. A. LEROY-BEAULIEU. Les fortunes en France d'après les déclarations successorales.

ITALY

A III. R. BENINI. Quote successorie di alcune specie di ricchezza.
A III. G. SOLINAS COSSU. Valore dei beni transferiti per successione e donazione nel quindicennio 1885–1899/1900.
A III. Relazione della Amministrazione del Demanio. *La Ricchezza in rapporto alle successioni e donazioni.*
A III. M. PANTALEONI. Dell' ammontare probabile della ricchezza privata.
B. LUIGI PRINCIVALLE. Alcune indagini sui passagi della proprietà fondiaria per causa di morte.

C 24. *Distinction between Capital and Income*

HORST F. MENDERSHAUSEN. The relation between income and savings of American Metropolitan families. *The American Econ. Review*, Sept. 1939.

See also A I*a*. COLIN CLARK. *National Income and Outlay.*
C 18. RAYMOND NEEDHAM. The distinction between capital and income.

C 25. *Treatment of changes in Capital Values*

UNITED STATES

See C 22. S. FABRICANT. *Revaluation of Fixed Assets*, 1925–1934.

C 26. *Change in Values of Stocks and Commodities: Inventories*

UNITED STATES

See C 17. S. FABRICANT. *Capital Consumption and Adjustment.*

D. SOURCES

United Kingdom

U.K. Return of the amount of property assessed to income and property tax under schedules A, B and D in each county, 1814 and 1842/3–1864/65. B.P.P. Session xxxix, 1866, Session xli, 1870. Schedules D and E, 1864/65–1869/70.

—— First Census of Production. Cd. 6320, Final Report, Tables, 1907.

—— Report on the Census of Production, 1907 (Sir Alfred Flux). B.P.P. 1912/13, cix.

—— Second Census of Production, 1912.

—— Third Census of Production, 1924.

—— Fourth Census of Production, 1930. Preliminary Survey.

—— Reports of the Commissioners of Inland Revenue annually from 1855/56.

—— Distribution by Counties to Assessments to Income Tax under Schedules A and B. B.P.P. 1912–13, xlix, 414.

—— Approximate distribution of the estimated amounts of taxable incomes. B.P.P. xxxii (Cmd. 224), 1919.

—— Treasury. Imperial Taxation on Real and Realised Personal Property. B.P.P. Session xlv, 1884/85.

—— Treasury. Select Committee on Income and Property Tax 1861. B.P.P. vii, 1861.

—— Treasury. Select Committee on Municipal Trading. B.P.P. vii, 1900; vii, 1903.

—— Supertax. Number of persons asked to make returns, number of persons who gave notice, number of persons who neglected to make returns for supertax 1909/10–1913/14. B.P.P. xxxviii, 36, 1914–16.

—— *Ministry of Labour Gazette.* Railway Returns, collected yearly, mostly September issue.

—— Ministry of Agriculture and Fisheries. The Agricultural Output of England and Wales, 1925. Cmd. 2815, 1927.

—— Ministry of Agriculture. The Agricultural Output of England and Wales, 1930–1931. B.P.P. Cmd. 4605, xxvi, 1933–34.

—— Ministry of Agriculture. The Agricultural Output of Scotland, 1930. B.P.P. Cmd. 4496, xxvi, 1933–34.

Australia

Bureau of the Census and Statistics:

G. H. Knibbs. *The Private Wealth of Australia and its Growth and Distribution.* Ed. M. Atkinson. Australia Economic and Political Studies. Melbourne, 1918.

Council for Scientific and Industrial Research. *Ten years of progress,* 1926–1936. Melbourne, 1936.

A. G. B. Fisher. *The Economic Record* (New Zealand), Nov. 1930.

Austria

C. J. v. Czoernig. *Statistisches Handbüchlein der Oesterreichischen Monarchie.* 1861.

J. Fillunger. *Vergleichende Statistik über die Real- und Produktionswerte der Landwirtschaft, der Montan-Industrie, der Verkehrs- und Communikations-Anstalten und des Staatshaushaltes im Oesterr. Kaiserstaat.* Wien, 1868.

Belgium

A. Quetelet. *Recherches Statistiques sur le Royaume des Pays-Bas*. Bruxelles, 1929.

France

Chambre de Députés. *Inventaire de la Situation finançière de la France au début de la 13iéme*. Législature présenté par M. Clémentel, 1924.

A. de Foville. La consommation nationale et l'exportation. *Économiste français*, 11 April 1891.

E. Michel. *Les habitants, démographie, salaires, corporations et syndicats, assistance, mutualité, épargne, prévoyance, impôts*. Paris-Nancy, 1910.

M. A. Neymarck. La statistique internationale des valeurs mobilières. *Bull. de l'Inst. Int. de Stat.* Vol. xx, Supplément, 1913.

Germany

F. C. W. Dieterici. *Statistische Uebersicht im preussischen Staat und im deutschen Zollverein*. 1831–1836/44. 4 Vols. edited between 1836 and 1846.

Die Einkommensbesteuerung vor und nach dem Kriege. *Einzelschriften zur Statistik des Deutschen Reichs*. No. 24.

H. G. Moulton. *The Reparation Plan*. New York, 1924.

Statistisches Reichsamt. *Statistisches Jahrbuch für das Deutsche Reich*. Berlin, annual from 1877.

W. Woytinski. *Die Welt in Zahlen*, Vol. i. Berlin, 1925–28.

Italy

G. Mortara. Numeri indici dello stato e del progresso economica delle regioni italiane. *Giornale degli Economisti*, Vol. xlvii, 1913.

—— Numeri indici delle condizioni economiche in Italia. 1920. *Bull. de l'Inst. Int. de Stat.* xx, 2.

United States

Brookings Institution. Institute of Economics, Publ. No. 55:

E. G. Nourse and Associates. *America's Capacity to Produce*. Washington, 1934. (Being Pt I of 'The Distribution of Wealth and Income'.)

E. E. Day and W. M. Persons. An Index of the Physical Volume of Production. *Review of Economic Statistics*, Supplement for 1920.

D. Friday. *Profits, Wages, Prices*. New York, 1920.

F. J. Guetter and A. E. McKinley. Statistical Tables relating to *The Economic Growth of the United States*. Philadelphia, 1924.

Moody's Manuals. Especially those for Public Utilities and those for Statistics. Different annuals.

U.S.A. Senate. 73rd Congress, 2nd Session, Document 124. *National Income, 1929–32*. Letter from the Acting Secretary of Commerce. Under supervision of S. Kuznets and R. F. Martin. Washington, 1934.

U.S.A. Federal Trade Commission. 69th Congress, 1st Session, 1926. *National Wealth and Income*.

U.S.A. Foreign and Domestic Commerce Bureau. Statistical Abstracts from 1923 onwards.

U.S. Treasury Department. U.S. Internal Revenue. Statistics of Income. Washington, yearly since 1917 to date, figures from 1919.

See also C 8. *Economist*. Regular analysis of companies' profits and losses.
C 7. H. J. H. Parker. *Income of small shopkeepers, etc.*

Japan

A I*a*. Charles V. Sale. Some statistics of Japan. *Stat. Journ.* 1911.

Index

CAMBRIDGE: PRINTED BY WALTER LEWIS, M.A., AT THE UNIVERSITY PRESS